CONVERSION AND THE POLITICS OF RELIGION IN EARLY MODERN GERMANY

SPEKTRUM: *Publications of the German Studies Association*

Series editor: David M. Luebke, University of Oregon

Published under the auspices of the German Studies Association, *Spektrum* offers current perspectives on culture, society, and political life in the German-speaking lands of central Europe—Austria, Switzerland, and the Federal Republic—from the late Middle Ages to the present day. Its titles and themes reflect the composition of the GSA and the work of its members within and across the disciplines to which they belong—literary criticism, history, cultural studies, political science, and anthropology.

Volume 1
The Holy Roman Empire, Reconsidered
Edited by Jason Philip Coy, Benjamin Marschke, and David Warren Sabean

Volume 2
Weimar Publics/Weimar Subjects
Rethinking the Political Culture of Germany in the 1920s
Edited by Kathleen Canning, Kerstin Barndt, and Kristin McGuire

Volume 3
Conversion and the Politics of Religion in Early Modern Germany
Edited by David M. Luebke, Jared Poley, Daniel C. Ryan, and David Warren Sabean

Conversion and the Politics of Religion in Early Modern Germany

Edited by

DAVID M. LUEBKE, JARED POLEY,
DANIEL C. RYAN, and DAVID WARREN SABEAN

Berghahn Books
New York • Oxford

First published in 2012 by
Berghahn Books

www.berghahnbooks.com

© 2012 David M. Luebke, Jared Poley, Daniel C. Ryan, and David Warren Sabean

Library of Congress Cataloging-in-Publication Data

German Studies Association. Conference (32nd : 2008 : St. Paul, Minn.)
Conversion and the politics of religion in early modern Germany / edited by David M.
Luebke ... [et al.].
    p. cm. — (Spektrum ; v. 3)
Includes bibliographical references (p.) and index.
ISBN 978-0-85745-375-4 (hardback : alk. paper) — ISBN 978-0-85745-376-1 (ebook)
1. Conversion—Christianity—History of doctrines—Congresses. 2. Germany—
Church history—Congresses. 3. Christianity and politics—Germany—Congresses.
I. Luebke, David Martin, 1960– II. Title.
    BT780.G47 2008
    248.2'409--dc23

                                                                    2011040622

British Library Cataloguing in Publication Data

A catalogue record for this book is available from the British Library

Printed in the United States on acid-free paper.

ISBN 978-0-85745-375-4 (hardback)
ISBN 978-0-85745-376-1 (ebook)

... our desire is heightened in conversion ... till it becomes a spontaneous activity of the self that constitutes a coherent new life.

—Friedrich Schleiermacher, *Der christliche Glaube* (1830)

~: CONTENTS :~

~: PREFACE :~

The phenomenon of religious conversion offers an attractive avenue for historical research, since religious change touches upon collective identity, communal boundaries, relationships between "secular" and "religious" concerns, and religious politics. This edited volume, which grew out of panels on the topic of conversion at an annual meeting of the German Studies Association, offers perspectives on the nature, meaning, and effects of conversion in the German-speaking lands in the wake of the Reformation. Contributors examine crucial topics such as the territorialization of confession, conversion and diplomacy, irenicist (tolerant) approaches to religious difference, conversion and notions of the self, and the changing meanings of "conversion" during a period of significant social, political, and legal transformation.

This volume shows how political authorities and subjects imbued religious confession with novel meanings during the early modern era. Generally, the contributors suggest ways that religious concerns overlapped with political and social matters. Religious transformation can be attributed to a variety of factors: coercive pressure, social change, political considerations, and the acceptance of new belief. And resistance to religious innovations could also have political, social, or theological roots.

The volume also offers insights into the historicity of the very concept of "conversion." One widely accepted modern notion of the phenomenon simply expresses denominational change, yet this concept had no bearing at the outset of the Reformation. Instead, a variety of processes, such as the consolidation of territories along confessional lines, attempts to ensure tolerance, and diplomatic quarrels helped to usher in new ideas about the nature of religious boundaries and, therefore, conversion. However conceptualized, religious change—conversion—had deep social and political implications for early modern German states and societies.

~:~

The editors would like to acknowledge not only the contributors to this volume but also all of the scholars who participated in the cycle of panels on "Conversion in the German-speaking Lands" at the 2008 German Studies Association meeting. We also wish to thank Carrie Sanders for compiling the bibliography, Ann De Vita for her editorial work, and Marion Berghahn for her support.

INTRODUCTION

The Politics of Conversion in Early Modern Germany

DAVID M. LUEBKE

In the beginning was a conversion—or, more precisely, the memory of a profound change, given clarity and meaning with each retelling through the years. Near the end of his life, in 1545, Martin Luther published an account of what came to be known as the "Tower Experience." After "meditating day and night" over the Epistle of Paul to the Romans, Luther arrived at the realization that his angry struggles to comprehend the meaning of divine righteousness were themselves the work of God within him. Like the Apostle Paul, Luther remembered the sensation that he "had entered paradise itself through open gates." To reinforce his new understanding, Luther turned to the writings of another famous convert, Saint Augustine of Hippo, who had likewise come to understand righteousness as a cloak "with which God clothes us."[1]

Whether the conversion occurred exactly as Luther remembered it, whether it happened in 1513 or 1515 or 1518, whether it was a single event or several that the reformer lumped together long after the fact—all these questions are less salient for present purposes than the political function of Luther's autobiographical sketch in mid-sixteenth-century Germany.[2] By then, what had begun as a noisy row among theologians was transforming into a seemingly permanent rift, setting the old faith against the new, Luther's adherents against the followers of Zwingli and Calvin, and rebaptizers against the world. In an environment of escalating confessional tensions, Luther's account aimed to mobilize his audience to think and act in particular ways.[3] By associating his own experience with the archetypal conversions of Paul and Augustine, Luther lay claim to the purity of the primitive church and raised the stakes of alignment in the confessional struggle to a matter of eternal life and death.

Luther's conversion narrative, in other words, was inescapably bound up with the formation of confessional blocs. So were the two conversion narratives of Jean Calvin. Though subtler in tone—nothing so dramatic as the Tower Experience marked Calvin's embrace of the new teachings—his accounts reveal the evolution of an even keener sense of confessional distinction. The first, written only six years after the fact in 1539, described a gradual process of discovery, spurred on by the stings of conscience and a fear of divine wrath that exposed "a very different form of doctrine … brought back to its fountainhead" and "restored to its original purity."[4] By contrast, Calvin's second account, contained in the preface to his *Commentary on the Psalms* (1557), recalled a "sudden conversion" that had brought his mind "into a teachable frame" (*subita conversio ad docilitatem*).[5] Looking back on the labors of twenty years, Calvin emphasized divine calling and metaphors of pilgrimage, intentionally "evoking images of Moses, David, Jeremiah and Paul."[6] Like Luther before him, Calvin now wrote as one who had come to regard himself a prophet of the true church and an instrument of the divine plan.[7]

Beyond their differences, the narratives of both reformers articulated a new type of religious conversion that burst the existing repertoire of meanings. As Duane J. Corpis and Eric-Oliver Mader remind us in their contributions to this volume, the "Pauline" or "Augustinian" trope of conversion—a numinous, revelatory experience, provoking a comprehensive change of belief—was by no means the only available definition. On the contrary, in the pre-Reformation era a rich field of signification surrounded *conversio* and its German counterpart, *Bekehrung*. This concept still could, of course, refer to movement from one distinct religion to another, as it had during the early medieval period of mass conversions to Christianity in western and northern Europe.[8] Of the available meanings, this came closest to the Augustinian model.[9] Closer to Luther's time, the term could describe a turning toward the God of Christian orthodoxy (and away from heresy). But the most common usage referred to a complex and gradual process of spiritual revitalization and intensification. Conversion in this sense might culminate in the taking of monastic vows. From the thirteenth century on, more and more converts traveled a path of spiritual intensification that ended outside the established religious orders. As John Van Engen has observed, conversions of this type were fraught with tension and, in the decades around 1400, nearly destroyed the systems then in place for accommodating such impulses.[10] But they did not rupture the categorical distinction between Christianity and its others. On the eve of Reformation, the most widespread notions of conversion denoted spiritual movement *within a single religion*.

The Reformation added a new archetype of convert, one who moves between the various forms of western Christianity *as if between one religion and another*. Or, to rephrase the point in terms borrowed from Duane Corpis, theologians on both sides of the confessional divide discarded the late medieval, "intrareligious" definition of conversion in favor of an "interreligious" meaning. The shift did not occur suddenly, nor did the older meaning disappear completely. Rather, the new definition emerged slowly, as hopes for the restoration of unity dimmed and as the reform movements consolidated into institutional churches, independent of Roman authority, under the tutelage of German princes and magistrates. "The confessions," writes Corpis, were "becoming distinct and rival religions."

Significantly, this new definition was articulated through a set of "territorial" metaphors that reproduced the increasingly spatialized structure and exercise of sovereign authority in the constituent states of the Holy Roman Empire. The shift in metaphors also coincided with a fundamental ecclesiopolitical shift: in 1555, the Imperial Diet achieved a settlement in the religious controversy by conferring the right to establish religion onto the sovereign princes and city-states of the realm. The options, to be sure, were limited to Catholicism and the religion described by the "Augsburg Confession"—the statement of fundamental Protestant beliefs compiled by Philipp Melanchthon in 1530. Nor was the peace of 1555 meant to be permanent; even so, the legal formula *cuius regio, eius religio*—"he who rules determines the religion"—was firmly in place by the end of the century.[11] By the late seventeenth century, as Corpis shows, polemicists had begun to speak of the boundaries between confessions as if they were political borders, with the mass of nonbelievers arrayed on the far side.[12]

The nine essays collected in this volume share a common concern with the changing relationship between conversion and the reconfiguring politics of the post-Reformation era. They are divided into three parts. The essays of Corpis and Mader comprise the first section and approach the relationship as a problem of theology. A second section, consisting of essays by Jesse Spohnholz, Ralf-Peter Fuchs, and Daniel Riches, delve into the politics of conversion at three levels—the local or civic, the imperial, and the diplomatic. The third set of essays, by Alexander Schunka, Benjamin Marschke, and Jonathan Strom, extends the topic to two new phenomena of the seventeenth and eighteenth centuries—the irenicist union movement and Pietism—and examine their relationship to conversion in the "interreligious" mode. A ninth and final essay by Douglas H. Shantz examines the extraordinary life of an eighteenth-century freethinker whose conversion took him out of organized religion entirely.

These essays build on a surge of scholarly interest in early modern conversion that has been gathering strength since the mid and late 1990s. As long as research on the Reformation era remained under the intellectual sway of narrowly denominational perspectives, historians showed little interest in conversion—paradoxically so, given its centrality both to the self-image of sixteenth-century reformers and to the politics of religion itself. Interest in conversion revived largely in response to a new interpretation of the relationship between church, state, and the reform of religion in the sixteenth century. Its proponents argued that reform in both camps, Protestant and Catholic, are best understood as the products of "confessionalization"—a transformation of culture and power on both sides of the religious divide, involving the codification and implementation of Catholic and Protestant doctrines, which was intended to ensure the homogeneity of belief and practice. The driving force behind this process was a close and mutually beneficial alliance between ecclesiastical authorities, who gained from it the wherewithal to suppress competing "heresies," and secular rulers, to whom the alliance promised new and potent sources of wealth and legitimacy.[13] As that alliance strengthened, the bond also tightened between orthodoxy and obedience toward the authority of princes and magistrates. Because early modern Europeans could not conceive of religion as a sphere separate from other domains of being, let alone imagine it as a category subordinate to society or politics, turning away from the faith of one's secular overlord meant, increasingly, to defy his authority or even to rise up against it.[14] Small wonder, then, that secular authorities often characterized religious minorities in terms plucked from the lexicon of slanders ordinarily reserved for rebellious peasants.[15] This link between state power and religious change has led many historians to proclaim that in sixteenth-century Germany, there was "no conversion without confession."[16]

How well or poorly does the assertion hold up? Anyone looking for conversions that took this form will find plenty of examples that confirm the paradigm. But like many historical catchphrases, this one raises as many questions as it purports to answer. What, for example, distinguished Protestant from Catholic understandings of conversion in the new, "interreligious" mode, and what impact did these differences have? Did the new archetype displace older modes, or did "intrareligious" modes of conversion persist as well? How did social ties such as kinship impinge on the politics of conversion, whether at the local level or on the plane of dynastic relations? Given the intensely social nature of conversion in the post-Reformation era, can we assume that religious persuasion was the only, or even the decisive, motivation behind affiliational change?

While none of the contributors to this volume would dispute the proposition that conversion took on new forms after Luther and Calvin, each calls into question the adequacy of "confession" as a conceptual frame of reference and of the "confessionalization" paradigm to explain the full complexity of its politics and social implications. One difficulty is chronological. As both Corpis and Mader argue, the notion of conversion-as-confessional-change presupposes the existence of clearly defined boundaries between the Christian denominations at a time when these were still forming—as if the outcome of confessionalization had been present from the beginning. As Corpis shows, the fully confessionalized, "interreligious" model of conversion did not become dominant until the late sixteenth and seventeenth centuries; Mader reminds us that the word *Konvertit* did not enter the German language until the late eighteenth century. Furthermore, forces other than state power shaped the metaphors that polemicists used to articulate the interreligious archetype. Corpis argues that the impact of encounters with non-Christian peoples in Asia and the Americas proved central to the new conceptualization of conversion. In order to define themselves more clearly against confessional foes, polemicists of all stripes drew on stereotypes of Turkish "Mohammedans" and pagan indigenes of the New World that had begun to form prior to the Reformation. The new politics of conversion, in short, reflected transformations that were unfolding on a global scale and quite independently of confessionalization.[17]

Eric-Oliver Mader relates the charge of anachronism to more fundamental criticism of the confessionalization thesis. In emphasizing the cultural strategies that characterized princes on both sides of the confessional divide, its proponents minimize those attributes of doctrine and religious practice that distinguished one faith from another. Mader seeks to explain a wave of conversions from Protestantism to Catholicism that gathered strength after 1550 and crested during the century after 1648. Along the way, he unpacks the radically dissimilar concepts of conversion developed within each camp. Lutheran theologians emphasized faith and divine agency but distinguished between sudden conversions in the Pauline mode and those that proceeded gradually through an awakening to divine grace. Catholic controversialists, by contrast, stressed active human agency; their insistence on individual volition, rather than divine agency, contributed to the Roman church's superior missionary zeal. Mader also argues that Catholicism's uncompromising insistence on an institutional monopoly over the means of salvation contributed to its success. In general, the distinctive properties of each theology—their *propria*—yielded highly divergent understandings of conversion, which in turn profoundly affected the ability of each confession to win converts to the "true" faith. By minimizing the importance of theological differences, the confessionalization paradigm too easily reduces conversion to nothing more than a function of state-building.[18]

The paradigm can also generate optical illusions. Specifically, its relentlessly statist point of view encourages the assumption that any large-scale conversion *must* have been driven by the high and mighty. In his study of confessional change in Wesel, Jesse Spohnholz shows that the town's drift toward Calvinism, long assumed to have been the result of proselytization and pressure from civic magistrates, resulted gradually from political circumstances and demographic forces, including an influx of Dutch refugees during the 1570s and 1580s. Throughout the transition, the Lutherans and Calvinists of Wesel cohabited more or less peaceably; churches remained supraconfessional, so as to accommodate the needs of a pluriconfessional population. The formal conversion of Wesel to the Reformed faith took place in 1609, when the Duchy of Cleves devolved to Johann Sigismund, the Elector of Brandenburg and a convert to Calvinism. Yet even then, it is likely that for many parishioners the adoption of Calvinism amounted to little more than recognition of a new master. The conversion of Wesel, in short, had less to do with the triumph of religious truths than broad structural transformations.

Like Corpis and Mader in the first section, Spohnholz shows that confessional categories took hold slowly and that at the local level, confessional boundaries remained flexible and porous for many generations after the "Luther Affair." His study also reminds us that religious movements did not always gain adherents because they were more persuasive on theological grounds, or because "converts" experienced a profound change of heart. This is not, of course, to deny that conversions in the Pauline mode could and did occur; rather it is to suggest that the full complexity of conversion in post-Reformation Europe cannot be grasped in theological terms alone. Finally, the gradual and relatively peaceable transition of Wesel from Lutheran to Reformed observance also undermines the widely held assumption that conversion on a large social scale was necessarily conflictual.

One could argue that this seemingly nonchalant attitude toward religious divisions reflected political weakness or indecision—that in the confessionally neutral Duchy of Cleves, the magistrates of a semiautonomous town could afford to distinguish civic concord from uniformity in religion and, in the interest of political self-preservation, stress the one over the other.[19] At the imperial level, the stakes remained incomparably higher because the formal conversion of any prince, whether or not his subjects followed him into the new fold, necessarily altered the distribution of military and diplomatic power among the confessional blocs within the Empire and, by extension, in Europe generally. At the imperial level, too, there was nothing ambiguous about confessional allegiances or the differences between Catholic, Lutheran, and Reformed.

Even so, it would be mistaken to assume that sharp distinctions always soured confessional relations. On the contrary, as Ralf-Peter Fuchs shows, the Empire's most effective means for containing the disruptive effects of princely conversion involved making confessional divisions *more* rigid, not less. This method involved "freezing" the official confessional status quo of each territory on the basis of a comprehensive legal settlement. The idea originated in the 1530s among Catholic princes who feared the cost of princely conversions in souls and properties lost to the Protestant churches. Originally conceived as a stopgap measure in anticipation of a negotiated reunification, "freezing" gradually transformed into a means of placing confessional divisions on a secure legal and political footing. An early example of freezing was the "ecclesiastical reservation" clause of the Religious Peace of 1555, which made permanent the Catholic status of prince-bishoprics and other ecclesiastical principalities. Another was the highly disruptive Edict of Restitution, promulgated by Emperor Ferdinand II in the throes of the Thirty Years' War, which sought to freeze the distribution of confessional power by negating all seizures of Catholic ecclesiastical principalities undertaken by Protestant princes since 1552.

The Peace of Westphalia finally ended the Thirty Years' War in 1648; it also generalized the principle of freezing by pegging the official religion of all the Empire's constituent states to the status quo of 1624, the so-called "normative year." Fuchs emphasizes that this solution by no means brought the politics of conversion to an end. On the contrary, quarrels over implementing the normative year persisted through the eighteenth century. As princely conversions to Catholicism increased after 1648, moreover, Protestant princes now found themselves defending the "frozen" status quo, just as Catholic princes had done a century earlier. On the whole, though, the normative year had a stabilizing effect. After 1648, disputes arising from princely conversion were adjudicated at the Imperial Diet or before tribunals of imperial justice, and only rarely on the field of battle. Over time the settlement established, willy-nilly, a de facto right to convert long before anyone considered religious pluralism a normative good.

The "normative year" achieved these effects by imposing limits on the right of princes to determine the official religion of their territories and to compel their subjects to worship only in the state-sanctioned church. Where such constraints were lacking, the nexus between religion and sovereignty remained volatile as ever. The second section concludes with Daniel Riches's analysis of a diplomatic scandal in 1690, in which the politics of conversion spun out of control and spoiled an alliance that both parties—the Calvinist Elector Friedrich III of Brandenburg-Prussia and the orthodox Lutheran King Karl XI of Sweden—otherwise found beneficial. The outrage centered on the ambiguous status of a Swedish noblewoman who, upon marrying the elector's ambassador, converted to Calvinism and was punished for her defiance. For Karl XI, the noblewoman's conversion represented an affront to his role as the royal guarantor of religious truth in Sweden; Friedrich III interpreted the woman's punishment as a violation of his paternalistic authority over the personnel of his diplomatic mission in Stockholm. Neither monarch could allow himself to be seen as indifferent to such insults. In this instance, the logic of absolutism exacerbated intra-Protestant confessional tensions and propelled both rulers to act contrary to their shared diplomatic interests.

These findings recommend a healthy skepticism toward the old notion that "absolutism" typically stabilized and eased religious tensions once confessional identities had taken root in the general population. So also does a controversy that erupted over an interconfessional dynastic marriage in 1708 between Elisabeth Christine of Braunschweig-Wolfenbüttel, a Lutheran, and Charles, the Catholic heir to the Habsburg crown lands. The fact that such an alliance was even imaginable politically registers the degree to which confessional tensions had diffused in the six decades since 1648. But to seal the alliance, Elisabeth Christine was required to convert to the religion of her husband. And so she did, on 1 May 1707.

As Alexander Schunka demonstrates, the controversy over her conversion interfered with the ongoing efforts of "irenicist" Protestant theologians to transcend confessional divisions on the basis of shared theological essentials.[20] Crossing as it did the divide between Protestant and Catholic, the dynastic marriage between Elisabeth Christine and Charles drove a wedge between the advocates of Lutheran/Catholic reconciliation, such as the Helmstedt theologian Johann Fabricius (1644–1729), and irenicists who, like the Prussian Daniel Jablonski (1660–1741), sought reunion only among the Protestant faiths as a means of bolstering the anti-Catholic coalition. Fabricius's commentary on the conversion, which played down disagreements between Lutherans and Catholics, ignited indignation throughout Protestant Germany. The ensuing pamphlet war had international repercussions as well. In England, Elisabeth Christine's conversion heightened popular opposition to the impending Hanoverian succession, and once George I had ascended the British throne, the controversy increased his obligation to demonstrate his anti-Catholic bona fides. In Germany, the affair sabotaged hopes for intra-Protestant reunion.

The theme of irenicism draws us into the third set of essays and a new combination of relationships between conversion and politics. In the sixteenth century, most secular authorities had sought to fashion confessionally homogenous populations; in the period after 1648, by contrast, German princes frequently deployed their power in a manner that encouraged the pluralization of faiths. At a minimum, the conversions of German princes to Catholicism—forty-two of them, according to one contemporary tally—legalized Roman observance at court while leaving Protestant state churches intact.[21] These included Duke Anton Ulrich of Braunschweig-Wolfenbüttel, who converted to Catholicism only two years after his daughter, Elisabeth Christine; another was Duke Carl Alexander of Württemberg (1733–1737). Others, such as Christian August of Pfalz-Sulzbach (1622–1708), introduced Catholic observance to formerly monoconfessional parishes.[22] While it is tempting to laud these interventions as triumphs for religious toleration, Schunka's study shows that princely conversions stirred up popular antipathy. If anything, the episode demonstrated the ongoing vitality of confessional identities.

So do the irenicist policies of King Frederick William I of Prussia (1713–1740), the subject of Benjamin Marschke's contribution to this volume. Since 1613, when Elector Johann Sigismund converted to Calvinism, the religion of Prussia's ruling dynasty had differed from that of its Lutheran subjects. The king's lineage also included several proponents of Protestant union. Unlike his predecessors, Frederick William was a "cafeteria Calvinist," as Marschke calls him, a genuine advocate of religious toleration who took what he liked and disregarded the rest. His ultimate goal was to unlock what confessionalization had joined: the bond between orthodoxy and obedience to secular authority. Unfortunately for irenicism, Frederick William also seems to have believed that he could erase confessional differences by decree—by forbidding confessional controversy, for example, or by banning liturgical practices that drew attention to confessional difference.

To succeed, Frederick William's irenic plans meant converting theologians across the Protestant spectrum to the notion that their differences were insubstantial. In resisting this proposition, none were fiercer than the greatest beneficiaries of Frederick William's favor, the members of the Pietist movement led by August Hermann Francke (1663–1727) and headquartered in Halle. Marschke's analysis of the Pietists' internal correspondence reveals a coordinated effort to thwart union between the Lutheran and Calvinist churches in Brandenburg-Prussia on the basis of irreconcilable theological and liturgical differences. From the Pietists' point of view, irenicism spelled forced conversion and the surrender of much that made their movement worthwhile—including, potentially, their control over the Prussian military chaplaincy.

It is ironic that a movement so opposed to theological dogmatism proved hostile to intra-Protestant reconciliation. Jonathan Strom's essay on the spiritual autobiographies of German Pietists offers one explanation for the Pietists' antipathy and attests, along the way, to the persistence of late medieval concepts of conversion as a form of spiritual intensification. Strom compares a set of conversion narratives from the region around Dargun, where the Pietist Princess Augusta of Mecklenburg-Güstrow held court, with a collection of narratives edited by the great Swabian jurist Johann Jacob Moser. Common to them all is a narrative of laborious progression from the recognition of sin to an attenuated "repentance struggle" (*Bußkampf*) and finally the enlightening "breakthrough" (*Durchbruch*) to "true" conversion. With their emphasis on spiritual autonomy and transformation, such conversions often threatened existing ecclesial authority—much as the pious movements of the late Middle Ages had done. The wave of conversions in villages around Dargun, for example, tore the fabric of parochial life and provoked the hostility of Mecklenburg's orthodox Lutheran state church. But as a form of spiritual intensification, Pietist conversions remained entirely within a Lutheran theological framework; if anything, Pietist conversions functioned to strengthen existing confessional identities, not weaken them. Here, then, was a form of conversion that did *not* entail confessional boundary-crossing but transpired entirely within a single faith. In this sense, therefore, Pietism revived the pre-Reformation, "intrareligious" mode of religious conversion. Small wonder that August Hermann Francke and his cohorts in Halle opposed the irenic schemes of King Frederick William so energetically: irenicism threatened to undo the very thing that Pietist conversions were meant to achieve.

The final contributor to this volume, Douglas H. Shantz, introduces a wholly new kind of conversion unique to the eighteenth century: neither "interreligious" nor "intrareligious," it took the convert out of established Christianity entirely and into an open-ended, Deist rationalism. The infamous subject of Shantz's essay, Johann Christian Edelmann (1698–1767), dedicated his prodigious intellectual energies to public critique, and even ridicule, of Christian dogma, earning him the abiding, pan-confessional hostility of ecclesiastical and secular authorities throughout the Empire. In the extremity of his radicalism, Edelmann cut a lonely figure: as is well known, the German *Aufklärung* as a whole never subjected Christianity to the kind of zealous, anticlerical scrutiny that characterized Enlightenment in Paris. In the German context, Edelmann was sui generis.

Yet not even Edelmann could escape the cultural templates of his youth and student years, when he dallied with mystics, Mennonites, and Pietists. As Shantz shows, the narrative structure of Edelmann's autobiography, published between 1749 and 1755, resembles nothing so much as the archetypal Pietist conversion narrative. The elements are all present: recognition of iniquity (in Edelmann's case, the tyranny of priests); an extended struggle (with the authority of faith); and, finally, a breakthrough to "the divinity of reason," which Edelmann described in terms that, stripped of its Christian content, could have been written by Francke himself—or perhaps even Luther.

Taken together, the contributions to this volume recommend a departure from interpretations of conversion in early modern Europe that stress rupture over continuity and the primacy of individual experience over social and political contingencies. To be sure, the debates that raged among theologians in the early sixteenth century injected a new concept of conversion into the religious culture of western Christianity, which the steady progress of confessionalization reinforced. Yet despite all the political force marshaled in its favor, the new concept was slow to take hold and, as the phenomenon of Pietism reveals, did not displace older understandings of conversion. By the same token, these essays argue that early modern conversion cannot be grasped solely as an individual, spiritual transformation apart from its social and political context. For many, perhaps most sixteenth- and seventeenth-century Germans, conversion did not entail a reorientation of belief as abrupt as Luther's or as profound as Calvin's; for some, such as Elisabeth Christine of Braunschweig-Wolfenbüttel or the wife of Brandenburg's ambassador to Sweden, conversion was primarily an obligation of marriage and therefore the expression of kinship, diplomacy, and gender relations, not an inward transformation. Needless to say, an approach that inquires solely after spiritual authenticity or doctrinal validity of individual conversions will miss the full complexity of these transactions.

In three ways, these essays also call into question the adequacy of "confessionalization" to explain the breadth and complexity of early modern conversion. In the first place, defining post-Reformation conversions a priori in confessional terms means excluding those forms of conversion that do not fit the bill—such as the Pietists' *Bußkampf* or Edelmann's conversion to Deist rationalism. Second, the paradigm's "top-down" perspective on conversion distracts from the demographic and communal forces that shaped religious identities "from below"—forces that, as the case of Wesel shows, were potent enough to effectuate conversions on a mass scale. Third, the paradigm diminishes effects of confessionalization that were unrelated to state-building. These essays show that the very attributes that made princely conversions destabilizing politically—such as the secularization of ecclesiastical goods and the transformation of religious orthodoxy into a mark of obedience—also stimulated negotiations that ultimately curtailed the right of magistrates and princes to determine the official form and doctrine of religious observance. Certainly, the process of confessionalization ossified religious identities and made converting more arduous; but it also created conditions for relatively stable cohabitation and the adjudication of conflicts that conversion generated.

Finally, the religious movements of the late seventeenth and eighteenth centuries point to a fundamental shift in the relationship between state power, conversion, and popular belief. By reviving conversion-as-spiritual-intensification *within* a Lutheran framework, the Pietists unwittingly registered the final success of confessional divisions: Pietist conversion was to the Lutheran "religion" as late medieval conversion had been to western Christianity as a whole. Confessional identities, in other words, had become so generally internalized that the Christian denominations operated as distinct religions. The failure of irenicism likewise registered the solidity of confessional mentalities. In the sixteenth century, converting the population at large to Lutheran, Calvinist, or Catholic orthodoxy had been the Sisyphean task of theologians, missionaries, and parish visitors. After the Peace of Westphalia, princes who converted to Catholicism, who encouraged Pietists, or who embraced irenicism found themselves promoting religious heterogeneity against the wishes of orthodox, monoconfessional clergy and parishioners. In the age of Enlightenment, confessional identities were entrenched in popular religiosity as never before. The circle of conversion was complete.

Notes

1. Martin Luther, "Vorrede zum ersten Bande der Gesamtausgabe seiner lateinischen Schriften" (1545), in *Martin Luthers Werke: Kritische Gesamtausgabe*, 65 vols. (Weimar, 1883–1966; reprint Weimar, 2000–2007), vol. 54, pp. 177–187; translated by Lewis W. Spitz as "Preface to the Latin Writings" (1545) in Jaroslav Pelikan and Helmut T. Lehmann, eds., *Luther's Works*, 55 vols. (Philadelphia, 1957–1986), vol. 34, pp. 327–343, here 336–337.
2. For an overview of the various datings see Marilyn J. Harran, *Luther on Conversion: The Early Years* (Ithaca, 1983), pp. 174–188; and a collection of essays devoted to this question, Bernhard Lohse, ed., *Der Durchbruch der reformatorischen Erkenntnis bei Luther: Neuere Untersuchungen* (Stuttgart, 1988). Harran advocates a date in 1518/19 in

Luther on Conversion, pp. 179–180, as did Heiko A. Oberman, *Luther: Man Between God and the Devil* (New York, 1989), pp. 152–156.

3. On conversion narratives as strategies of mobilization, see Dana Anderson, *Identity's Strategy: Rhetorical Selves in Conversion* (Columbia, SC, 2007).

4. John C. Olin, ed., *A Reformation Debate: Sadoleto's Letter to the Genevans and Calvin's Reply* (New York, 1966), pp. 81–84. On Calvin's conversion narratives, see most recently Bruce Gordon, *Calvin* (New Haven, 2009), pp. 33–35; and Wilhelm H. Neuser, *Johann Calvin: Leben und Werk in seiner Frühzeit, 1509–1541* (Göttingen, 2009), pp. 38–42.

5. Gordon, *Calvin*, p. 34; Neuser, *Johann Calvin*, p. 38; Heiko A. Oberman, "*Subita conversio*: The Conversion of John Calvin," in his *John Calvin and the Reformation of the Refugees* (Geneva, 2009), pp. 131–148.

6. Gordon, *Calvin*, p. 34.

7. Neuser, *Johann Calvin*, pp. 39–40.

8. On early medieval conversions, see most recently Daniel König, *Bekehrungsmotive: Untersuchungen zum Christianisierungsprozess im römischen Westreich und seinen romanisch-germanischen Nachfolgern (4.-8. Jahrhundert)* (Husum, 2008); and the articles assembled in James Muldoon, ed., *Varieties of Religious Conversion in the Middle Ages* (Gainesville, FL, 1997).

9. To be sure, the Augustinian model departed from the Pauline precedent in important ways. Unlike Paul, Augustine's conversion was intellectual and predicated more on reading than revelation; he was also a serial converter, arriving at Christianity only after embracing Manichaeism and neo-Platonism. See Frederick H. Russell, "Augustine: Conversion by the Book," in Muldoon, *Varieties of Religious Conversion*, pp. 12–30 and Karl F. Morrison, *Conversion and Text: The Cases of Augustine of Hippo, Herman-Judah, and Constantine Tsatsos* (Charlottesville, 1992), pp. 1–38.

10. John Van Engen, "Conversion and Conformity in the Early Fifteenth Century," in Kenneth Mills and Anthony Grafton, eds., *Conversion: Old Worlds and New* (Rochester, 2003), pp. 30–65.

11. Bernd Christian Schneider, *Ius reformandi: Die Entwicklung eines Staatskirchenrechts von seinen Anfängen bis zum Ende des Alten Reiches* (Tübingen, 2001), pp. 218–228, 256–268, 316–320.

12. See also Kim Siebenhüner, "Glaubenswechsel in der Frühen Neuzeit: Chancen und Tendenzen einer historischen Konversionsforschung," *Zeitschrift für historische Forschung* 34, no. 2 (2007): 243–272.

13. Among the first to connect conversion and confessionalization was Ute Mennecke-Haustein, "Konversionen," in Wolfgang Reinhard and Heinz Schilling, eds., *Die katholische Konfessionalisierung* (Gütersloh, 1995), 242–257. Since then, several edited volumes have examined the topic: Friedrich Niewöhner and Fidel Rädle, eds., *Konversionen im Mittelalter und in der Frühen Neuzeit* (Hildesheim, 1999); Heinz Duchhardt and Gerhard May, eds., *Union—Konversion—Toleranz: Dimensionen der Annäherung zwischen den christlichen Konfessionen im 17. und 18. Jahrhundert* (Mainz, 2000); and Ute Lotz-Heumann, Jan-Friedrich Mißfelder, and Matthias Pohlig, eds., *Konversion und Konfession in der Frühen Neuzeit* (Gütersloh, 2007).

14. The best statement of the confessionalization thesis remains Wolfgang Reinhard, "Zwang zur Konfessionalisierung? Prolegomena zu einer Theorie des konfessionellen Zeitalters," *Zeitschrift für historische Forschung* 10 (1983): 257–299; translated as "Pressure toward Confessionalization? Prolegomena to a Theory of the Confessional

Age," in C. Scott Dixon, ed., *The German Reformation: Essential Readings* (Oxford, 1999), pp. 172–192. Since the early 1980s, the confessionalization thesis has generated a vast literature. For the best recent overviews of this literature, see Thomas A. Brady, Jr., "Confessionalization: The Career of a Concept," in John M. Headley, Hans J. Hillerbrand, and Anthony J. Papalas, eds., *Confessionalization in Europe, 1555–1700: Essays in Honor and Memory of Bodo Nischan* (Aldershot, 2004), 1–20; and Stephan Ehrenpreis and Ute Lotz-Heumann, *Reformation und konfessionelles Zeitalter* (Darmstadt, 2002).

15. See, for example, Martin Scheutz, "Die 'fünfte Kolonne': Geheimprotestanten im 18. Jahrhundert in der Habsburgermonarchie und deren Inhaftierung in Konversionshäusern (1752–1775), *Mitteilungen des Instituts für österreichische Geschichtsforschung* 114 (2006): 326–380.

16. See Ute Lotz-Heumann, Jan-Friedrich Mißfelder, and Matthias Pohlig, "Konversion und Konfession in der Frühen Neuzeit: Systematische Fragestellung," in Lotz-Heumann et al., *Konversion und Konfession in der Frühen Neuzeit*, pp. 11–32, here p. 15.

17. In a similar vein, Carina Johnson argues that Protestant reformers deployed new concepts of heathen idolatry in their attacks on Roman Christianity, which had the effect of blurring distinctions between pagans and non-Protestant Christians; see her "Idolatrous Cultures and the Practice of Religion," *Journal of the History of Ideas* 67 (2006): 597–621. See also Christine R. Johnson, *The German Discovery of the World: Renaissance Encounters with the Strange and Marvelous* (Charlottesville, 2008).

18. This critique was first advanced against confessionalization theory as a whole by Thomas Kaufmann, "Die Konfessionalisierung von Kirche und Gesellschaft: Sammelbericht über eine Forschungsdebatte," *Theologische Literaturzeitung* 121 (1996): 1008–1012 and 1112–1121.

19. On the politics of confessional neutrality in Jülich, see most recently Antje Flüchter, "Konfessionalisierung in kulturalistischer Perspektive? Überlegungen am Beispiel der Herzogtümer Jülich-Berg," in Barbara Stollberg-Rilinger, ed., *Was heißt Kulturgeschichte des Politischen?* (Berlin, 2005), pp. 225–252.

20. On irenicism see most recently the essays collected in Duchhardt and May, *Union—Konversion—Toleranz*; and in Harm Klueting, ed., *Irenik und Antikonfessionalismus im 17. und 18. Jahrhundert* (Hildesheim, 2003).

21. Johann Stephan Pütter, *Historische Entwickelung der heutigen Staatsverfassung des Teutschen Reichs*, 3 vols. (Göttingen, 1786–1787), vol. 2, pp. 336–341.

22. Volker Wappmann, *Durchbruch zur Toleranz: Die Religionspolitik des Pfalzgrafen Christian August von Sulzbach, 1622–1708* (Neustadt an der Aisch, 1995).

CHAPTER ONE

Paths of Salvation and Boundaries of Belief

Spatial Discourse and the Meanings of Conversion in Early Modern Germany

DUANE J. CORPIS

Both Catholic and Lutheran writers in the Holy Roman Empire articulated the concept of conversion after the Reformation with a cluster of related words and expressions. *Conversio* was the main Latin word for conversion, and its most common German equivalent was *Bekehrung*. *Bekehrung* itself possessed several nuanced meanings, denoting both the process of internal spiritual renewal experienced by a true convert and the external act of formally changing from one religion to another. But beyond *Bekehrung*, early modern German possessed a rich vocabulary to describe the act of conversion. One could, for example, "change" religion (*die Religion wechseln* or *verändern*); "move from one religion over to another" (*von einer Religion zu einer anderen übertretten*); or "take on" a new faith (*eine neue Glaube annehmen*).

These terms articulated a range of meanings that overlapped one another yet occupied discrete positions in the theological grammar of post-Reformation Christianity. In this essay I focus on two meanings at play in the texts of Catholic and Lutheran authors who concerned themselves with conversion and the nature of religious identity in early modern Germany. These positions corresponded roughly to a basic distinction between "intrareligious" and "interreligious" conversion. The former signifies the inner spiritual change that makes the "convert" a more committed believer but without a change of institutional religious affiliation; the latter refers to a person's movement from one religious community to another. In this case, the convert's choice to "take on" a new religion was typically accompanied by assertions of a profound spiritual transformation but was institutionally marked by the adoption of a new religious creed and identity.

These two meanings of conversion had existed since the early Church. Although the various terms used in German to describe conversion might refer to either of these two modalities of religious experience (or to both at the same time), the conceptual compartmentalization of the two meanings of intrareligious and interreligious conversions had become so commonplace that the distinction made its way into Johann Heinrich Zedler's *Universal-Lexicon aller Wissenschaften und Künste* (Universal Lexicon of All the Sciences and Arts), an eighteenth-century encyclopedia. The *Universal-Lexicon* included two entries, one for *Bekehrung* and one for *Religions-Veränderung*. The description for *Bekehrung* offers a particularly Protestant perspective. When a person "is converted to God" (*zu GOtt bekehret wird*), the conversion "awakes faith in Christ the savior."[1] The act of conversion "produces a transformation (*Veränderung*) within the person" such that "what previously had existed [i.e., sin], is now erased, and what was once lacking [i.e., faith], is now generated."[2] As a result of this divine gift, the convert now (and only now) acquires the capacity to perform good works. The impact of this inner rebirth is so profound that a true convert "can be certain of his conversion, for whoever is converted will notice many changes in his soul."[3] The entry for *Bekehrung* nowhere mentions that the process might involve a change of confessional, denominational, or religious status or identity. Conversion, in this sense, meant the act of spiritual transformation that brought a person, any person, closer to Christ through the awakening of true faith.

While the word *Veränderung*—change or transformation—is used repeatedly in the definition for *Bekehrung*, the entry *Religions-Veränderung* offers a quite different take on an act that we today would also typically call a conversion. Immediately following the term *Religions-Veränderung*, the entry lists several synonyms: *Religions-Änderung*, *Mutatio Religionis*, and *Mutatio Sacrorum*. The text defines a *Religions-Veränderung* as a moment "when someone moves (*übertritt*) from one religion to another, and professes himself to another religion after [his] renunciation and abjuration of the religion, to which he had previously been affiliated."[4] In language that is confessionally neutral, the entry notes that such an act is fully protected by the "freedom of conscience" (*Gewissens-Freyheit*) promised by the Peace of Westphalia, so long as the new religion chosen by the convert was one of the three tolerated confessions of the realm, "namely the Catholic, Lutheran, or Reformed," and that such a change should be permitted "without diminishing a person's honor (*Ehre*) or dignity (*Würde*)."[5] The entry then proceeds to discuss the problem of those people who abandon one religion for another due to secular inducements such as "money or other worldly advantages or motives," but while it questions the authenticity of such conversions, the text never challenges the fundamental legal or religious legitimacy of multidirectional conversions among the three official confessions.[6]

Thus, by the eighteenth century the *Universal-Lexicon* distinguished between the two core meanings of conversion: an internal spiritual awakening that could take place within a person who presumably might already be a member of a Christian church, and a change of affiliation that transferred a person across a distinct religious boundary. Of course, both meanings had existed since the early Church. However, in the sixteenth century, two circumstances—the fragmentation of western Christendom and increased European contact with non-Christian cultures around the world—reconfigured these meanings in important ways. What changed was the way in which the two primary typologies of conversion were weighted in relationship to one another and the manner in which they were used to characterize relations both between Catholics and Protestants and between Christianity and the non-Christian religions of the world.

These changes played out in two stages. As the first part of this chapter shows, Lutheran reformers initially mobilized a preexisting, Catholic sense of religious conversion—essentially the "intrareligious" type of conversion—even as they reformulated the theological explanation for what initiated and caused a person to convert. The reformers offered a new model for how a person arrived at conversion, but they did not change what a true conversion fundamentally was or ought to be: it remained a movement toward God and godliness, a renewal of the soul that altered the convert's orientation to divine grace, justification, and salvation. The more Luther's movement became institutionalized, however, the more an "interreligious" meaning of conversion came to predominate. I argue that this shift took root partly within the context of the confessional formation that began in the latter half of the sixteenth century. Indeed, the growing discursive preeminence of interreligious conversion was itself a central part of the process of confessionalization. After the Peace of Augsburg (1555) and even more so after the Peace of Westphalia (1648), increasingly rigid confessional boundaries separated religious camps while also instantiating the possibility for interreligious conversion *within* Christianity, the crossing over from one Christian denomination to another.

This process of differentiation did not transpire only in the context of interconfessional polemics; rather, the polarized confessional divide that emerged between Protestantism and Catholicism also reflected Europeans' efforts to comprehend the experience of global expansion in the early modern period. Specifically, the process of confessional differentiation unfolded within two intertwined contexts: Christendom's own internal religious fragmentation and Europe's intensified encounters with the broader, non-Christian world. The complex geopolitical dimensions of these two contexts produced an imaginary religious landscape filled with religious "Others" demarcated from one another by expanding and contracting borders. The second part of this chapter shows how the competing Christian confessional communities imagined religious difference in terms of a larger, worldwide struggle between the "one true faith," whether Protestant or Catholic, and the multiple "false" religions at home and around the globe.

Conversion as Spiritual Transformation

In the Middle Ages, the concepts of intra- and interreligious conversion existed side by side. The interreligious conversion of pagans, Jews, and Muslims to Christianity entailed the adoption of new beliefs, rites, and a new institutional source of religious authority. But the broader meaning of conversion was that of intrareligious conversion, which described a Christian's spiritual movement closer to God, culminating in the transformation and reorientation of the soul, a spiritual epiphany, or in its most extreme cases mystical contact with the divine. This definition explains why *conversio* was also the term used to describe the specific act of taking monastic vows and leaving the decadent, profane world behind for the spiritual refuge of the monastery.

The idea of conversion as an inner journey of spiritual renewal and movement toward God also influenced a range of medieval movements that sat precariously on the edge of Christian orthodoxy, among them the Brethren of the Free Spirit, the Beguines, and the Brethren of the Common Life. The type of inner conversion professed by members of these movements had the potentially transgressive effect of decoupling the convert from the ecclesiastical authority of the church. Karl Morrison concludes that because of its mystical dimensions, this radical model of conversion "was not bound to formal, institutional obedience"; therefore "it frequently proved subversive of formal obedience and custom."[7] Such was the case with Protestant reformers, whose understanding of inner conversion was inextricably embedded within their critiques of official church doctrine.

To blunt this critical edge, medieval authors tried to secure the orthodoxy of inner conversion through constant reference to the convert's obedience to God and to the divinely ordained order of earthly authority. Indeed, to describe the act of taking monastic vows as *conversio* was itself a means to contain the threat of religious conversion by drawing the process back under the institutional church's control. This was the case when Bernard of Clairvaux preached a sermon on conversion in 1140, which purportedly led to the spiritual conversion of over twenty men who immediately joined Bernard's own Cistercian Order.[8] Similarly, Guibert de Nogent consistently labels as converts those men who joined his monastery and led exemplary ascetic lives.[9] Likewise, the fourteenth-century Dominican nun Margaret Ebner explained her gradual movement toward mystical union with Christ through the cultivation of monastic ideals such as simplicity, patience, and compassion.[10] The fusion of monastic life with conversion tamed the potential threat inherent in personal spiritual experience and revelation. This union of intense, inner conversion with complete submission to the institutional authority of the church would continue in the writings of sixteenth-century Catholic figures such as Teresa of Avila and Ignatius of Loyola.

Martin Luther derived his primary understanding of conversion from medieval tropes focused on the inner transformation of the soul, even if *leaving* rather than entering the monastery became the symbolic act of conversion for cloistered monks who joined the reform movement. Although Luther's usage of the term conversion changed over the course of his career as a reformer, he primarily thought about the concept in relationship to his understanding of justification by faith alone, which he posited as the sole route to salvation. For Luther, conversion was not a choice made by a person or the result of human works; it was initiated by God alone as an undeserved gift. Accordingly, a person did not convert simply by rejecting papal authority, repudiating Purgatory and the cult of the saints, or taking communion in both kinds. By themselves, these outward acts did not indicate inner conversion to God, although anyone who had in fact been converted by the grace of God would perform them as a consequence of their conversion.[11]

For Luther, the conversion of Paul served as an exemplary instance of *Bekehrung*. So important is the narrative of Paul's conversion that Luther recommended preaching about it "at least once a year.... For here one sees a miraculous act above all miracles, in that Christ converted his worst foe."[12] Despite humanity's inherited state of damnation, even Saul, the archenemy of God himself, could through divine grace find himself on the path to salvation. Luther contrasts Paul's conversion from a persecutor of God to a follower of the Gospels with the "papists" who continued to persecute "true Christians" seeking reform.

Luther's interpretation of Saul's conversion emphasizes the doctrine of salvation, *sola fidei*, which emerges as one of the key dividing points between Luther's soteriology and the sixteenth-century Catholic Church's renewed emphasis on free will and good works. To the extent that *sola fidei* and intrafaith conversion were not fundamentally new concepts, Luther did not represent his teachings as a new religion but as a superior explanation for the process by which God effects spiritual regeneration in the lives of Christians. But despite his shifts away from Catholic theological orthodoxy, Luther still emphasizes conversion as a movement of the soul toward God and godliness. He uses the well-known narrative of Saul's experiences on the road to Damascus as a spatial metaphor for conversion, in which God as prime actor reorients Saul's soul and conscience toward God; thenceforth the reborn man adopts the new name Paul and begins to walk a lifelong path of righteousness. Luther then contrasts Paul's rebirth to the stubborn failures of the contemporary Catholic Church, which, lacking true faith in God's grace, could not follow the reformed Christian down the same road of righteousness.[13] Thus, the story of the road to Damascus offered Luther a simple way to describe inner conversion as a journey along a singular path, a movement between sinfulness and godliness, error and truth, damnation and eternal salvation.

Luther's successors continued to describe conversion in similar ways. In 1566, Joachim Magdeburg published a treatise that explained conversion (*Bekehrung*) as a spiritual rebirth initiated not by an individual's personal power (*Kraft*), but through the preaching of the Gospels. The Word of God acts as a conduit for grace, but only God controls who receives it. Conversion is thus a movement toward God, but initiated externally. In contrast, Catholic teaching is a "pure fiction" (*ein lauter gedicht*) and stems from the devil.[14] Catholicism is seen not as a rival religion but simply a form of error—a historical reversion away from God. In Magdeburg's conception, the convert moves not from one religion to another, but from a state of sin to one of grace, in which the soul is filled with the Holy Spirit. Magdeburg's strict adherence to Luther's theology is no place clearer than when he states "that the natural man is neither able nor capable of achieving his conversion and true godliness from his own natural power, that he can do nothing toward his own conversion, that he in his conversion is purely passive (as Luther explained) and not at all active."[15]

A generation after Luther, the spiritualist Lutheran minister Valentin Weigel explained that the purpose of his treatise *Von der Bekehrung des Menschen* (On the Conversion of Man, 1570) was to teach Christians "what … conversion (*Bekehrung*), or new birth is … [and] what sin, old birth, or apostasy (*Abkere*) from God is."[16] The opposition between the linguistically related German words *Bekehrung* and *Abkere* signals that Weigel understood conversion and apostasy in the medieval sense of the soul's movement along a path between redemption and damnation. *Bekehrung*, made possible by Christ's sacrifice, took the form of complete obedience to God, while *Abkere*, the first instance of which was Adam's fall, represented defiance of God, which he labels with the following litany of terms: "sin, disobedience, self-will, old Adam, transgression, a bite from the apple."[17] Both Weigel and Magdeburg speak of the process of conversion using stark binaries that position the soul moving between diametrically opposed poles—God and Satan, heaven and hell, obedience and willfulness, grace and damnation. Weigel's references to the expulsion from Paradise more explicitly express these oppositions through a spatialization of conversion's bidirectional, axial movement—either to or from a state of grace. Consequently, neither author understood conversion as a choice between two doctrinally different confessions or religions, even though by the time these two wrote their treatises, the Lutherans had already authored the Augsburg Confession and the Council of Trent had formulated and codified the doctrine of the Counter-Reformation Church.

The Catholic Church also did not initially view the heresies of the reformers as distinct religions. Unlike Jews and Muslims, who threatened Christendom because they were religious outsiders beyond the community established by the sacramental rites of the Church, the heresies of Martin Luther and his fellow reformers were insidious threats from within the body of Christianity. The reformers spread error (*Irrthum*) and false teachings (*Irrlehre*) as if they were a cancer (*Krebs*) or poison (*Gift*) that destroyed the true Church from within. Catholics called Protestant theology a *Mißbrauch*, literally a "misuse" of biblical teachings. Those who accepted the error of the reformers had therefore not adopted a new religion but distorted the one true faith, resulting in their fall from God and the Church.

One of the first Catholic authors to articulate a concept of conversion responding to Protestantism was Johannes Mensing. In his 1528 critique of Luther's doctrine of justification by faith alone, Mensing asserted the orthodox Catholic position that humans possess the capability to earn righteousness by good works. In the eyes of God, justification necessitated a deliberate rejection of evil acts. Beyond the theological differences, however, Mensing's spatialized metaphors for the process of salvation resonated with the interior model of conversion seen in both prior medieval texts and the Reformation's earliest writings. The convert must use "all of his power to abandon all things, which are not of God, to point himself towards God (*noch zu Got weysen*) ... and to stand oneself before God (*richtet sich auff zu Gott*), and to be willingly obedient to Him in all of one's life, thoughts, desires, words, and works."[18] This personal act is at the very heart of inner conversion: in turning away from evil toward God, "we convert ourselves" (*wir vns bekeren*). Significantly, the biblical passage he quotes, "Kerend euch zu mir, so kere ich mich zu euch," translates literally as "*Turn* yourselves to me, so I will *turn* myself to you."[19] Mensing consciously employs etymologically related words—*sich bekehren* and *sich kehren*—as synonyms to infuse conversion with a sense of motion and movement. Faith, for Catholic theologians, was therefore a precondition, not a product, of conversion, and justification required a person to make the first move in order to walk the path of redemption: "Whoever wishes to come to God must believe that God exists and that God is the redeemer that he has sought."[20]

As Eric Mader explains in the following chapter of this volume, important theological differences existed between Lutherans and Catholics about whether God alone initiated the process of conversion or whether a person had some agency to shape his or her own spiritual rebirth. Still, the authors discussed so far would have agreed that conversion was primarily an inward experience that touched upon the soul's orientation and movement toward God. Likewise, neither Catholics nor Luther's followers deployed an *interreligious* concept of conversion to comprehend the fragmentation of Latin Christianity during the early sixteenth century. Indeed, we should be careful when speaking of conversion *from* Catholicism *to* Lutheranism or *from* Lutheranism *to* Catholicism in the early stages of the Reformation, because we are not yet dealing with religious camps that self-consciously understood themselves as formally distinct, institutionalized religions. The reformers did not describe their conversions or the conversions of their followers in terms of the formal adoption of an alternative faith, for their goal was not the founding of a new religion. Instead, it was an internal reform movement aimed at returning the church to its apostolic foundations.[21] As such, the conversion sought by Luther and other reformers typically aimed at the redemption, regeneration, and liberation of the human soul from sin and error.

Despite the eventual hardening of theological differences, the early debates over Christian doctrine and rites did not result in institutionally distinct confessions. Instead, the Luther Affair unleashed a frenzied cacophony of theological positions and with it a momentary space of open-ended doctrinal and liturgical possibility. The early Lutheran and Catholic emphasis on intrareligious conversion is best understood in the context of this explosion of religious alternatives, which several historians have described as a phase of "wild growth" (*Wildwuchs*).[22] Inner conversion—the turning of a person toward a more godly life in accordance with the dictates of the Gospels—was one of the core issues in this turbulent, early phase. Each new voice in the debate claimed to show the best path of conversion, away from the depravity of sin and toward a more fully Christian life justified in the eyes of God.[23]

Whether that inner transformation required human will or stemmed purely from God's gift of grace, whether it demanded a reform of Christian sacraments, whether transformation could be achieved within the existing ecclesiastical hierarchy—all these questions remained open. Luther and his followers formed but one faction in these debates, yet all parties to it described conversion along similar lines, as spiritual movement from a state of sin toward God through an inward revitalization of faith.[24] These notions of intrareligious conversion mobilized metaphors of space and movement along an axis drawn between the poles of salvation and damnation. But this conceptualization of space was one-dimensional, a single line drawn between God and the devil, heaven and hell; it was not yet drawn in physical space with two-dimensional territorial boundaries. That came with the shift toward an interreligious concept of conversion, itself the product of consolidated confessional institutions and territories.

Conversion as a Boundary Crossing

The early sixteenth-century model of conversion never disappeared entirely. Well into the eighteenth century, both Lutherans and Catholics continued to speak of the inner spiritual transformation of converts as a unilinear movement of the soul toward God. But over time, a different kind of spatialized language emerged, one that described conversion as the transgression of a confessional boundary in physical space, a border-crossing between territorially defined, rival religious communities. This territorialization of conversion discourse became ever more pronounced after the repeated attempts to consolidate the confessional landscape of the Holy Roman Empire, first in 1555 with the Peace of Augsburg and then again in 1648 with the Peace of Westphalia. As the dominant confessions began to coalesce in the empire and to clarify their boundaries, the space for alternative theological visions began to narrow, and the religious *Wildwuchs* of the early Reformation began to dry up. In its place arose three highly organized, hierarchically structured confessions, each with their own understandings of theological doctrine, religious practice, and ecclesiastical institutions. In the seventeenth and eighteenth centuries, the notion of *interreligious* conversion, infused with an explicitly territorial metaphorical language, became more prominent among Catholics and Lutherans. Increasingly, the spatial contours of conversion were mapped in two dimensions across the religiously diverse but territorially compartmentalized landscape of the Holy Roman Empire, Europe, and the globe.

This tendency highlighted, in turn, the degree to which the various Christian confessions had begun to see one another as irreconcilable enemies, separated by both theological and geopolitical boundaries. The confessions, in other words, were in the process of becoming *distinct and rival religions*, not merely alternative teachings that shared a common theological ground and institutional framework. To be sure, the confessions recognized aspects of similitude and even equivalence, but they did not see one another as equals. Each confession regarded the alternative Christian faiths as heretical, and the conditions of inclusion and exclusion grew more stringent in tandem with confessional differentiation.

The growing emphasis on conversion as boundary-crossing was linked to the consolidation of confessional authority in the Holy Roman Empire as cities and states institutionalized their choice either to adopt Protestant reform, to remain loyal to Rome, or in rare cases to formulate a multiconfessional compromise.[25] The changed meanings of conversion also drew upon the intellectual struggles of Catholics and Lutherans to comprehend European interactions with the non-European world in the early modern period. Specifically, theologians of all camps began drawing parallels between the confessional divisions within Christendom and their experience with non-Christian religions, including Islam and the various forms of paganism Europeans came into contact with as a result of colonial and commercial expansion. The meanings they ascribed to Germany's division into territorially distinct confessional blocs reflected the impact of cultural encounters that were unfolding on a global scale.

Just as late medieval concepts of conversion persisted long into the sixteenth century, these reimagined associations were not entirely new.[26] Since the 1520s, reformers and Catholic authors alike had deployed the indigenous peoples of the New World, Turkish "Mohammadans," and Jews living within the Latin West as foils to define their own sense of Christianity in opposition to a demonized religious Other. These non-Christian religions served as literary *topoi*, providing a range of protean cultural meanings during the Reformation. Islam and Judaism offered a set of readily available, preexisting stereotypes, which both Protestants and Catholics mobilized as fungible cultural signifiers against one another. The triangulated comparisons between Lutheranism, Catholicism, and various non-Christian religions resulted in a tendency to conflate inter-Christian confessional divisions at home with distinctions among the various religions around the world. In essence, the discourse of *interreligious* conversion *between* Lutheranism and Catholicism gained a discursive logic and acquired coherence as the two confessions institutionalized their mutual self-understandings as separate and distinct churches, and in turn conversion discourses reinforced this distinction through a series of textual comparisons and conflations that organized the conceptual relationships between Protestant and Catholic confessions and various non-Christian world religions.

Confessional polemics produced these conceptual relationships in part by defining Catholics and Lutherans as competitors for converts among non-Christians outside Europe. Missionary successes signified proof of superiority: as one anonymous Catholic author wrote in the late seventeenth century, "recently the conversion of pagans is authentic proof of the truth of Catholicism."[27] The author contrasted the successful Catholic missions with his Protestant rivals, declaring that "in contrast, not a single pagan village, let alone any countries, have been converted by Lutheran preachers."[28] By framing Lutheranism as a rival for pagan souls, the author ascribed to it a structural similarity with paganism as one religion among many, all competing with the one true religion. The author reinforced this parallelism by asserting that it was not only pagans who had converted, but also German elites, including territorial princes "[who] have left Lutheranism and other sects to become Catholic." To explain these converts from Protestantism, the author points to the persuasive force exerted by the fact that "only [the Catholic Church] has spread throughout the world" and that it "alone has converted the pagans."[29]

A sermon by Johann Bodler, published in 1683, likewise used Catholic global mission work as propaganda against Protestantism. The sermon distinguished between three groups: "unbelieving pagans" (*unglaubige Heyden*), the adherents of "obstinate false-believing [Christian] Sects" (*aigensinnig-mißglaubige Secten* and *mißglaubige Christen*), and "wicked Christians" (*glaubige* but *boßhaffte Christen*). All three risked damnation. In order to guide these people to the true faith, Bodler invoked the successful missions of Francis

Xavier, who arrived "among the pagans like a light in the dark night of the Orient." Xavier's pious work returned to the Occident, for through the example of his conversions abroad, "he brought many [Protestant] sectarians … to true knowledge" despite the entrenched errors of Luther and Calvin.[30] To be sure, Bodler acknowledges a civilizational boundary between Christianity and the pagan Other, whom he describes as "wild barbarians and brutes" (*wilde Barbaren und Unmenschen*).[31] Here, a secular notion of difference intrudes upon the primary difference rooted in religion that Bodler is trying to map. But despite the inferior qualities of pagans, Bodler believed that Francis Xavier's work had spread the truth across the world in an even and steady process of global conversion, like "a sun spreading its full brilliance from one end of the world to another, through so many lands."[32] The geography of Catholic conversion expanded with Xavier's own travels, which started in Europe and then proceeded "over the great ocean, to Africa to Goa, from there over Malaca to far off Japan and the city of Meacum, from there back again over the sea to the Chinese coast—in all, many hundreds and thousands of miles in addition to still many more travels."[33]

Xavier's territorial expansion of Catholicism is a recurring trope in Catholic literature. In 1787, for example, an anonymous Catholic polemic reported that "already in the year 1501, many years before there existed even a single Protestant Christian on God's earth, the Catholic religion was spread across both Indies by various monastic orders. After that time, specifically around the year 1540, after Luther and Calvin, along with their other associates, caused the greatest confusion in Germany, and led a great many into apostasy (*Abfall*) from the Catholic Church, the world-famous missionary, the saintly Franz Xavier from the Society of Jesus, was sent to the Indies and then to Japan by the pope, to preach the Gospels to the pagans and idol worshippers."[34] According to the text, Xavier had succeeded tremendously in acquiring converts: "Not only had he baptized with his own hands twelve kings and queens, but he also lit the light of true belief in entire principalities, entire kingdoms and empires." In such a territorialized missionary discourse, the boundaries may expand or contract, but the description of global conversions repeatedly drew sharp lines between the truth of Catholicism and the falsehood common to Protestantism and non-Christian religions. Such conversion narratives emphasized the boundaries of confessional inclusion and exclusion—who was "inside" and "outside" of the imagined religious community—rather than the process of an individual's movement toward salvation. The territoriality of this notion of conversion trumped the personal dimensions of changing faith; Xavier had, after all, not only baptized with his own hands individual kings and queens but, as the writer emphasizes, had converted entire principalities, kingdoms, and empires.

The author did not focus solely upon Francis Xavier; he also included a list of successful Catholic missions from all over the world, including Monomotapa, Brazil, Peru, New France, and the Philippines.[35] The text then lists various Protestant princes and dynasties of the Holy Roman Empire that converted from 1629 to 1707, when Elisabeth Christine of Braunschweig-Wolfenbüttel became Catholic in order to marry the future Emperor Charles VI. The author triumphantly declares that "the number of those who in various parts of the world have joined the Roman Catholic Church exceeds greatly the number who have left it in Europe. The city of God will never end, but wanders from one land and kingdom to another."[36] Thus the territorial gains made by Protestantism in Europe are reversed and trumped by the expansion of Catholicism around the world, as well as by key conversions at home. Such language clearly indicates the central role played by conversion in a Catholic discourse of geopolitical competition and dominance both in Europe and abroad. As represented in the flood of similar Catholic missionary texts, converts won at home and around the globe, regardless of their religion of origin, were visible proof that God favored the Roman Catholic Church as the one true faith.

Catholics, however, were not alone in their attempt to use the converted non-Christian as a sign of religious truth. Lutheran commentators also developed this strategy, albeit somewhat later than their Catholic counterparts. As noted above, the first generation of Lutheran reformers had already begun to collapse distinctions between their Catholic rivals and non-Christian religions in order to expose and condemn what they saw as papist heresy.[37] Early reformers readily compared the Catholic Church and its veneration of images to the stubborn Jews who clung to the empty formalism of the Old Law and to pagan idolaters of the New World.[38] And although the Catholic Church had earlier contacts outside Europe due to the early missionary work of Franciscans, Dominicans, and Jesuits, Lutherans also started to incorporate foreign missions into their polemical writings.

We can see growing concern over the struggle for non-Christian converts as early as 1618, when the Kempten preacher Georg Zeaeman wrote a sermon challenging Catholic claims to success in missionary work. Specifically, Zeaeman attacked Jesuit stories of miracles performed in the New World, which reportedly had encouraged multitudes of Native Americans to convert. Such miracles, Zeaeman charged, were the products of deception and manipulation: monks had rigged images of the saints so that they appeared to cry, and some had even made pacts with the devil and used black magic to fool the indigenous peoples.[39] According to Zeaeman, the Scriptures made clear that the Antichrist would lead people astray with false signs and miracles.[40] Those who succumbed to such diabolical trickery were therefore not true converts. While the Jesuits mobilized New World miracles and conversions as proof of Catholicism's truth, Zeaeman dismisses them both, since false miracles produced false conversions, which in fact proved that the Jesuits were the "servants of the Antichrist."[41]

Zeaeman's rhetoric was defensive, aiming to discredit Catholic missionary successes rather than promote a Lutheran project to convert non-Christians. But by the early eighteenth century, German Lutheranism began to express its own missionary consciousness with greater confidence, demonstrating that post-Reformation Lutherans also developed a territorially expansive concept of interreligious conversion. Like their Catholic counterparts, Lutherans articulated this territorialized dimension of conversion by triangulating relationships among Lutheranism, Catholicism, and other religions. One example comes from a Lutheran history published in Augsburg on the centennial of the Peace of Westphalia. Structured in a catechistic question-and-answer format, the text asks how Lutherans in Augsburg might help their coreligionists outside of the local community (in der Ferne) and advises the reader to aid the missions in India, to provide support for Jewish and Muslim converts, and to encourage the spread of Lutheranism among members of the Greek Orthodox Church.[42] Later, the text warns readers not to forget about their religious opponents (Religions-Gegentheil)—the Catholics. Lutherans should pray for Catholics and, whenever possible, guide them to the truth.[43] In terms of both the rhetorical structure of the text and its explicit content, the project of converting Catholics becomes indistinguishable from the conversion of Muslims, Jews, or even members of the Greek Orthodox Church.

This rhetoric of globalizing conversion efforts became more and more common in eighteenth-century Lutheran discourse. For example, in a prayer book published in Kempten in 1794, the "First Prayer in the Usual Early Bed Hour" makes explicit the global dimensions within which German Lutherans had come to think of conversion: "We ask you on behalf of all the people of the earth, let the light of truth shine over them, and teach them all to recognize yourself, the only true God, and the one you have sent, Jesus Christ. Destroy all unbelief and superstition, and let the true ... Christianity become ever more universal and potent."[44]

In their sermons and letters, the Lutheran clergy in Augsburg forged an imaginary link between converts won at home and those made through missionary work in India. In 1732, for example, they organized a collection in support of a Lutheran mission in Tharangambadi (Tranquebar), India. Months later, the pastors read to their parishioners the lengthy letter they had received from the missionaries, thanking them for their generous donation. The clergy wrote in response that God's power would prevail "against the great resistance of both the papists and the pagans."[45] Furthermore, the pastors wrote, they hoped that the missionaries in Tharangambadi would "rejoice with us here over the departure of many thousands of Salzburgers from papism."[46] Here the pastors were referring to the flight of the crypto-Lutheran Salzburgers, whom the archbishop of Salzburg had exiled from his territory in 1731–1732. Not only did the Augsburg pastors represent the Salzburgers as heroic converts who had defied papism; they also imagined a connection between the project of supporting the Salzburg immigrants at home with the conversion of pagans in India. Both were part of the unfolding of God's plan, in which "the Antichrist would be destroyed and our great Jesus would alone be honored in all lands."[47]

Such post-Reformation texts demonstrate the degree to which the meaning of "conversion" had shifted. The word still retained its medieval meaning of a movement toward God or union with the divine. A person could still have a conversion experience within one of the Christian confessions without adopting a new religion. But in general, Catholicism and the Protestant confessions had come to see one another as institutionally, theologically, and historically separate religions that occupied distinct terrains and territories, so much so that the difference between Protestant and Catholic marked a conceptual distance not unlike the one separating Christians from non-Christians. Consequently, individuals who moved from one Christian confession to another were portrayed as similar to converts from non-Christian religions. As the competing Christian confessions began to view themselves as distinct religions, the emphasis shifted from intrareligious to interreligious conversion. To convert meant to change religions and to cross a boundary defined by territorial, institutional, and doctrinal logics. When religious authors conflated the differences between the conversion of Christians belonging to heretical confessions and the conversion of Jews, Turks, and pagans, they inadvertently collapsed the absolute distinction between Christianity and non-Christian religions. Successful interreligious conversions became proof of divine sanction for Catholicism and Lutheranism alike. Consequently, the growing emphasis placed upon interreligious conversion—in the context of Christian confessions at home and other non-Christian religions around the world—reflected both the conceptual and institutional fragmentation of Christianity, even as it buttressed the reconsolidation of Christianity along sharp confessional divisions.

Notes

1. Johann Heinrich Zedler, *Grosses vollständiges Universal-Lexicon aller Wissenschafften und Künste, welche bishero durch menschlichen Verstand und Witz erfunden und verbessert worden*, 64 vols. (Leipzig and Halle, 1731–1754), vol. 3, col. 515, p. 261, Bayerische Staatsbibliothek Digitale Bibliothek, http://www.zedler-lexikon.de (accessed 25 January 2011). The passive voice of the phrase "zu GOtt bekehret wird" suggests a Pauline model of conversion initiated by God rather than the convert her- or himself.
2. Zedler, *Universal-Lexicon*, vol. 3, col. 516, p. 261.
3. Zedler, *Universal-Lexicon*, vol. 3, col. 517, p. 262. Protestants, especially Lutherans, were more inclined to claim that certain knowledge of one's salvation could be achieved through the powerful workings of faith, while Catholic theologians tended to doubt the possibility of absolute certainty in this matter.

4. Zedler, *Universal-Lexicon*, vol. 31, col. 523, p. 275. "Religions-Veränderung, Religions-Aenderung, *Mutatio Religionis* oder *Sacrorum*, ist, wenn jemand von einer Religion zur andern übertritt, und mit Verläugnung oder Abschwörung derjenigen, welcher er vorher zugethan gewesen, sich zu einer andern bekennet."

5. Zedler, *Universal-Lexicon*, vol. 31, col. 523, p. 275.

6. Zedler, *Universal-Lexicon*, vol. 31, col. 523, p. 275.

7. Karl F. Morrison, *Understanding Conversion* (Charlottesville, 1992), p. 186.

8. Bruce Hindmarsh, *The Evangelical Conversion Narrative: Spiritual Autobiography in Early Modern England* (Oxford, 2005), p. 23.

9. John F. Benton, ed. *Self and Society in Medieval France: The Memoirs of Abbot Guibert of Nogent* (Toronto, 1984).

10. Leonard P. Hindsley, "Monastic Conversion: The Case of Margaret Ebner," in James Muldoon, ed., *Varieties of Religious Conversion in the Middle Ages* (Gainesville, 1997), pp. 31–46.

11. Marilyn J. Harran offers an in-depth treatment of Luther's theology of conversion in *Luther on Conversion: The Early Years* (Ithaca, 1983). For an important theological intervention on Harran's work, see Jonathan D. Trigg, *Baptism in the Theology of Martin Luther* (Leiden, 1994), pp. 154–171.

12. Martin Luther, "Von der Bekehrung Pauli," in *Martin Luthers Werke. In einer das Bedürfniß der Zeit berücksichtigenden Auswahl*, vol. 9, 2nd ed. (Hamburg, 1828), p. 86.

13. Luther, "Von der Bekehrung Pauli," pp. 85–93.

14. Joachim Magdeburg, *Widerlegung, Des Grewlichen unnd Gottslesterlichen Papistischen Irthumbs, vom Merito Congrui, oder Freyen Willen, welchen nu die Synergisten mit ihrer Lehre von der mit Mithülffe des Menschen inn der Bekehrung als vom Todt widerumb aufferwecken, und in die Kirchen einfüren wollen* (Regensburg, 1566), p. H-iii, H-iv.

15. Magdeburg, *Widerlegung*, p. H-iv.

16. Winfried Zeller, ed., *Zwei nützliche Tractate, der erste von der Bekehrung des Menschen, der andere von der Armut des Geistes oder wahrer Gelassenheit (1570)* (Stuttgart–Bad Cannstatt, 1966), p. 9.

17. Zeller, *Zwei nützliche Tractate*, p. 10.

18. Johannes Mensing, *Bescheidt Ob der Glaube alleyn, on alle gute wercke dem menschen genug sey zur seligkeyt etc.* (n.p., 1528), p. 9-r.

19. Mensing, *Bescheidt*, p. 9-r. The biblical quote is Zechariah 1:3.

20. Mensing, *Bescheidt*, p. 9-r.

21. As Steven Ozment has noted, the reformers were "preoccupied far more with problems of continuity and order than with ways to bring about change." See Ozment, *Protestants: The Birth of a Revolution* (New York, 1991), p. 23. See also Bruce Gordon's "The Changing Face of Protestant History and Identity in the Sixteenth Century," in Bruce Gordon, ed., *Protestant History and Identity in Sixteenth-Century Europe*, vol. 2, *The Later Reformation* (Aldershot, 1996), pp. 1–22.

22. Franz Lau, "Anbruch und Wildwuchs der Reformation," in Franz Lau and Ernst Bizer, eds., *Reformationsgeschichte Deutschlands bis 1555*, 2nd ed. (Göttingen, 1969), pp. 17–43.

23. Scott Hendrix, "Rerooting the Faith: The Reformation as Re-Christianization," *American Society of Church History* 69, no. 3 (2000): 558–577.

24. As Andrew Pettegree points out, even an indoctrination tool like the catechism could experience its own *Wildwuchs*. Luther's *Deutsch Catechismus* and *Kleine Catechismus*

"stimulated an enormous outpouring of compositional energy, as local pastors through-out Germany turned their attention to the needs of their particular communities. This was laudatory, but risked a bewildering confusion of voices: at one point in the century, there were at least fifty catechisms circulating in the single city of Hamburg. The second half of the century brought an attempt to enforce greater uniformity by teaching only from Luther's Short Catechism, which thus acquired canonical status." Andrew Pettegree, *Reformation and the Culture of Persuasion* (Cambridge, 2005), p. 189.

25. On "confession building," see Ernst Walter Zeeden, *Die Entstehung der Konfessionen Grundlagen und Formen der Konfessionsbildung im Zeitalter der Glaubenskämpfe* (Munich, 1965) and *Konfessionsbildung: Studien zur Reformation, Gegenreformation und katholische Reform* (Stuttgart, 1985).

26. Carina L. Johnson, "Idolatrous Cultures and the Practice of Religion," in *Journal of the History of Ideas* 67 (2006): pp. 597–621; Thomas Kaufmann, "*Türckenbüchlein*": *Zur christlichen Wahrnehmung "türksicher Religion" in Spätmittelater und Reformation* (Göttingen, 2008); and Adam S. Francisco, *Martin Luther and Islam: A Study in Sixteenth-Century Polemics and Apologetics* (Leiden, 2007). Christine R. Johnson discusses the explosion in interest among German authors and readers with European expansion in *The German Discovery of the World: Renaissance Encounters with the Strange and Marvelous* (Charlottesville, 2009).

27. *Evangelischer Wanders-Mann, Aufzeichnend, Was Recht-glaubige Wanders-Leuth Auß der Irr-Glaubigen Predigen zu lehrnen haben, so wol zu Hauß, als draus, Lutherisch- als Catholischen, zu sicherm Nachricht, nutzlich, und lustig zu gebrauchen* (Augsburg, 1692), p. 258.

28. *Evangelischer Wanders-Mann*, p. 256.

29. *Evangelischer Wanders-Mann*, p. 261.

30. Johann Bodler, *Fest- und Feyr-täglicher Predigen CURS Als in einem Wett-Rennen zu dem Ring der glückseeligen Ewigkeit* (Dillingen, 1683), p. 563.

31. Bodler, *Fest- und Feyr-täglicher Predigen*, p. 564.

32. Bodler, *Fest- und Feyr-täglicher Predigen*, p. 567.

33. Bodler, *Fest- und Feyr-täglicher Predigen*, p. 567.

34. *Von merkwürdigen Bekehrungen zur katholischen Kirche, vom sechszehenten bis achtzehenten Jahrhundert; sammt einigen Grundsätzen, die für Rechtglaubigen sehr tröstlich sind,* in *Neueste Sammlung jener Schriften, die von einigen Jahren her über verschiedene wichtigste Gegenstände der Wahrheit im Drucke erschienen sind,* vol. 33 (Augsburg, 1787), pp. 11–12.

35. *Von merkwürdigen Bekehrungen zur katholischen Kirche*, p. 13.

36. *Von merkwürdigen Bekehrungen zur katholischen Kirche*, pp. 15–16.

37. Hendrix, "Rerooting the Faith," pp. 561–565.

38. Johnson, "Idolatrous Cultures," pp. 607–608.

39. Georgius Zeaeman, *Drey Evangelische Jubel- und Danckpredigen* (Kempten, 1618), pp. 102–103.

40. Zeaeman, *Drey Evangelische Jubel- und Danckpredigen*, p. 97.

41. Zeaeman, *Drey Evangelische Jubel- und Danckpredigen*, p. 105.

42. *Nöthiger und kurtzgefaßter Unterricht Theils von der Historie und Innhalt Des Auf einen dreyßig jährigen Krieg endlich in dem Jahre 1648. erfolgten und durch GOttes Gnade bereits hundert Jahre daurenden Westphälischen Friedens, Besonders auch zu Ansehung der hieran Theil nehmenden des H.R.R. Freyen Stadt Augspurg, Und der darinnen, Krafft solchen Friedens und dessen Executions-Recesses, auf immer vestgestellten Regiments-Paritaet:*

Theils von Christschuldiger Begehung Eines auf den 8ten August. 1748. als auf das ohnehin wegen dieses Friedens jährlich gewohnliche Evangelische Friedens-Fest Obrigkeitlich verordneten Hunderjährigen Jubel-Angedenckens zum Besten anderer, sonderlich der Lateinischen und Deutschen Schulen unsers Evangelischen Augspurgs, abgefasset (Augsburg, 1748), p. 58.

43. *Nöthiger und kurtzgefaßter Unterricht*, pp. 58–59.

44. *Handlungen und Gebete bey dem öffentlichen Gottesdienste der evangelisch lutherischen Gemeine in der Reichsstadt Kempten* (Kempten, 1794), p. 156.

45. St. Anna, Wesensarchiv, Fasz. 20, Sonderakten II, Nr. 10, Letter from the Lutheran clergy of Augsburg to missionaries in East India, 20 November 1732, in response to a letter from the missionaries on 15 October 1731.

46. St. Anna, Wesensarchiv, Fasz. 20, Sonderakten II, Nr. 10.

47. St. Anna, Wesensarchiv, Fasz. 20, Sonderakten II, Nr. 10.

CHAPTER TWO

Conversion Concepts in Early Modern Germany
Protestant and Catholic

ERIC-OLIVER MADER

Conversion Research

Religious conversion has emerged as an attractive field for historical research. In the last few years, the number of articles, special periodical issues, research projects, monographs, and conferences has increased significantly, opening up whole new areas to historical research on the early modern period. Historians interested in conversion have been developing new concepts and methods in discussion with other disciplines. The most current research has adopted a critical stance toward the older tradition of conversion historiography, which approached the subject with confessional biases or focused on prominent cases, asking only whether conversion was motivated primarily by religion or politics. Taking a quite different approach, current researchers look at conversion in its more complex cultural and social contexts and conceive of it as a process of interaction, considering the convert as both an object of ministration and a subject making his or her own decisions.[1]

Methodologically, current historical research draws on debates among sociologists and psychologists about how to conceptualize conversion while also utilizing approaches associated with the "New Cultural History."[2] While sociological research has proved helpful for analyzing the process of religious decision-making, the cultural history approach reminds us to keep the broad field of political, social, and cultural contexts in mind when researching religious turns. Among the many new aspects of the subject that have been considered are issues of social and geographic mobility, confessional indifference, and the construction of conversion narratives.[3] Many researchers have taken up issues of gender and other social categories in order to grasp how various religious and confessional understandings of the very nature of conversion differentiate people socially and culturally. Studies have also examined conversions over long time spans and, in the context of "New World History," cross-cultural exchange and syncretism.[4]

We begin by exploring the conceptual categories used to understand early modern conversion. While we do not know a great deal about how contemporaries understood conversion, reconstructing the divergent meanings of conversion as they existed in the early modern period will help delineate specific confessional profiles. This essay seeks to understand why Catholicism attracted German Protestants, other Europeans, and non-Europeans between 1550 and 1750.

Early Modern Conversion Concepts

The arguments produced by Ute Mennecke-Haustein, Laetitia Boehm, and some of the contributors to the recently published volume *Konversion und Konfession in der Frühen Neuzeit* (Conversion and Confession in the Early Modern Period) are particularly important to this discussion of the early modern understanding of conversion.[5] In their discussion, these scholars have pointed to a fundamental change in the understanding of conversion from the medieval notion of *"conversio."* Most of the other work on the subject has sought to map the interpretations of the different confessions, although attention has been mostly drawn to Catholic ideas, while research on Lutheran and Calvinist conceptions remains sparse.[6]

The scholarship on *conversio* indicates that in the medieval period, the term described the free decision to enter a monastery or the conversion of pagans or heretics. With the Reformation and the new confessions, however, *conversio* informed the notion of a new type of convert. Luther and other monks who left monasteries offer an example of how conversion operated in a transformed context. There were also lay humanists like Melanchthon or Calvin, who experienced the Reformation as *conversio*, a fundamental change based on religious insights and demanding new forms of conduct.[7] After the Council of Trent, the wave of conversions unleashed by the Reformation led to a countermovement—a phase of return to Catholicism by first-generation reformers like Valentin Paceus and Georg Witzel. In some of the recent studies, they count as the first early modern converts, although such an interpretation fails to make an intrinsic connection between conversion and confession.[8]

Other scholars focus on the return of theologians like Friedrich Staphylus or Martin Eisengrein, who worked at the Jesuit University of Ingolstadt and were connected to Peter Canisius; for these authors, these were the first real converts.[9] Because the post-Tridentine Catholic campaign to turn the tide of

Protestantism succeeded in returning princesses and princes, scholars, politicians, and subjects in Bohemia, the Holy Roman Empire, Hungary, Poland, and France to Catholicism, historians have called the seventeenth century the age of conversion.[10] Since these conversions appeared at the same time that confessional identities were forming, they are interpreted largely in terms of confessional change. Such a position assumes that confessional identities were already fixed and that confession is central to the notion of conversion. Indeed, the mantra has emerged: "without confession no conversion."[11] This interpretation also assumes that contemporaries were incapable of perceiving the new type of confessional conversion and still appealed to the medieval notions of "*Bekehrung*" (turning, conversion) from "heretical apostasy." Only by the end of eighteenth century is this supposed to have changed, with the entry of the notion "*Konvertit*," derived from the English word "convert," into the German religious vocabulary to denote the change of confessional affiliation.[12]

Conversio in Protestant and Catholic Contexts

The master narrative that has now come to dominate discussion takes sources from the mid sixteenth century as its touchstone and relies on the "confessional paradigm" developed in the 1990s. But the paradigm can be criticized on several grounds. First of all, it seems presumptuous to utilize a twentieth-century construction of confession as the criterion for "conversion" in a proper sense. This anachronism restricts the broad semantic field of early modern notions of conversion. Indeed, it poses problems for explaining inner-confessional conversions and—as recent studies have even done—leads to the conclusion that founders of religions could not be counted as converts. Another problem with tying conversion to confession is accounting for religious reorientations experienced as *confessio* by individuals such as Johann of Nassau-Hadamar, who turned from Calvinism to Catholicism in Vienna in 1629. His confession to Catholicism was characterized by deep insight into theological controversy even as it was still based on specifically Calvinist interpretations of belief.[13] This problem of interpretation can perhaps be solved by differentiating between individual levels of confession on the one hand and confession as a normative, official set of beliefs on the other. Nonetheless, the prescribed concept leaves other early modern notions of conversion, such as those marked by political or juridical concerns, unconsidered. When contemporaries referred to the effects that ruling princes' conversions had on the constitution of the Holy Roman Empire or on their lands, they spoke about "*Religionsänderung*" (change of religion) or "*mutatio religionis*" rather than about "conversion."[14]

In the following discussion, I do not want to pursue these problems or explore the broad semantic field of "*conversio*" in early modern Germany but will rather focus on the close connection between contemporary understandings of conversion and ideas of (re)turning to God (*Bekehrung*), mission, and heretical apostasy.

Conversio ad deum / Conversion of a Sinner

In Lutheran dogmatic theological tracts, the discourse about "turning to God" is omnipresent, the two key terms being *Bekehrung* in German and *conversio* in Latin texts.[15] However, in most of the Protestant treatises a semantic field underlies these notions; taken from Scripture, it combines theological concepts of sin and repentance. Johannes Musaeus, for example, interpreted "conversio" in the context of the Old Testament Hebrew word שוב (shub) and the New Testament Greek word μετάνοια (metanoia). Each indicates a slightly different path sinners can take in returning to God.[16] In his Wittenberg disputation dealing with the connection between free will and conversion, Johann Lucius from Dresden tied "conversion" to the idea of spiritual renascence or the regeneration of a sinner toward God.[17] Both the ideas of regeneration and movement toward God were widely held concepts throughout the eighteenth century, and they can still be found in theological encyclopedias of recent times.[18]

Early modern Lutheran dogma distinguished two ways to process a conversion: "transitive" and "intransitive." While the transitive "conversio" of a sinner was understood as a conversion effected directly by God and performed suddenly, the intransitive type was conceptualized as a process.[19] For the discussion here, the intransitive conversion of a sinner is the most interesting, since this was a pattern often displayed in concrete conversion processes. An excellent example is Count Johann of Nassau-Saarbrücken-Idstein's reaction to the conversion of his son Gustav Adolph to Catholicism. Extremely angry about the turn to Catholicism under the influence of two Jesuits and the Elector Philipp of Schönborn in Regensburg in 1653, Johann wrote two letters, which later were published. Reviling his son for leaving the true Lutheran religion "in a dishonorable, frivolous, and self-perjuring manner" and calling him a victim of Jesuit traitors and the devil, he expressed the hope that God would make his son suffer from his state of sin, presuming that this would be the only way to redirect him to Lutheranism and salvation:

> And because I now see that all my honest and heart-felt fatherly admonitions to you were of no avail, I therefore surrender you to the judgment of God and bid Him fervently to give the Devil power over you so that ... like the incestuous pervert (*Blutschänder*) whom Paul surrendered to Satan your flesh will be tortured and your body chastised so that your soul may yet be saved. But should you still not wish to turn (*kehren*) yourself then let [your soul] revert to the eternal court of God, which will surely give you your due.[20]

A closer look at the intransitive concept in Lutheran dogmatics shows it to have been deeply tied to the Lutheran theology of grace. Conversion was thought to be effected by God, who through the medium of the Holy Spirit transmits his grace to the heart or soul of a sinner, thus creating the insight that sin is a painful state.[21] To put this in more concrete terms: to perform a conversion, the Holy Spirit first has to affect the soul of the sinner in such a way as to induce insight into his sins. The sinner begins to suffer but also to develop confidence in the grace of God, which open up the possibility of escaping the state of sin through penance and contrition. The phrase "confidence in the grace of God" is important as a link to the Lutheran concept of grace and to Luther's answer to the central question: How do I obtain a gracious God? Indeed, as Luther argued against Erasmus, human will plays no part in God's decision to give or to withhold his grace.[22]

In 1567 the Jesuit Eduard Thorn became a Lutheran, receiving a stipend at Lauingen in the county of Pfalz-Neuburg. His apology shows how the Lutheran conception was spelled out in a concrete case. To confirm his turn to Lutheranism, Thorn had to give answers to a list of questions. He had to admit that from the bottom of his heart he felt the errors he lived in while he was a Jesuit. He also had to confess that he was enlightened by the grace of God, which gave him insight into both the religious errors committed as a Jesuit and the acceptance of the true words written in the Holy Scripture. Thorn's response to the fourth question, on how a human being attains redemption, directly appeals to the Lutheran conversion concept: humans achieve forgiveness not through works or merit but solely through faith from the sheer grace and mercy of God by means of the singular obedience and merit of Jesus Christ.[23]

"Fiducia," or faith, in God's grace is a necessary element in a Lutheran understanding for an ongoing conversion. Contemporaries would brand those lacking faith as "*verstockt*"—obdurate—a term indicating a human being's inability to gain insight into his or her painful state of sin and thus his or her inability to convert.[24] Turned the other way round, the conversion process starts at the moment the sinner, through divine intervention, realizes his painful state of sin. There were disputes about whether this was the point (*terminus a quo*) at which conversion starts, with some authors seeing the beginning of conversion as an act initiated when the sinner shows remorse (*Reue*). And there was also the problem of whether the process of "conversion" should be conceptualized as a steady process of repentance. Considerable intra-Protestant debate was devoted to the part human volition plays within the conversion process. Despite prominent quarrels, such as that over "synergism" between Flacius Illyricus and his school and critics like Christoph Lasius, Victorin Strigel, and Johann Pfeffinger in the sixteenth century, the Protestant concept of "conversion" was completely different from the Catholic.[25]

Both Lutheran and Catholic theologians marked this difference. François de Coster, a Catholic controversialist and professor at the Jesuit University of Cologne, put it this way:

> But with regard to the inner condition of the man who is just before God, they [the Lutherans] cannot agree with us. For they do not accept that through justification man can be truly justified in his soul but [believe that] by a cloak draped upon him [man] only seems pure, whole, and pious while he is inwardly no less abominable, somnolent, and godless than he was before justification. However Catholic faith teaches us, true to Holy Scripture that a justified man is no longer turned away from God but toward Him and clings to Him through inner will and love.... Because justification alters the will of the sinner, he looks toward God, converts (*bekehret*) to God, and is inwardly transformed: from which results a most admirable beauty in the soul.[26]

Johann Lucius, the Wittenberg disputant, arguing against François de Coster and Robert Bellarmine, strikingly pointed out that Catholics do not view "conversion" as illumination of the human spirit or correction of human will or human heart.[27] They believe that human beings are naturally inhabited by a light originally received from God and therefore are able to recognize the mysteries of true belief and with an innate dynamic potential can adopt or reject true Christian faith.[28]

For Reformed Protestants, the idea of conversion was bound up with John Calvin's doctrine of predestination. Defined as "the eternal decree of God by which He has determined in Himself what He willed to become of each man," predestination implies a twofold decree of the election unto holiness and salvation and of reprobation unto death on account of sin and guilt. This doctrine affirms the total passiveness of man, who is neither able to freely consent nor to resist God's election or reprobation: "The counsel of God, as far as it concerns the elect, is founded on his gratuitous mercy, totally irrespective of human merit; but to those whom he devotes to condemnation the gate of life is closed by a just and irreprehensible, though incomprehensible judgment." Consequently, conversion is not understood as an act of human volition but of God's grace.[29]

Man's passiveness was also stressed by later Calvinist federal theologians and perhaps most prominently expressed by Johannes Coccejus (1603–1669). In his *Summa Theologiae*, Coccejus conceived of predestination as a subcategory under the doctrine of divine decrees, which included both God's decree to show grace to some and his decree to leave others under wrath. Thus the reprobate is included in God's providence, by which he sustains his creation and the world. The reprobate lives under God's goodness but falls outside the grace of the Redeemer. Coccejus, like other federalists, thought that a fallen sinner is chosen *through* Christ. This, however, does not mean that he is chosen *on account of* Christ. The ground of election is rather God's eternal good-pleasure.

The elect are chosen, not predestined, in Christ, but still a determined number of the elect are known from eternity. Moreover it is the Father who, in his sovereign determination, decides to save miserable sinners through Christ.[30]

Conversion and Mission

Putting the Calvinist and Lutheran positions aside and concentrating on the fundamental dissimilarity of Protestant and Catholic conceptions, one could say that Protestants viewed a convert rather as a passive object driven by immediate or intermediate intervention or predestination of God, while Catholics stressed the role played by human intellect and will. In other words, in the Catholic view *conversio* was something in which human will had a part, whereas for Protestants it tended to remain an act of God. Consequently, a proper conversion to Catholicism could occur when the convert came to the decision that the Roman Catholic Church offered the most convincing arguments that it was the legitimate church of Christ. Indeed, many examples of intellectual conversions to Catholicism occurred not only among scholars like Christoph Besold, Lukas Holstenius, and Nils Stenson, but also among princes like Jakob III of Baden-Hachberg or, outside Germany, Queen Christina of Sweden.[31]

Even further, it seems to be not by accident that early modern Catholicism developed rather strong missionary activity all around the globe and that conversions in the seventeenth century were predominantly Catholic. Mission policy—in contemporary terms, the "methods to gain converts"—were theoretically spelled out in political and theological tracts, institutionally backed up in the Congregation for Propagating the Faith (established in 1622), and carried out by members of the new religious orders, Catholic princes, their advisors, and finally by such converts as members of the Pfalz-Neuburg dynasty and the many scholars who reverted to the Church.[32]

Catholic intellectuals developed a wide range of strategies to achieve conversion, and many of them, such as Molanus, Bellarmine, and perhaps most elaborately, Gabriele Paleotti, developed theories of visual persuasion.[33] To regain heretical Germany, Minuccio Minucci, adviser to Wilhelm V of Bavaria and foreign policy expert at the German Congregation of the Holy See founded by Pope Gregory XIII in 1572, thought the key strategy would be to convert the princes. Here he had recourse to the principle of *cuius regio eius religio* from the Peace of Augsburg in 1555. The point was to acquire princes not only as individual converts, but also as protagonists to help multiply the process of reconversion to Roman Catholicism. Princes should recatholicize their own territories. By inciting members of their families as well as other princes to adopt the true faith, one hoped to create a domino effect that would lead to the conversion of Germany as whole.[34]

In his *Ten Books on Politics*, the Jesuit Adam Contzen, confessor of Count Palatine Maximilian of Bavaria, developed a more concrete method to convert heretics all over Europe. He mixed softer and stronger versions of persuasion, pointing for example to the role that "musica pia" could play for a conversion, but he also did not refrain from advising the forcible conversion of subjects.[35] In his *Relationi Universali*, the Italian ex-Jesuit Giovanni Botero expressed the hope of regaining heretically infected Germany, pointing to the achievements of the Jesuit fathers. The Jesuits, he suggested, tried to convert the hearts of the people not through violence but by preaching truth, engaging in disputation, expounding the catechism, and supervising minds in schools, colleges, and seminaries.[36] But Botero also observed the status of the Christian religion on a worldwide level and pointed to conversions throughout all parts of the world. Meanwhile a lively publication of tracts examined mission activity in different regions of the world.[37]

Contemporaries already recognized the fact that these kinds of activity, reflection, and organization could not be observed within early modern Protestantism. Catholic tracts opposing heresy bolstered the idea of Roman Catholicism as the only true church by pointing to the lack of missionary success among Protestants. The very idea of a world community developed as one of the criteria of the true church, and Catholic apologists found one sign of Lutheran, Calvinist, Anabaptist, and Donatist heresy to be their restriction to particular regions or countries.[38]

Arguing against the Lutheran controversialist Andreas Osiander, the Jesuit hardliner Georg Scherer pointed in this same direction:

> Verily, in fifteen hundred years' time not one heathen emperor or empress, king or queen, prince or princess, has allowed himself to be baptized by you or has turned to you in matters of faith as even today none do. But in our own time, many idolatrous and heathen kings and princes have converted and still do turn toward our Catholic religion, specifically those of Japan, Peru, and India, for only in the year just passed the respectable and most powerful king and princes in Japan have sent their legates to Rome and the Apostolic See as a sign and proof of their obedience and subservience toward the Roman church.[39]

Indeed, Lutherans hardly reflected upon how to incite conversions, and they built no institutions with a missionary impulse. Certainly they stressed reading the Bible and preaching for access to religious truth. In the Formula of Concord— accepted by three electors, twenty dukes and princes, twenty-four counts, four barons, thirty-five free imperial cities, and over eight thousand pastors—preaching from the Bible was understood as the prime medium for conversion.[40]

Lutherans also pointed to the role of religious disputations and private discussion in persuading heretics. Apart from trying to achieve conversions of Jews and a few remarks that can be found in Lutheran literature on this idea, systematic missionary activity equal to the Catholic conversion offensive after the Council of Trent did not develop until the Danish-Pietistic mission in Tharangambadi (Tranquebar) at the beginning of eighteenth century.[41] It underlines the argument that one of the reasons for the differences in the seventeenth century may well have had to do with how "conversion" was conceived. Eighteenth-century Lutheran missionary activity represented a new conceptualization of conversion arising within Pietism, which emphasized subjectivity, individual religious experience, and human volition.[42]

Conversion and Heresy/Apostasy

"*Conversio*" could indicate both apostasy and heresy, in the sense of either turning away from true belief or returning to the true faith. Within Protestant traditions, aggressive insults were leveled at those who left the Protestant fold. In the sixteenth century, converts like Staphylus, Valentin Paceus, and Stephanus Agricola were derided as "Mamlukes," "Jewish Cattle," "weathercocks," and "tottering pipes." Converts were also perceived as victims of crass manipulation or even as unwitting tools of the "devil."[43] Protestant controversialists held that salvation could be achieved only within the Protestant confession, while apostates, having turned to the state of sin, would lose salvation and could regain it only through a reconversion. We have seen this view expressed in the reaction of Johann of Nassau-Saarbrücken, but it was typical of Protestant polemic aimed at other princely converts to Catholicism in seventeenth-century Germany.[44]

In the first half of the seventeenth century, however, the hotly disputed idea arose in unionist circles that salvation could be achieved within all Christian confessions. Although the influential Helmstedt professor Georg Calixt did not wish to imply approval for conversions to Catholicism, he did stress that within all Christian confessions, someone unaware of confessional issues could be redeemed. In the theological understanding of heresy and apostasy, Calixt shook up the categories by making the issue of religious consciousness explicit. For many converts to Catholicism, however, such an idea was a central motive arguing in favor of conversion. Some fifty years later, Protestant professors at Helmstedt went even further, allowing conversion to Catholicism under special circumstances. The matter came up with the conversion of the fiancée of the Holy Roman Emperor, Elisabeth Christine of Braunschweig-Wolfenbüttel.[45] What is interesting for our discussion is that Helmstedt professors held it for a fact that Catholicism and Protestantism share all essential issues of belief. To make sure that Elisabeth Christine would not lose her salvation, some supposed she would only have to concentrate on central issues of belief and to refrain from Catholic errors. Distinguishing between *adiaphora*[46] and essential articles of faith was a tried and true method in Protestant theology. Until the eighteenth century, however, no one had struck upon the idea of turning this argument upside down and justifying a conversion to Catholicism by accepting errors in adiaphora. This indeed implies a completely different conception of conversion—a conception where the idea of heresy is reduced to Catholic errors in adiaphora.

While such ideas in the long run tended to undermine the Protestant confessional profile and shift the weight of apostasy in the conceptualization of conversion, Catholics continued to maintain that belonging to the Catholic Church would be the only way to earn salvation. Consequently, every form of Christian confession formulated outside official Catholicism would count as heresy. Theologians never tired of drawing up catalogues to define different types of heresies, including all the reforming sects turning up since the fifteenth century as well as the older Christian schisms.[47] Heresy or apostasy, caused by a loss of authority, was treated as a disease metastasizing like a cancer. Reestablishment of the authority of the Church was necessary to heal it.

The Inquisition was established to ensure purity of belief, and it possessed the authority to absolve heretics and reincorporate them into the Catholic Church. In practice, however, the ability to absolve heretics, i.e., to reincorporate converts to Catholicism, was given as well to the religious orders, cardinals, and bishops. The formal status of a heretic as well as the formal process of conversion were and still are prescribed by canon law.[48] Conversion here indicates a gradual process of turning back to the Catholic Church that finally leads to the formal reception of a convert. Canon law therefore demands the recognition of the Catholic confession of faith, the seven sacraments, and the pope as head of the Church, as well as an abjuration from heresy, which in seventeenth-century practice was not always performed. Those already baptized were to be supervised in Catholic catechism before receiving their reception, the catechism of Peter Canisius being the most often used. In official Catholicism, conversion from the Catholic Church to other religions or confessions is still treated as heresy and not brought under a neutral idea of conversion. This means that a heretic remains, within certain boundaries, part of the Catholic Church—according to canon law it is impossible to leave it. This implies that Catholicism only recognizes the return of heretics or conversion of pagans to Catholicism and continues to claim to be the sole representation of true Christianity. Against this background it is hardly surprising that Catholics answered Protestant irenicism in terms of a politics of conversion.

Conclusion

As I have tried to show, Catholic and Protestant conversion concepts can be distinguished within three different contexts. Catholics conceived conversion as something that can be effected by men, while Protestants referred to God's direct intervention as an element necessary for a sinner to experience a conversion. This might have been one of the reasons for the development of divergent policies of missionary activity emerging within Lutheran and Catholic milieus. While Catholics developed a theoretically reflective and institutionally buttressed missionary activity in the sixteenth and seventeenth centuries, such efforts were almost fully lacking among Lutherans until the beginning of eighteenth century. Examining *"conversio"* as spelled out within the scheme of heresy and apostasy, we have seen that Catholicism claimed the monopoly of representing true Christianity. Lutherans, however, developed ideas that held it possible to achieve salvation within all Christian religions and under certain circumstances even allowed conversions to the Catholic Church. Such ideas, which tended to undermine confessional differences, seem also to have paved the way for a neutral understanding of conversion as a mere change of confessional affiliation.

Both forceful Catholic missionary activity since the second half of sixteenth century and irenic ideas as pursued by Protestants beginning in the mid seventeenth century are important factors that explain the success of early modern Catholicism. This attraction was expressed in a wave of conversions to the Roman Catholic Church, observable not only among German Protestant princes but also among scholars, political advisors, and even theologians. The wave of reconversion to Catholicism had enormous impact on early modern Germany. It changed the country's confessional map, since Catholic princes' turns to Catholicism brought the Counter-Reformation to the territories of the Pfalz-Neuburg dynasty and of Nassau-Siegen. Furthermore, it affected the confessional balance in the Holy Roman Empire and thus the basis of its complex constitutional system. When August of Saxony, for example, turned Catholic to attain the crown of Poland, an absurd situation occurred at the Imperial Diet in Regensburg: the "Corpus evangelicorum" had a Catholic head. Finally—and far beyond implications for the Holy Roman Empire—the fact that early modern Catholicism gained converts all over the globe while Protestantism had only partial international success seems to have been due to a prior conception of conversion that took human participation into account and was oriented toward effecting religious "turns" through persuasion and intellectual insight.

Notes

1. Recent publications devoted to the subject of conversion include a special issue (vol. 15, no. 2) of the journal *Aschkenas: Zeitschrift für Geschichte und Kultur der Juden* (2005), edited by Jutta Braden and Rotraud Ries; a special issue (vol. 7, no. 2) of the *Wiener Zeitschrift zur Geschichte der Neuzeit* (2007), edited by Marlene Kurz and Thomas Winkelbauer, entitled "Juden—Christen—Juden-Christen: Konversionen in

der Frühen Neuzeit"; and a special issue (vol. 15, no. 1) of *Historische Anthropologie* (2007), edited by Ute Luig and Edith Saurer. Recent books, chapters, and articles on the topic include Duane J. Corpis, "Mapping the Boundaries of Confession: Space and Urban Religious Life in the Diocese of Augsburg, 1648–1750," in Will Coster and Andrew Spicer, eds., *Sacred Space in Early Modern Europe* (Cambridge, 2005), pp. 302–325; Jörg Deventer, "Zu Rom übergehen: Konversion als Entscheidungshandeln und Handlungsstrategie. Ein Versuch," in Rudolf Leeb et al. (eds), *Staatsmacht und Seelenheil: Gegenreformation und Geheimprotestantismus in der Habsburgermonarchie* (Vienna, 2007), pp. 168–180; Frauke Volkland, *Konfession und Selbstverständnis: Reformierte Rituale in der gemischtkonfessionellen Kleinstadt Bischofszell im 17. Jahrhundert* (Göttingen, 2005); Heike Bock, *Konversionen in der frühneuzeitlichen Eidgenossenschaft: Zürich und Luzern im konfessionellen Vergleich* (Epfendorf, 2009); Jan N. Bremmer et al., eds., *Cultures of Conversions* (Louvain, 2006); Jan N. Bremmer et al., eds., *Paradigms, Poetics and Politics of Conversion* (Louvain, 2006); and Ute Lotz-Heumann et al., eds., *Konversion und Konfession in der Frühen Neuzeit* (Gütersloh, 2007). Classic works on conversion include Friedrich Wilhelm von Ammon, ed., *Gallerie der denkwürdigsten Personen, welche im XVI., XVII. und XVIII. Jahrhunderte von der evangelischen zur katholischen Kirche übergetreten sind* (Erlangen, 1833); and Andreas Räss, *Die Convertiten seit der Reformation nach ihrem Leben und aus ihren Schriften dargestellt*, 13 vols. (Freiburg, 1866–1880).

2. Monika Wohlraab-Sahr, "Religiöse Bekehrung in soziologischer Perspektive: Themen, Schwerpunkte und Fragestellungen der gegenwärtigen relgionssoziologischen Konversionsforschung," in Hubert Knoblauch, Volkhard Krech, and Monika Wohlrab-Sahr, eds., *Religiöse Konversionen. Systematische und fallorientierte Studien in soziologischer Perspektive* (Konstanz, 1998), pp. 7–43; Steve Bruce, "Sociology of Conversion: The Last Twenty-Five Years," in Bremmer et al., *Paradigms, Poetics and Politics*, pp. 1–12; Detlef Pollack, "Überlegungen zum Begriff und Phänomen der Konversion aus religionssoziologischer Perspektive," in Lotz-Heumann et al., *Konversion und Konfession*, pp. 33–58. On the "new cultural history," see Rudolf Vierhaus, "Die Rekonstruktion historischer Lebenswelten: Probleme moderner Kulturgeschichtsschreibung," in Hartmut Lehmann, ed., *Wege zu einer neuen Kulturgeschichte* (Göttingen, 1995) pp. 7–28; Ute Daniel, *Compendium Kulturgeschichte: Theorien, Praxis, Schlüsselwörter* (Frankfurt, 2001). For a recent overview, see Stefan Jordan, *Theorien und Methoden der Geschichtswissenschaft* (Paderborn, 2009), pp. 148–213.

3. Alexander Schunka, *Gäste, die bleiben: Zuwanderer in Kursachsen und der Oberlausitz im 17. und frühen 18. Jahrhundert* (Münster, 2006), pp. 308–351; Ricarda Matheus, "Mobilität und Konversion. Überlegungen aus römischer Perspektive," *Quellen und Forschungen aus italienischen Archiven und Bibliotheken* 85 (2005): 170–213; Kim Siebenhüner, "Glaubenswechsel in der Frühen Neuzeit. Chancen und Tendenzen einer historischen Konversionsforschung," *Zeitschrift für Historische Forschung* 34, no. 2 (2007): 243–272; Eric-Oliver Mader, "Fürstenkonversionen zum Katholizismus in Mitteleuropa im 17. Jahrhundert: Ein systematischer Ansatz in fallorientierter Perspektive," *Zeitschrift für Historische Forschung* 34 no. 3 (2007): 403–440; Kim Siebenhüner, "Conversion, Mobility and the Roman Inquisition in Italy around 1600," *Past & Present* 200 (2008): 5–35.

4. Friedrich Niewöhner and Fidel Rädle, eds., *Konversionen im Mittelalter und in der Frühneuzeit* (Hildesheim, 1999); Kenneth Mills and Anthony Grafton, eds., *Conversion: Old Worlds and New* (Rochester, 2003).

5. Ute Mennecke-Haustein, "Konversionen," in Wolfgang Reinhard and Heinz Schilling, eds., *Die katholische Konfessionalisierung* (Gütersloh, 1995), pp. 242–257; Dieter Breuer, "Konversionen im konfessionellen Zeitalter," in Niewöhner and Rädle, *Konversionen im Mittelalter*, pp. 59–69, here p. 60; Laetitia Böhm, "Konversion. Einige historische Aspekte aus der christlichen Frömmigkeitsgeschichte mit Beispielen von Professoren der alten Universität Ingolstadt," in Klaus Krämer and Ansgar Paus, eds., *Die Weite des Mysteriums: Christliche Identität im Dialog* (Freiburg, 2000), pp. 522–548; Ute Lotz-Heumann, Jan-Friedrich Mißfelder, and Matthias Pohlig, "Konversion und Konfession," in Lotz-Heumann, Jan-Friedrich Mißfelder, and Matthias Pohlig, *Konversion und Konfession* (Gütersloh, 2007) pp. 11–32.

6. Ute Mennecke-Haustein, "Die Konversion des Friedrich Staphylus (1512–1564) zum Katholizismus—eine *conversio?*," in Niewöhner and Radle, *Konversionen*, pp. 71–84.

7. Johannes Schilling, *Gewesene Mönche. Lebensgeschichten in der Reformation* (Munich, 1990).

8. G. L. Schmidt, *Georg Witzel, ein Altkatholik des XVI. Jahrhunderts* (Vienna, 1876); Barbara Henze, *Aus Liebe zur Kirche—Reform: Die Bemühungen Georg Witzels (1501–1573) um die Einheit der Kirche* (Münster, 1995); H. G. Voigt, "Valentin Paceus: Seine Entwicklung vom protestantischen Führer zum altgläubigen Konvertiten," *Zeitschrift des Vereins für Kirchengeschichte der Provinz Sachsen* 22 (1926): 1–25; Werner Kathrein et al., eds., *Im Dienst um die Einheit und die Reform der Kirche: Zum Leben und Werk Georg Witzels* (Frankfurt, 2003).

9. Ute Mennecke-Haustein, *Conversio ad ecclesiam: Der Weg des Friedrich Staphylus zurück zur vortridentinischen katholischen Kirche* (Heidelberg, 2003).

10. Hans Schmidt, "Konversion und Säkularisation als politische Waffe am Ausgang des konfessionellen Zeitalters. Neue Quellen zur Politik des Herzogs Ernst August von Hannover am Vorabend des Friedens von Nymwegen," in *Francia* 5 (1977): 183–230; Breuer, "Konversionen im konfessionellen Zeitalter."

11. Lotz-Heumann, "Konversion und Konfession," p. 15.

12. Mennecke-Haustein, "Konversionen."

13. Michel Walter, "Die Konversion des Grafen Johann Ludwig von Nassau-Hadamar im Jahre 1629," *Archiv für Mittelrheinische Kirchengeschichte* 20 (1968): 71–102.

14. Johann Stephan Pütter, *Historische Entwickelung der heutigen Staatsverfassung des teutschen Reichs*, 3 vols. (Göttingen, 1786–1787), vol. 2, pp. 334–356.

15. See for example Daniel Cothenius, *Disputatio Catech. XVIII. De Poenitentia seu Conversione Hominis peccatoris ad Deum, ejusque partibus ... Sub praesidio Reverendi & clarissimi viri Dn. Davidis Rungii SS Theologiae doctoris et Proefessoris Wittebergensi publici...* (Wittenberg, 1602); Johann Lucius, *Disputatio de arbitrii servitute circa conversionem hominis, aliosque actus spirituales, in inclyta Witteberg. Academia ad disputandum proposita sub Praesidio Balth. Meisneri...* (Dresden and Wittenberg, 1615); Johannes Musaeus, *De Conversione Hominis Peccatoris ad Deum Tractatus Theologicus quo de Conversionis appelationibus, natura, actibus, & speciatim de actibus fidei...* (Jena, 1659); Johannes Hulsemann, *Disputatio Theologica de vocatorum conversione per poenitentiam, quam in collegio Theologico publice aperto...* (Leipzig, 1706); Johannes Fridericus Eichfeld, *De Ordine Modoque Gratiae Divinae in Conversione Hominis Occupatae Aphorismi Theologici ... Praeside Johanne Fechtio* (Rostock, n.d.).

16. Musaeus, *De Conversione Hominis Peccatoris*, Disp. I, Cap. I.: "De voce Conversionis & Verbo Ebraeo בוש." I thank Asaph Ben-Tov for his thoughtful explanations on the Hebrew context of שוב (shub).

17. Johann Lucius, *Disputatio de arbitrii*, Quaestio III, xix: "Cum principaliter quaeretur, quid possit arbitrium in conversione hominis, ante omnia sciendum, quid sit Conversio, & quomodo sumatur. Est autem nihil aliud, quam motus quidam spiritualis, per quem homo renascitur & regeneratur, atque ad Deum, à quo apersus erat convertitur. Solet autem modis accipi 1. proprie pro ipsa mutatione spirituali, qua homo propter peccatum omnino aversus Deo, per fidem, Christi meritum apprehendentem ad Deum convertitur. 2. nonnihil latius, pro ipsa simul conversionis continuatione, & quotidiana adauctione: Illius subjectum sunt hominis peccatores..."

18. E. Walter, "Konversion," in Josef Höfer and Karl Rahner, eds., *Lexikon für Theologie und Kirche*, 2nd ed., 11 vols. (Freiburg, 1957–1965), vol. 6 (1961), pp. 520–521; Art. "Konversion," in Gerhard Müller, Horst Balz, Gerhard Krause, eds., *Theologische Realenzyklopädie*, 36 vols. (Berlin, 1977–2007), vol. 19 (1990), pp. 559–578; Ilona Spangenberger-Riedel, "Konversion, Konvertiten," in Walter Kasper, ed., *Lexikon für Theologie und Kirche*, 3d ed., 11 vols. (Freiburg, 1993–2001), vol. 6 (1997), pp. 338–340; Otto Bischofberger et al., "Bekehrung, Konversion," in Hans Dieter Betz et al., eds., *Religion in Geschichte und Gegenwart*, 9 vols. (Tübingen, 1998–2007), vol. 1 (1998), pp. 1228–1241.

19. Most explicitly by Musaeus, *De Conversione*, Disp. I, Cap. I: "Conversio hominis peccatoris accipi solet duplici significatu: uno transitivo, pro conversione, qua Deus hominem peccatorem convertere, & peccator ab ipso converti denominatur. Altero intransitivo, pro conversione, qua peccator se convertere dicitur. Utrumque enim usu loquendi receptum est, ut Deus peccatorem, & peccator se convertere dicatur."

20. "Und weil ich nuhmehr sehe, dass alle väterliche trewhertzige Erinnerung an dir vergebens, als übergebe ich dich, nach Gottes Gerichte, und bitte denselben inbrünstig dass er dem Teufel über dich macht gebe, gleich wie über dem Blutschänder, welchen Paulus dem Satan übergeben...auch dein Fleisch quähle, deinen Leib züchtige, ob etwan noch die Seele möchte errettet werden. Wiltu dich aber an gar nichts kehren, so sey es Gottes ewigen Gerichte nochmahlen befohlen, der gewisslich deiner nicht fehlen wird." *Wahrhafftiger Abdruck Des von hochgebornem Grafen und Herrn Herrn Johanßen Grafen zu Nassaw zu Saarbrücken und Sarwerden...vom dato Itzstein den 19. Septembris 1653 an seinen zur Römisch. Päbstischen Religion getretenen Sohn Gustavum Adolphum nacher Regensburg gethanen Schreibens...* (n.p., 1653), quote. *Wahrhafftiger Abdruck dehren von dem hochgebornem Grafen und Herrn Herrn Johanßen Grafen zu Nassau Saarbrücken und Sarwerden...den 10. und 14. Octobris des 1653 Jahrs an seinen zur Röm. Päpstischen Religion getretenen Sohn Gustav Adolphum* (n.p., 1654); Christel Lentz, "Das kurze dramatische Leben des Grafen Gustav Adolph von Nassau-Saarbrücken-Idstein (1632–1664): Erbgraf, Konvertit und Türkenkämpfer," in *Nassauische Annalen* 116 (2005): 281–300.

21. Hulsemann, *Disputatio Theologica*, II, fol. A 3: "Primum itaque medium acquirendi salutem per Christum partam, ex parte hominis, est agnitio, dolor & detestatio peccati."

22. Peggy Cosmann, *Zur Geschichte des Subjektivitätsbegriffs im 19. Jahrhundert* (Würzburg, 1999), pp. 75–84. For Luther on human will, see *D. Martin Luthers Werke, kritische Gesamtausgabe*, vol. 18, (Weimar, 1908), pp. 600–787; Robert Kolb, *Bound Choice, Election, and Wittenberg Theological Method: From Martin Luther to the Formula of Concord* (Grand Rapids, 2005).

23. "Der Mensch erlangt vergebung one seine Werck und verdienst auß lauter Gnaden und Barmhertizgkeit Gottes, umb des einigen gehorsams unnd verdiensts willen Jesu christi, allein durch den Glauben"; Tilemannus Heshusius, *Dancksagung zu Gott für die*

Bekehrung Eduardi Thorni auß Engellandt bürtig, welcher die Gotteslesterliche Sect der Jesuiter, öffentlich verworffen, und mit warer Bekanntnuß zu der heyligen Kirchen Jesu Christi getretten ist. In welcher der Leser finden wird eine kurtze und gegründete Widerlegung, der fürnembsten Irrthümer der Jesuiter" (Lauingen, 1567), p. 24.

24. See for example Andreas Kessler, *Methodus Haereticos convertendi: Außführlicher Tractat von der Ketzer Bekehrung, in zweyen Theilen verfasset...* (Coburg, 1631), p. 126.

25. Karl Friedrich Ulrichs, "Johann Pfeffinger," in Traugott Bautz, ed., *Biographisch-Bibliographisches Kirchenlexikon,* 14 vols. (Hamm and Herzberg, 1975–1998), vol. 7 (1994), pp. 413–416; Irene Dingel, *Concordia controversa. Die öffentlichen Diskussionen um das lutherische Konkordienwerk am Ende des 16. Jahrhunderts* (Gütersloh, 1996); Ernst Koch, "Victorin Strigel (1524–1569): Von Jena nach Heidelberg," in Heinz Scheible, ed., *Melanchton in seinen Schülern* (Wiesbaden, 1997), pp. 391–404; Thomas Kaufmann, "Matthias Flacius Illyricus," in Werner Freitag, ed., *Mitteldeutsche Lebensbilder. Menschen im Zeitalter der Reformation* (Cologne, 2004), pp. 177–199.

26. "Aber von dem innerlichen Zustand deß Menschen so vor Gott gerecht ist, kommen sie [i.e., the Lutherans] mit uns nit über ein. Dann sie wollen nicht, daß der Mensch durch die Rechtfertigung wahrhafftig an der Seelen verendert werde, sondern nur durch ein angelegtes Kleid, auswendig und rein, gesund und fromm scheine, da er innwendig nit weniger scheußlich, schläferich und gottlos ist, als er für der Rechtfertigung war. Der katholische Glaub aber lehret, uns, wahrhafftig aus der Schrifft, das ein gerechter Mensch nit mehr von Gott abgewant, sondern zu Gott gewant sey, denselben durch innerlichen Willen und Liebe anhange...Weil nemblich der Sünder durch die Rechtfertigung den willen verendert, Gott ansehet, sich zu Gott bekehret, unnd innwendig verendert wird: Aus welchen in der Seelen eine vortreffliche schönheit folgt..." François de Coster, *Enchiridion controversiarum: Das ist stretiger Religionspunckten kurtzer Begriff ... aus dem lateinischen ins Deutsch bracht und in Druck verfertiget durch Guilelmum Maionem Saxum* (Cologne, 1595), p. 172.

27. "Coster, Franz," in Rochus Liliencron et al., *Allgemeine Deutsche Biographie,* 56 vols. (Leipzig, 1875–1912), vol. 4, p. 515.

28. Lucius, *Disputatio de arbitrii,* xxii.

29. John Calvin, *Institutes of the Christian Religion,* ed. by John T. McNeill, transl. by Ford Lewis Battles, 2 vols. (Louisville: 1960, reissued 2006), vol. 1, 3, 21, pp. 615ff; Charles Partee, *Calvin and Classical Philosophy* (Leiden, 1997), pp. 27–94; Paul Helm, *John Calvin's Ideas* (Oxford, 2004), pp. 157–183.

30. Willem van Asselt, *The Federal Theology of Johannes Coccejus (1603–1699)* (Leiden, 2001), pp. 220–223. On Reformed federal theology in general, see Jan Rohls, *Geschichte der Ethik,* 2nd ed. (Tübingen, 1999), pp. 342–348.

31. Johann Pistorius and Jakob von Baden-Hachberg, *Vnser, Von Gottes Genaden, Jacobs, Marggrafen zu Baden vnd Hachbergk...Christliche erhebliche vnd wolfundirte Motifen, warumb wir auß einigem eifferigen trib vnsers Gewissens...nicht allein für vnser Person die Lutherische Lehr verlassen vnd zu dem Catholischen Immerwehrenden vnd allein seligmachenden Christlichen Glauben Vns notwendig begeben, Sondern auch vnser von Gott anbeuohlene Land zu ebenmessiger warhaffter Religion anweisen vnd reformieren lassen müssen* (Cologne, 1591); Hans-Jürgen Günther, *Die Reformation und ihre Kinder dargestellt an Vater und Sohn Johannes Pistorius Niddanus: Eine Doppelbiographie J. Pistorius d. Ä. (1502–1583) und J. Pistorius d. J. (1546–1608)* (Nidda, 1994); Oskar Garstein, *Rome and the Counter-Reformation in Scandinavia: The Age of Gustavus Adolphus and Queen Christina of Sweden, 1622–1656* (Leiden, 1992); Susanna Åkerman, *Queen Christina*

of Sweden and Her Circle: The Transformation of a Seventeenth Century Philosophical Libertine (Leiden, 1991).

32. Josef Schmidlin, "Die Gründung der Propagandakongregation," Zeitschrift für Missionswissenschaft 12 (1922): 1–14; Hermann Tüchle, Acta SC de Propaganda Fide Germaniam spectantia: Die Protokolle der Propagandakongregation zu deutschen Angelegenheiten 1622–1649 (Paderborn, 1962); Joseph Metzler, ed., Sacrae Congregationis de Propaganda Fide memoria rerum, vol. 2, 1622–1700 (Rome, 1971); Hermann Tüchle, Die Protokolle der Propagandakongregation zu deutschen Angelegenheiten 1657–1667. Diasporasorge unter Alexander VII (Paderborn, 1972); Garstein, Rome and the Counter-Reformation, pp. 3–17. For the role of the Pfalz-Neuburg dynasty in the recatholicization of Germany, see Eric-Oliver Mader, "Konfessionalität im Hause Pfalz-Neuburg: Zur Bedeutung des Faktors 'Konversion' für das konfessionelle Profil einer Herrscherdynastie," in Benedikt Mauerer et al., eds., Barocke Herrschaft am Rhein um 1700: Kurfürst Johann Wilhelm und seine Zeit (Düsseldorf, 2009), pp. 95–115.

33. Christian Hecht, Katholische Bildertheologie im Zeitalter der Gegenreformation und Barock. Studien zu den Traktaten von Johannes Molanus, Gabriele Paleotti und anderen Autoren (Berlin, 1997); Jens Baumgarten, Konfession, Bild und Macht: Visualisierung als katholisches Herrschafts- und Disziplinierungskonzept in Rom und im habsburgischen Schlesien (1560—1740) (Hamburg, 2004); Holger Steinemann, Eine Bildtheorie zwischen Repräsentation und Wirkung: Kardinal Gabriele Paleottis "Discorso intorno alle imagini sacre e profane" (1582) (Hildesheim, 2006).

34. Cornel Zwierlein, "'convertire tutta l'Alemagna'–Fürstenkonversionen in den Strategiedenkrahmen der römischen Europapolitik um 1600: Zum Verhältnis von 'Machiavellismus' und 'Konfessionalismus,'" in Lotz-Heumann et al., Konversion und Konfession, pp. 63–105.

35. Adam Contzen, Politicorum Libri Decem, in quibus De Perfectae Reipubl. Forma, Virtutibus, Et Vitiis, Institutione civium, Legibus, Magistratu Ecclesiastico, civili, potentia Reipublicae; itemque Seditione et bello, ad usum vitamque communem accomodatè tractatur, 2nd ed. (Cologne, 1629), pp. 103–109; Eric-Oliver Mader, "Adam Contzen, S.J. (1571–1635)," in Richard Golden, ed., Encyclopaedia of Witchcraft: The Western Tradition, 4 vols. (Santa Barbara, 2006), vol. 1, pp. 214–215.

36. Giovanni Botero, Relationi Universali di Giovanni Botero Benese, Di novo da lui reviste, & in puo luoghi ampliate (Vicenza, 1595), part 3, book 1, fol. 5r–v.

37. DHI Rom, Minucciana VII, 82r–84v and 91r–92r (= Del Prè Lorenzo Maggio); fol. 500r–506r (=Del card. Madrucci sopra la ridutione del duca di Sassonia); DHI Rom, Minucciana IX., fol. 281r–289v (=Considerationi date all'Illmo S.^{re} Card^{le} Borromeo Per proporre alla Santa memoria di Gregorio XIII Nel initio dell' anno 1591) and ibid. fol. 290r–294v; For Minuccio Minucci, see Cornel Zwierlein, "'convertire tutta l'Alemagna,'" pp. 63–105; also Jonas Heinrichson, Consilium Politicorum. De ratione et via regiones septentrionales ad cultum sedis romanae reducendi: item causis propter Daniae suspecta esse debet Regnorum Poloniae et Suetia coniuncto (1604); Contzen, Politicorum libri decem, pp. 731–744. For catalogues of converts pointing to the gobal success of early modern Catholicism, see Christoph Ott, Historia Nova Seculi Nostri Decimi Septimi, Ferreo- Aurei, Complectens Gesta per Imperium Romano- Germanicum, sub Rudolpho II. Matthia I. Ferdinando II. Ferdinando III. Impp. Austriacis ... (Innsbruck, 1682); Christoph Ott, Unvergleichliche Ehren-Cron Welche Der Roemischen Catholischen Kirchen in disem sibenzehenden Welt-Gang auß allen vier Theilen der Welt Als Europa, Asia, Africa und America, Durch Ihr Bekehrung zu dem Catholischen Glauben vil gecroente als

Kayserliche Koenigliche Churfuerstliche Fuerstliche Und andere hoch-achtbare Persohnen auffgesetzt (Dillingen, 1686–1702).

38. Coster, *Enchiridion controversiarum*, pp. 62–61.

39. "Warlich, es hat innerhalb fünffzehen hundert Jahren, auff der gantzen rundscheibigen Welt, kein einiger Heydnischer Kayser oder Kayserin, König oder Königin, Fürst oder Fürstin, sich von euch tauffen lasen, oder bey euch sich deß Glaubens halben angemeldet, es thuts auch noch keiner. Zu unser Catholischen Religion aber, bekennen und melden sich noch dieser zeit an, vil Abgöttischer, Heydnischer König und Fürsten, nemblich, in Iapon, Peru unnd India, wie dann allererst im nechst verflossenen Jar, ansehnliche, großmächtige König und Fürsten auf Japonia, ihre Legaten zu Rom, bey dem Apostolischen Stul, zum Zeichen unnd Beweis ihres Gehorsams und Underthänigkeit gegen der Römischen Kirchen, gehabt haben." Georg Scherer, *Rettung der Jesuiter Unschuld wider die Giftspinnen Lucam Osiander* (Ingolstadt, 1586), pp. 55–56. Scherer advances the same argument in *Ursachen der Bekehrung der Herrschaft Haußeck im hochlöblichen Ertzherzogthumb Oesterreich under der Enß...* (Ingolstadt, 1586), pp. 2–10. With reference to Scherer, see also Sixt Vischer, *Lützelburgische Bekehrung, Das ist: Etliche gruendtliche und so gar auch den einfaeltigen verständliche Ursachen Warumb sich die Pfarrmenig zu Luetzelburg vom Luthertum zur alten Catholischen Roemischen Kirchen und Glauben recht und billich begeben hab...* (Munich, 1608), p. 9.

40. Manfred Roensch, "Die Konkordienformel in der Geschichte des deutschen Luthertums," *Lutherische Theologie und Kirche* 2, no. 79 (1979): 37–52; Irene Dingel, *Concordia controversa*.

41. Anders Nørgaard, *Mission und Obrigkeit. Die Dänisch-hallische Mission in Tranquebar 1706–1845* (Gütersloh, 1988); and Arthur Bogner, ed., *Weltmission und religiöse Organisationen. Protestantische Missionsgesellschaften im 19. und 20. Jahrhundert* (Würzburg, 2004).

42. Walter Wendland, "Die Pietistische Bekehrung," *Zeitschrift für Kirchengeschichte* 38 (1920): 193–238; Johann Henrich Reitz, *Historie der Wiedergebohrnen: Vollständige Ausgabe der Erstdruck aller sieben Teile der pietistischen Sammelbiographie*, ed. Hans-Jürgen Schrader, 4 vols. (Tübingen, 1982).

43. Zacharias Rivander, *Fest-Chronica* (Erfurt, 1591), fos. 80r–82v.

44. For example, the reaction of Jacob Heilbrunner to the conversion of Count Palatine Wolfgang Wilhelm of Pfalz-Neuburg; see Staatsarchiv Amberg, Pfalz-Sulzbach, Geheime Registratur, 153, pp. 188ff.

45. Wilhelm Hoeck, *Anton Ulrich und Elisabeth Christine von Braunschweig-Lüneburg-Wolfenbüttel: Eine durch archivalische Dokumente begründete Darstellung ihres Übertritts zur römischen Kirche* (Wolfenbüttel, 1845); Wilhelm Gottlieb Soldan, *Dreißig Jahre des Proselytismus in Sachsen und Braunschweig: Mit einer Einleitung* (Leipzig, 1847), pp. 183–216; Ines Peper, *Konversionen im Umkreis des Wiener Hofes um 1700* (Munich 2010), pp. 143–236.

46. The notion "adiaphora" originated in the older Stoa and, with a different meaning, turns up in Lutheran ethics from the mid sixteenth century on. Adiaphora here means actions that are ethically indifferent and not essential for the definition of the true confession.

47. Bernardus Lutzenburgensis, *Catalogus Haereticorum omnium penè, qui ad haec usque tempora passim literarum monumentis proditi sunt, illorum nomina errores, & tempora quibus vixerunt ostendens...* (Cologne, 1522); Caspar Franck, *Catalogus haereticorum, das ist: warhafftige Erzelung der namhafften Irrthumb und Ketzer, welche von Anfang der*

Welt biß auff unsere Zeit entstanden... (Ingolstadt, 1576); Johannes Pontanus, *Catalogus Praecipuorum, Apud Veteres Et Recentiores, quorum, in Augustana confessione, Formula Concordiae, in Ecclesiis & Scholis, crebra fit mentio, Haereticorum...* (Frankfurt, 1600); Francescus van Ranst, *Historia haereticorum, et haeresum anteá inscripta lux fidei, seu D. Thomas doctor Angelicus omnium errorum ante vitam, in vita, & post vitam...* (Venice, 1720).

48. Ilona Riedel-Spangenberger, "Konversion, III. Kath.," in *Lexikon für Kirchen- und Staatskirchenrecht*, (Paderborn, 2004), pp. 638–639; Elmar Güthoff, "Kanonistische Erwägungen zur eigenständigen Bedeutung der Apostasie," in Winfried Aymans, et al., eds., *Iudicare inter fideles: Festschrifts für Karl-Theodor Geringer zum 65. Geburtstag*, (St. Ottilien, 2002), pp. 109–119; Helmut Pree, "Die Konversion als Rechtsakt," in Rüdiger Althaus, et al., eds., *Kirchenrecht und Theologie im Leben der Kirche: Festschrift für Heinrich J. F. Reinhardt zur Vollendung des 65. Lebensjahres*, (Essen, 2007), pp. 347–353. See also the paper of Rüdiger Althaus, *Abfall vom Glauben oder Freiheit des Glaubens?* http:www.theo.uni-trier.de_downloadsAlthaus.pdf.

CHAPTER THREE

Turning Dutch?
Conversion in Early Modern Wesel

JESSE SPOHNHOLZ

Following the collapse of the Augsburg Interim in the summer of 1552, magistrates and clergy in the Rhineland town of Wesel adopted religious standards that affiliated the city with the recently triumphant Lutheran party in the religious conflicts then plaguing Germany. Within two generations, though, this town had become a bastion of Calvinism. According to most historical accounts of this transformation, Calvinism's triumph in Wesel was the result of a successful missionary campaign by the town's foreign-born Calvinist population, which had arrived just as Wesel was splitting from Rome and beginning to build its new church. This article reconsiders this version of Wesel's Reformation. It argues that the town's transition from Lutheranism to Calvinism was not so much the deliberate product of religious conversion as the unintended result of the profound instabilities of the era—in political order, in demographics, and even in the very nature of faith itself. The implications of this reevaluation go far beyond the history of this one German city. This chapter suggests that though the Reformation was in a very real sense an era of conversion, understanding the religious changes during this period primarily through this lens can perpetuate assumptions about the static nature of early modern confessional categories that, once challenged, reveal their remarkably flexible and dynamic character. Conversion, thus, was not necessarily the result of a campaign to transform inner convictions. In this case, it was instead the accidental result of the dramatic demographic and political changes of the Reformation era.

Conversion, as a model for understanding religious change, can describe two quite different phenomena. First, it can suggest a person's internal transformation from one religious paradigm to another. Scholars sometimes call this "genuine conversion." For Christians, this model of conversion often explicitly follows a narrative of spiritual advancement on the model of Saul of Tarsus's transformation on the road to Damascus, by which an individual comes closer to divine truth.[1] Few would deny that thousands of Germans living through the Reformation experienced powerful spiritual transformations of this sort as they abandoned old understandings of faith and adopted new models of piety. Yet historians should not assume that all Reformation-era conversions followed this model. The fact that sixteenth-century theologians often used unambiguous rhetoric to describe the confessional categories of the era does not necessarily mean that ordinary people understood those categories in the same way. Because there is so little evidence that illuminates the spiritual lives of most Reformation-era Germans, identifying and measuring this kind of spiritual conversion on a widespread level is remarkably difficult.

A second type of conversion, defined as shifting one's membership from one religious institution to another, is easier to measure. Such a move, however, need not entail a spiritual transformation. Beat Hodler, for instance, has studied cases of conversion in the seventeenth-century Swiss Confederation, where people often switched from one confession to another in exchange for the non-spiritual benefits that church membership provided. For Hodler, the very frequency with which people switched churches only highlights the inability of clergy to imbue their flocks with a coherent and mutually exclusive understanding of confessional identity, a point similarly made by Nicole Grochowina for Reformation-era Emden and Frauke Volkland regarding seventeenth-century Bischofszell.[2] In these cases, changing church membership occurred all the more frequently in places where confessional identity was the weakest and where historians therefore find few examples of "genuine conversions."

We can find examples of both kinds of conversion in those places in the Holy Roman Empire that moved from Lutheran to Reformed in the late sixteenth and early seventeenth centuries—a pattern often called the "Second Reformation."[3] Most commonly, adoption of the Reformed faith followed the conversion of a prince who attempted, often with limited success, to impose his new religion on his subjects.[4] Many individuals who changed churches under these conditions were not motivated by a spiritual transformation but by political pressures. Yet when Wesel's magistrates officially adopted the Reformed church in 1612, most residents received the change warmly. After all, by that year a substantial portion of the population had already submitted to the discipline of the town's Reformed consistory, and many officials even actively colluded in protecting Calvinists from harassment at the hands of ducal agents.[5] The first Calvinists in Wesel, however, were not state or municipal officials but religious refugees from the neighboring Low Countries who had fled from the persecution they faced back home. Many Reformed Protestants living in cities like Antwerp, Oudenaarde, Ghent, and 's-Hertogenbosch escaped to borderland cities of the Empire, like Wesel, that would tolerate their viewpoints. Their presence in the city first became significant in the early 1550s, though immigration continued for fifty years. At the time of their arrival, Wesel was formally a Lutheran city with a Catholic minority. The town's new Calvinist population thus initially had to learn how to survive as a religious minority in its new home.[6]

A critical feature of Wesel's religious landscape that made this coexistence possible was the fact that, while the town had approved the Augsburg Confession, official standards of belief and practice provided a relatively broad institutional framework that could accommodate people with a remarkably wide range of viewpoints. The town's new church ordinance, the *Einfältiges Bedenken* (The Simple Deliberation), was not characterized by orthodox Lutheranism but by confessionally ambiguous language. The work had been produced in 1543 by the archbishop of Cologne, Hermann von Wied, in cooperation with Martin Bucer and Philip Melanchthon, after Wied had abandoned his long-standing efforts to reform the Catholic Church from within.[7] Wied had been a strong supporter of Christian unity at the failed Regensburg Colloquy of 1541. The *Einfältiges Bedenken* represented his effort to continue striving for a broad Christian unity, even if it meant breaking with Pope Paul III to do so. Though his proposed church ordinance looked Lutheran in structure, its language emphasized liturgical expressions of unity more than theological clarity. After Wied was excommunicated and deposed, his *Einfältiges Bedenken* lived on in Wesel, as did its spirit of accommodation between Lutheran reforms and Catholic liturgical traditionalism and its avoidance of dogmatism. Under Wesel's new church ordinance, all members of the parish were required to worship together in most rites, regardless of their confessional inclination.

The initial influx of Calvinist refugees from the Low Countries in the 1550s briefly challenged this state of affairs, but by the mid 1560s the magistrates had reinstituted this broadly conceived church, which left room for the participation of the town's Catholics and Lutherans as well as the foreign Calvinist population.[8] This supraconfessional church remained in place into the early seventeenth century. Church authorities sought to avoid the inevitable confessional conflicts by allowing individuals to celebrate rituals in slightly different ways. Communicants could choose, for instance, between receiving the Eucharist under one or both forms. They were also allowed to take the wafer in their hands in accordance with Reformed practice or have the pastor place the host in their mouths as Lutherans and Catholics preferred. Catholics also sang Latin Mass hymns and burned holy candles before the high altar during these shared communion services.[9] The town's Catholics, Lutherans, and Calvinists also buried their dead in the same cemeteries, married in the same churches, and used the same baptismal fonts. This situation was not, in fact, unprecedented in northwest Germany. In cities, towns, and villages of Cleves, Berg, and Münsterland, neighbors of different confessions worshipped alongside one another in hybrid or accomodationist services, in some cases into the seventeenth century.[10] Historians' use of confessional categories to describe churches like those in Reformation-era Wesel thus tends to simplify a more complicated religious landscape.

Yet the dominant narrative presented by previous historians who have studied this city centers upon the residents' gradual conversion from Lutheranism to Calvinism. In this view, widespread internal spiritual conversion had happened in the hearts and minds of residents long before 1612. Earlier scholars have assigned the Dutch refugees, and particularly their consistory, tremendous influence in converting residents to the Reformed faith, a process that we might call "Turning Dutch."[11] Nineteenth-century church historians advanced this account, and the narrative of conversion that it rests on has remained largely the same in the hands of more recent historians.[12] A central problem of these studies is that their authors have not sufficiently proven that Weselers converted from Lutheranism to Calvinism in the first place. They have, rather, correlated Wesel's emergence as a Calvinist stronghold with the arrival of the Dutch refugees and inserted a plausible causal explanation. Historians have provided a variety of dates for Weselers' "conversion." Various commentators cite particular years—1564, 1565, 1566, and 1568—as the key turning point.[13] Others describe the conversion of Weselers as taking place sometime in the 1570s.[14]

The language used by historians who have studied Wesel highlights this tendency to gloss over a more complicated picture of events. Johannes Hillmann's words in 1896 demonstrate the contortions this could require: "Calvinism was victorious in the year 1578—but if one of our readers [today] could have seen the religious services then, he would hardly believe that was true, because the external form of worship was wholly Lutheran, and it would remain so for roughly the next twenty years."[15] In 1972 Heinz Schilling claimed that by 1570 Wesel's church was Reformed in its "essential faith" (*Glaubensubstanz*) and that its outward Lutheran trappings and liturgy were merely a political convenience. Even in the early twenty-first century David Fors Freeman described the city as "more or less, officially Calvinist."[16] Given the supraconfessional nature of the city's churches, efforts to describe them using confessional language have thus required some measure of elusiveness.

Similar problems await those attempting to categorize individuals who presided over Wesel's churches. Many studies describe the ministers Heinrich Rollius (served 1559–1565) and Gerhard Veltius (served 1566–1593) as Calvinists, despite the fact that both were appointed by the Catholic duke of Cleves, publically professed the Augsburg Confession, and served individuals with a variety of beliefs.[17] Similarly, Herbert Kipp calls Gerhard Venraid, who served in Wesel from 1571 to 1578, the first minister who "clearly belonged to the Reformed confession."[18] Yet Venraid's biography belies this categorization. Venraid converted to Lutheranism in 1547 in Orsoy; he took a post in Catholic Sonsbeck in 1563 but was removed from office for his evangelical position. He later attended the Calvinist Convent of Wesel in 1568. The following year he was again administrating Mass *sub una specie* in Königswinter, where he again swore allegiance to Rome.[19] When he took his post in Wesel, Venraid ministered to the town's Dutch Calvinists, but also to Lutherans and Catholics. There were, in fact, many confessionally ambiguous ministers on the Lower Rhine. Scholars describing such flexible attitudes and behaviors often suggest that people's confessional identities were confused, stunted, or ill-informed.[20] But that is to impose standards predicated on confessional identities that developed only much later.

When we consider how contemporaries in sixteenth-century Wesel described their church, we do not see evidence of "confusion." On the contrary, ministers clearly and fervently defended their positions. When they did so, they demonstrated not naiveté but rather a self-conscious and assertive denial that confessional categories could fully encompass the boundaries of their church. In 1564 Heinrich Rollius explained that "by nature I shy away from accusations and, since I was not baptized in the name of Calvin, Beza, Bullinger, Luther etc., but in the name of the Son of God, why is it necessary to rage against this or that person?"[21] His successor, Gerhard Veltius, used the very same language. In 1568 he appealed to St. Paul's letter to the Corinthians to warn against letting confessional divisions tear apart Christian unity: "St. Paul himself forbade that we should be Paulist, Cephalist, or Appolonian and similarly Luther [asked] that we should not be Lutheran, since none of these men died for anyone ... it is enough that they were called Christians."[22] Similarly, in a carefully worded letter of November 1580 to their Catholic duke, the town pastorate claimed, "We were not born Calvinists or Lutherans, we are not baptized in their name and they did not die for us."[23] Further, though the ministers' language was implicitly Protestant, they used the very same message of Christian unity to defend the participation of Catholic monks in the town's communion services.[24] While elsewhere in Reformation Germany clergy often emerged as defenders of totalizing, confessional models of piety, in Wesel the opposite was true. There, a parishioner could participate in the rites of a supraconfessional civic church without fully conforming in matters of doctrine. In such a context, the "Pauline" model of conversion cannot fully account for religious change.[25]

Although earlier historians have not adequately explained how or why Weselers converted, they have offered some evidence to prove that residents were largely Reformed decades before the town's official adoption of Calvinism. This evidence, however, is far from clear. Consider the claim that Wesel's church was Calvinist because the town hosted the so-called Convent of Wesel in November 1568.[26] The convent was supposedly a meeting of Dutch Calvinist leaders who sketched out a tentative church order to prepare for what they hoped would be their imminent takeover of the Low Countries. J.P. van Dooren hypothesized, however, that the meeting did not even take place in Wesel.[27] Even if van Dooren was wrong, the fact that the convent took place hardly offers proof that magistrates and other residents had converted. Municipal records provide no evidence that town officials even knew about the convent, let alone approved of its resolutions. The only hint that they might have learned about it was that early the next year they fired a minister who had signed the convent's articles.[28] This is hardly a convincing sign of their support for the Reformed faith.

Historians pointing to Weselers' unofficial conversion to Calvinism have also highlighted incidents of iconoclasm and image removal that illustrate deeply felt objections to "idolatry" characteristic of Reformed Protestantism.[29] The strongest examples of attacks on Catholic devotional images are those that took place in the late 1560s, coinciding with the arrival of large-scale waves of Dutch refugees.[30] Looking only at the *removal* of images, though, has resulted in exaggeration of Calvinists' influence. First, isolated incidents of image removal only highlight that most of the traditional imagery went untouched. The fact that church officials had St. Jorien's altar broken up in 1585 might be a marker of their Calvinist leanings, but it might just as well serve as a reminder that the twenty-three other altars in St. Willibrord's churches remained in place.[31] Second, churchwardens' account books record the replacement or repair of damaged images, suggesting that town officials' commitment to iconography had not simply vanished.[32] Calvinist refugees' ongoing complaints about religious imagery in the churches, which they saw as unwelcome remnants of the town's Catholic past, only corroborate this point.[33] Certainly there was a degree of compromise—the miracle-working image of St. Anthony housed in St. Nicholas's church was relocated to a less prominent location, but it was also left undamaged, and both churches continued to house altars, images of saints, and other traditional ornamentation.[34]

A third sign that Wesel "turned Dutch" was the town's hiring of the Dutchman Herman Herbertz, later pastor of the Reformed church in Gouda, as assistant minister in 1571. Historians have described a special relationship that developed between the Calvinist consistory and Herbertz, even suggesting that he served as a leader for the Dutch Reformed.[35] Yet the consistory's records rarely mention Herbertz. In May 1575 an elder was instructed to ask him to lead a prayer for a noblewoman. In February 1576, one of the elders suggested talking to Herbertz about the catechism that he used, though they left no record of the content of this conversation.[36] Herbertz never participated in the consistory, nor did he attend the meetings of the Reformed classis.[37] Even the fact that he later took a post in the Dutch Reformed Church is a red herring. In Gouda, Herbertz came under constant attack from orthodox Calvinists for his nonconformist views and was only protected by those magistrates who were strongly resistant to Calvinism. Herbertz instead promoted a nondogmatic civic church, following the so-called libertine party that clashed with Calvinists across the Dutch Republic.[38] In this light, Herbertz reflected the same strand of non-confessional Christianity that characterized Wesel's churches.

Historians have also suggested that Wesel was Calvinist because some of the clergy attended meetings of the Calvinist Classis of Cleves, which took place at the house of one of Wesel's Dutch elders twice yearly.[39] Johannes Heidfelt first came at the elders' invitation in October 1578, and in later years other ministers, including Johannes Havenburg and Godfried Breuccerus, appeared. Wesel's clergy occasionally even chaired the classis.[40] The chair (*voorsitter*) opened the meeting with a set list of questions prescribed by the national synods and called on attendees who wanted to speak. Surely this is evidence of cooperation between clergy and the Calvinist refugees. Still, the chair neither set the agenda nor advised in matters of theology. Rather, the ministers' participation was largely passive. The classis occasionally consulted pastors on matters they were deliberating, particularly when they sought common cause.[41] Yet, tellingly, even when they acted as chair, ministers often did not stay through the entire meeting. Chief Pastor Gerhard Veltius first appeared at a classis meeting only in April 1583 but left before it ended and did not return for nearly a decade.[42] Claims that the pastors' attendance proves that they were leaders of the Calvinist church conflates cooperation with conversion while ignoring the ministers' compromises with the town's Lutherans and Catholics. The fact that the classis decided in April 1580 to send a delegation to convince Wesel's ministers to abandon baptismal exorcisms only reaffirms the fact that ministers did not participate in many of the classis's discussions, and the fact that ministers did not ban exorcisms only reinforces the fact that the Calvinists' influence remained limited.[43]

Ministers could even emerge as potent critics of the Reformed community. Johannes Heidfelt criticized the operations of the classis as petty and trivial from the pulpit in May 1582, causing Calvinist elders to complain that he had "blasphemed the synod and the Christian meeting of the ministers and elders."[44] In February 1577 Gerhard Veltius expressed his desire to eliminate the consistory's influence over whether Reformed refugees attended communion.[45] When elders asked Heidfelt and Breuccerus to submit to consistorial discipline in December 1579, the ministers refused, though they did continue to advise the consistory.[46] Not all the ministers were even this accommodating. Rudolph Wullen and Casper Sticker suggested that cooperating with elders would bring "damage to their church."[47] Magistrates were likewise cautious about cooperation between the local church and Calvinists. When they learned in 1582 that some of Wesel's clergy attended classis meetings, they passed a resolution barring them from doing so in the future.[48] Despite the undisputable cooperation taking place, we cannot describe the clergy or the town's magistrates as having converted to Calvinism.

The strongest evidence that Weselers converted comes from the accusations of Lutherans who lambasted local preachers as Calvinists because they would not denounce Calvinism from the pulpit.[49] Here the best evidence comes from the pen of Otto von Bellinckhoven, a strident Lutheran and a member of one of Wesel's leading families. Unconvinced by fellow magistrates' assurances that the pastors' sermons conformed to the Augsburg Confession, in 1578 Bellinckhoven refused to attend communion.[50] Another Lutheran patrician, Herman Schwager, similarly denounced a minister as Calvinist in 1580 because he deviated from orthodox Lutheranism.[51] Given what we know about Wesel's religious compromise, it should be fairly clear that ministers' refusal to denounce Calvinism does not prove that they were Calvinists but instead only confirms their self-conscious distancing from confessionally divisive language. The rhetoric of these angry Lutherans simply does not provide a translucent window into the souls of those they were criticizing.

Furthermore, evidence from the records of the Calvinist consistory does not support the conclusion that elders were converting Weselers in significant numbers. The elders did decide, on 16 March 1579, to approach citizens whom they knew "to be of good will" to find out what it would take to convince them to accept the consistory's supervision.[52] The actual focus of their efforts, however, was not Weselers; the elders largely targeted the wives and children of Dutch Calvinist men. On 2 March 1579, elders resolved to visit "all women whose husbands are under the discipline to present and read them the confession of faith."[53] Consistorial records indicate that they followed through.[54] They also urged children to follow the example of their Reformed fathers. Of the six people who submitted to the Calvinist discipline in April 1590, for example, four were the children of refugees, and one was a Calvinist immigrant from Jülich. Only one came from a Wesel family.[55] Elders were also preoccupied with fellow refugees who maintained eccentric religious views.[56] In total, elders spent much more time trying to convince their countrymen to conform to Calvinism than they ever did attempting to convert Weselers.

Another demographic segment that was ripe for integration into the Reformed community was made up of refugees from neighboring German lands. The small population of Calvinists in Cleves faced mounting hostilities from the ducal government, local officials, and Catholic townspeople in the 1570s and 1580s. Similar conditions existed in the neighboring territories of Jülich, Mark, Berg, and the Archbishopric of Cologne.[57] Many of these people made their way to Wesel, which had earned a justified reputation for welcoming dissenters. Some, like Meriken Bogmans from Jülich and Kasper Rosenthal from Düsseldorf, joined the Calvinists on their own accord, but elders visited others at home to encourage them to join up.[58] Although in the previous decades the Calvinist community had been almost exclusively Netherlandish, between 1578 and 1600 as many as 12 percent of the 833 Calvinists living in Wesel whose origin is known came from German lands.[59]

Weselers, however, rarely appear as targets of elders' efforts. One exception is the elders' attempt in 1579 to convince Arnd de Scheper to submit to the Calvinist discipline. Their failure to do so, even after five months of pressure, highlights the fact that by and large, Weselers were not converting.[60] Even by the last decade of the sixteenth century, Weselers made up just 2 percent of the town's Calvinists as a whole. The local youth Philip Klayssen, who converted in July of 1578, and the innkeeper Willemar Seler, who joined in 1581, were among the few exceptions. As late as 1590, the elders still referred to their community as the "foreign church," "the Netherlandish Reformed Church within Lower Wesel," "the reformed church in Wesel," and the "church of Netherlandish strangers."[61] The fact that Weselers tolerated Calvinists, therefore, did not mean that they were adopting their religion.

The claim that most Weselers converted from Lutheranism to Calvinism over the second half of the sixteenth century rests on the assumption that confessions were mutually exclusive categories of faith. Therefore, if magistrates and pastors rejected papal authority, refused to sign the Lutheran Formula of Concord, and refused to denounce Calvinists from the pulpit as heretics, then they *must* be Calvinists. Recent critics of the confessionalization paradigm, however, have begun to suggest that confessional models of faith were not as normative as once imagined.[62] Many have emphasized the role of ordinary people in selecting only those elements of confessional churches that fit local needs.[63] Others have emphasized the diversity within confessions themselves and the persistent ability of individuals to cross confessional lines when it suited them.[64] Recent research has therefore urged that we understand confessions, and the boundaries that divided them, as historically contingent, and thus only understandable within specific localized contexts.[65] The complexity of Wesel's religious landscape certainly confirms this. As a result, understanding the meaning of religious change also demands making sense of the specific political, social, and cultural contexts of that change.

For too long scholars have tried to use confessional categories to describe events that took place during a period when confessions remained undeveloped. It is therefore understandable why modern scholars have so readily told the story of Wesel's slide toward Calvinism as one of conversion. That said, the fact remains that Wesel did indeed emerge as a bastion of Calvinism by the second decade of the seventeenth century. Though no evidence survives that proves most Weselers converted, in fact no evidence is needed to explain the change: the religious transformations that took place were the result of dramatic demographic shifts that took place between 1586 and 1612, as well as the political and military changes that brought those shifts about.

The first factor that contributed to Wesel's shift toward Calvinism was the religious wars in this area of the Empire. Starting in 1579, war in the Low Countries began spilling over into northwest Germany, while in 1582 a conflict erupted over control of the Archbishopric of Cologne.[66] The combination of the Dutch Revolt and the Cologne War polarized the region between Catholic and Protestant blocs. In addition, soldiers on both sides plundered the coun‧tryside, killing those who resisted, cutting off food supplies, and making travel exceedingly dangerous.[67] Matters became even more dire when Spanish troops began a four-year long siege of Wesel starting in the fall of 1586. Climbing mortality rates were exacerbated by the near simultaneous outbreak of the plague. Contemporaries bemoaned the death of "many thousands of humans and animals."[68] As Arnold von Anrath, who lived through this period, described it, "it was such a horrible time, that many thousands of people did not know what to say, because they had blurred eyes."[69] So many people died that burial plots were introduced into the schoolyard, the streets, and a public garden.[70] Magistrates calculated that between August 1586 and March of the following year, 10,600 people died.[71] Churchwardens reported that the number of people who had bells tolled at their funerals increased in the first year of the siege by over 500 percent before the bells cracked from incessant ringing.[72] Meanwhile, as Weselers died, the town continued to receive new streams of Calvinist immigrants from neighboring German lands.

The economic crash that followed compounded the problems. Particularly urgent was the scarcity of food: not only had Spanish troops trampled most of the local fields, but they also harvested the remaining crops for themselves.[73] Calvinist elders wrote in March 1587 that after eight months of siege they had no money or food left, while the numbers of hungry were still increasing.[74] The only people who were able to retain access to grain markets were wealthy Dutch merchants, who paid private mercenaries to protect their shipments. Men like Rudolf van Leyen and Claissen van Wesick provided virtually the only supplies that residents saw in these years.[75] Because they were also leaders of the Calvinist community, their ability to provide some relief for Wesel's miserable population enormously benefited its repute in the town.

The siege, which finally ended in the spring of 1590, created an atmosphere in which residents cheered on Dutch military advances, which further aided the standing of Dutch Calvinists within Wesel's walls.[76] Weselers celebrated after Calvinists at Nijmegen launched the revolt against the Spanish, and again when Dutch troops captured Rheinberg. Arnold von Anrath recorded a song of praise for the Dutch commander Marten Schenk van Niddigen, which portrayed him as a hero who relieved the region from Spanish oppression "in God's name."[77] Funds for rebuilding the town that were sent by the government of the fledgling Dutch Republic no doubt strengthened the ties between Dutch Calvinists living in Wesel and the local population.[78]

Another consequence of the siege was that as members of the town's traditional ruling elite died, many of their posts were taken by leaders of the Reformed community. This is not to say that local families and Lutherans were hit harder by the war, disease, and famine of these years, but that the siege simply made it impossible for the old guard to staff civic offices. To fill these positions, citizens began electing wealthy Dutch merchants and businessmen. No doubt the key role these men had served in supplying desperately needed food to residents encouraged their rise to political prominence. But this did not mean that most men with voting rights were now Calvinists: Lutheran leaders also continued to be elected to civic offices alone. By 1590, Lutherans still retained strong representation on the town council, but Calvinists had made inroads among other municipal offices, such as the so-called "Friends of the Commune," who represented the burghers' interests before the magistrates.[79]

In terms of Wesel's church life, the pivotal change came with the death of Gerhard Veltius, the town's chief pastor. Veltius had always maintained a safe distance from the Reformed community, and when he died in the summer of 1593, collaboration between the consistory and ministers increased; by the end of that year, the consistory had begun holding its meetings in the sacristy of the central parish church.[80] Within a month, the ministers subjected themselves to the strictures of Calvinist discipline, though since the consistory's authority was informal this was probably largely only a symbolic gesture. By August 1594 Peter Nettesheim, the elder from Düsseldorf, ceded his presidency of the consistory to a new minister at St. Willibrord's, Daniel Nellius, who had himself been raised in the refugee community. These changes did not lead to major liturgical reforms, though they did make it possible for an open and forthright debate on issues long of interest to Calvinists, such as the use of devotional candles, church organs, and the propriety of taking communion before the high altar. By the early seventeenth century, cooperation had increased between the Calvinists and the town's civic and ecclesiastical leaders, particularly in matters of poor relief.[81] Still, though Calvinists protested, conservatives maintained their dominance and worship services retained their supraconfessional character.[82]

The final conversion of Wesel, however, took a shift in the political situation. When the duke of Cleves, Johann Wilhelm, died without heirs in March 1609, the scramble to secure succession led to a military showdown. The claimants to the throne fell in line behind two confessional blocs. Elector of Brandenburg Johann Sigismund became the Calvinist favorite, while Elector of Palatine-Neuburg Wolfgang Wilhelm gained the backing of Spain, Bavaria, and the Catholic Church.[83] The provisional Treaty of Dortmund, signed in June 1609, granted the territorial cities freedom of worship until the proper succession was determined. This meant that Wesel now had legal permission to establish a Reformed church. Almost immediately, consistory elections took place for the first time in St. Willibrord's church, though its organization still remained separate from parish administration. It was only in 1612, after the succession crisis had been resolved, that Margrave Ernst, the younger brother of Johann Sigismund, arrived in Wesel to oversee the town's official adoption of Calvinism. He ordered that "the altars in the churches here be removed" because they "encouraged idolatry."[84] He even cemented the relationship between the new Brandenburg court and the town government by serving as a godparent for the mayor's newborn child.[85] Under Ernst's supervision, the Heidelberg Catechism was adopted and the commune elected a new municipal consistory. By June of that year the refugees' consistory had held its last meeting, and Calvinists took over all public religious observances. Plain bread replaced the host in communion services, and an ordinary table replaced the old high altar.[86] A municipal commission established that year took two years to complete its reorganization of the town's religious life, but by 1614 the Spanish ambassador could complain with relative accuracy that Wesel had become "a second Geneva."[87] The town's adoption of Calvinism was therefore not the result of a successful missionary campaign but of war, which transformed the town's demographics, polarized religious viewpoints, and introduced a new political authority in the duchy of Cleves.[88]

❦∴❦

There is no doubt that the confessional era saw profound religious transformations in the hearts and minds of Germans all across the Empire. Tens of thousands of men and women experienced what can rightfully be described as religious conversions as they abandoned the faith of their birth and adopted new models of piety. There are examples of such conversion in Wesel as well.[89] Yet, as this essay has argued, looking at the city's turn away from Lutheranism and its adoption of Calvinism through the lens of conversion misrepresents what was taking place for two reasons. First, conversion in either of the two ways that scholars usually measure it describes a shift between two well-defined categories. The story of Saul's transformation into Paul implicitly assumes that different religions offer mutually exclusive cosmologies. Similarly, measuring conversion through changes in church membership presupposes that one institution is distinct from another—membership in the Roman Catholic Church, for instance, precludes membership in the Anglican Church. In sixteenth-century Wesel, however, religious categories, whether measured ideologically or institutionally, were simply too blurry and overlapping for the language of conversion to suffice. Indeed, this was an era in which the nature of faith itself was in a state of flux, and individuals were often unclear or divided about how deeply and in what ways confessional disagreements really divided Christians. Second, hastily adopting a language of conversion obscures the importance of the profound political and demographic changes for communities living through the Age of Religious Wars. That is, it overlooks the fact that the residents of Wesel who welcomed the Elector of Brandenburg in 1612 were a fundamentally different group of people facing dramatically different choices compared to those who had adopted the *Einfältiges Bedenken* following the collapse of the Augsburg Interim. In both moments, Weselers took their faith quite seriously. Yet, in order to understand the meaning of those changes, historians need to understand the nature of that faith from the perspective of their subjects. The language of conversion can help in this effort, but as this essay has shown, it can just as easily obscure it.

Notes

1. See the contribution of Duane Corpis to this volume. For general treatments of conversion, see Lewis Rambo, *Understanding Religious Conversion* (New Haven, 1993) and Karl F. Morrison, *Understanding Conversion* (Charlottesville, 1992).
2. Beat Hodler, "Konfessionen und der Handlungspielraum der Untertanen in der Eidgenossenschaft im Zeitalter der Reformierten Orthodoxie," in Heinrich R. Schmidt et al., eds., *Gemeinde, Reformation und Widerstand: Festschrift für Peter Blickle zum 60. Geburtstag* (Tübingen, 1998), pp. 281–291; Nicole Grochowina, "Bekehrungen und Indifferenz in Ostfriesland im 16. Jahrhundert," in Ute Lotz-Heumann et al., eds., *Konversion und Konfession in der Frühen Neuzeit* (Gütersloh, 2007), pp. 243–270; and Frauke Volkland, "Konfession, Konversion und soziales Drama: Ein Plädoyer für die Ablösung des Paradigmas der 'konfessionellen Identität,'" in Kaspar von Greyerz et al., eds., *Interkonfessionalität – Transkonfessionalität – binnenkonfessionelle Pluralität: Neue Forschungen zur Konfessionalisierungsthese* (Gütersloh, 2003), pp. 91–104.
3. On the "Second Reformation" in general, see Heinz Schilling, ed., *Reformierte Konfessionalisierung in Deutschland: Das Problem der 'Zweiten Reformation'* (Gütersloh, 1986). For a discussion of the limitations of this term, see Harm Klueting, "Problems of the Term and Concept 'Second Reformation': Memories of the 1980s Debate," in John M. Headley et al., eds., *Confessionalization in Europe, 1555–1700: Essays in Honor and Memory of Bodo Nischan* (Aldershot, 2004), pp. 37–49.
4. Bodo Nischan, *Prince, People and Confession: The Second Reformation in Brandenburg* (Philadelphia, 1994); and Heinz Schilling, *Konfessionskonflikt und Staatsbildung: eine Fallstudie über das Verhältnis von religiösem und sozialem Wandel in der Fruhneuzeit am Beispiel der Grafschaft Lippe* (Gütersloh, 1981).
5. Jesse Spohnholz, *The Tactics of Toleration: A Refugee Community in the Age of Religious Wars* (Newark, 2011), chap. 3.
6. Spohnholz, *Tactics of Toleration*, chap. 2.
7. *Reformation d. Hermanni Archiepiscopi Coloniensis* (Marburg [Cologne], 1543). Evangelisches Kirchenarchiv Wesel (henceforth cited as EKAW) Gefach 21,1; Gefach 65,1,34–6 fols. 103–105. On Hermann von Wied and his efforts at reform in Cologne, see J.F.G. Goeters, "Der katholische Hermann von Wied," *Monatshefte für Evangelische Kirchengeschichte des Rheinlandes* 35 (1986): 1–17; August Franzen, *Bischof und Reformation: Erzbischof Hermann von Wied in Köln vor der Entscheidung zwischen Reform und Reformation* (Münster, 1971); and Mechtild Köhn, *Martin Bucers Entwurf einer Reformation des Erzstiftes Köln* (Witten, 1966). On the implementation of Wied's Reformation in Wesel, Walter Stempel, "Die Einführung der Kölner Reformation in der Stadt Wesel," *Monatshefte für Evangelische Kirchengeschichte des Rheinlandes* 34 (1985): 260–268.

8. Calvinist immigrants initially resisted Wesel's religious compromise, prompting magistrates to experiment with imposing Lutheran orthodoxy in 1561. By 1565 the hostilities this engendered had grown so severe that magistrates abandoned these efforts and reinstituted Wesel's supraconfessional church; Spohnholz, *Tactics of Toleration*, chap. 1.

9. Periodic complaints about this shared ritual were handled with relative success by religious and political officials. See Jesse Spohnholz, "Multiconfessional Celebration of the Eucharist in Sixteenth-Century Wesel," *Sixteenth Century Journal* 39 (2008): 705–729.

10. On Xanten in the Duchy of Cleves, see Heinrich Kessel, "Reformation und Gegenreformation im Herzogtum Cleve (1517–1609)," *Düsseldorfer Jahrbuch* 30 (1920): 16–17. On Berg, see Stefan Ehrenpreis, '*Wir sind mit blutigen Köpfen davongelaufen...*': *Lokale Konfessionskonflikte im Herzogtum Berg 1550–1700* (Bochum, 1993), pp. 101, 120–127, 161. On the city of Münster, see R. Po-Chia Hsia, *Society and Religion in Münster, 1535–1618* (New Haven, 1984), pp. 123–124. On the prince-bishopric of Münster, see David M. Luebke, "Confessions of the Dead: Interpreting Burial Practice in the Late Reformation," *Archiv für Reformationsgeschichte* 101 (2010): 55–79. I would like to thank the author for sharing an earlier draft of this article with me before its publication. On the imperial city of Dortmund, see Heinz Schilling, "Dortmund im 16. und 17. Jahrhundert – Reichstädtische Gesellschaft, Reformation und Konfessionalisierung," in *Dortmund: 1100 Jahre Stadtgeschichte* (Dortmund, 1982), p. 162.

11. The term is adapted from Thomas Brady's book *Turning Swiss: Cities and Empire, 1450–1550* (Cambridge, 1985). I have borrowed it from David Fors Freeman, "Wesel and the Dutch Revolt: The Influence of Religious Refugees on a German City, 1544–1612" (Ph.D. dissertation, Emory University, 2002), p. 17.

12. Albert Wolters, *Reformationsgeschichte der Stadt Wesel* (Bonn, 1868); Johannes Heidemann, *Vorarbeiten zu einer Geschichte des höheren Schulwesens in Wesel*, 2 vols. (Wesel, 1853–1859), vol. 2 (1859), pp. 44–47; Johannes Hillmann, *Die Evangelische Gemeinde Wesel und ihre Willibrordkirche* (Düsseldorf, 1896), pp. 109–123; Heinz Schilling, *Niederländische Exulanten im 16. Jahrhundert* (Gütersloh, 1972); Achim Dünnwald, *Konfessionsstreit und Verfassungskonflikt: Die Aufnahme der Niederländischen Flüchtlinge im Herzogtum Kleve 1566–1585* (Bielefeld, 1998), pp. 136, 143–146, 155; and Herbert Kipp, "*Trachtet zuerst nach dem Reich Gottes*": *Landstädtische Reformation und Rats-Konfessionalisierung in Wesel (1520–1600)* (Bielefeld, 2004).

13. For 1564, see Kipp, *Landstädische Reformation*, pp. 362–363. For 1565, see Heidemann, *Vorarbeiten*, vol. 2, pp. 46–47. For 1566, see Freeman, "Wesel and the Dutch Revolt," p. 260. For 1568, see Justus Hashagen, *Der rheinische Protestantismus und die Entwicklung der rheinischen Kultur* (Essen, 1924), p. 130; and Wolters, *Reformationsgeschichte*, pp. 314–332.

14. Dünnwald, *Konfessionstreit und Verfassungskonflikt*, pp. 174–76; Schilling, *Niederländische Exulanten*; Hillmann, *Evangelische Gemeinde Wesel*, pp. 109–110; and Walter Stempel, '*Unnder beider gestalt*': *Die Reformation in der Stadt Wesel* (Wesel, 1990), p. 59. Only the 1913 Göttingen dissertation by Wilhelm Martens emphasizes the ecclesiastical and political shifts of the seventeenth century; see his *Das Kirchenregiment in Wesel zur Zeit der letzten klevischen und der ersten brandenburgischen Fürsten* (Göttingen, 1913). Relying on local studies, broader histories of the Reformation have replicated this confusion. For 1564, see Henry J. Cohn, "The Territorial Princes in Germany's Second Reformation, 1559–1622," in Menna Prestwich, ed., *International Calvinism, 1541–1715* (Oxford, 1985), p. 136; Mark Greengrass, *The Longman Companion to*

the European Reformation, c.1500–1618 (New York, 1998), p. 74; and F.L. Carsten, *Princes and Parliaments in Germany: From the Fifteenth to the Eighteenth Century* (Oxford, 1959), p. 274.

15. Hillmann, *Evangelische Gemeinde Wesel*, p. 109.
16. Schilling, *Niederländische Exulanten*, pp. 91–93; and David Fors Freeman, "'Those Persistent Lutherans: The Survival of Wesel's Minority Lutheran Community, 1578–1612" in Wim Janse and Barbara Pitkin, eds., *The Formation of Clerical and Confessional Identities in Early Modern Europe* (Leiden, 2006), p. 398. For similar examples: Stempel, *Reformation in der Stadt Wesel*, p. 59; Kipp, *Landstädtische Reformation*, pp. 362–363; Dünnwald, *Konfessionsstreit und Verfassungskonflikt*, p. 155.
17. Wilhelm Rotscheidt, "Übergang der Gemeinde Wesel von dem lutherischen zum reformierten Bekenntnis im 16. Jahrhundert," *Monatshefte für Rheinische Kirchengeschichte* 13 (1919): 225–256; Kipp, *Landstädtische Reformation*, pp. 66, 70, 166–169; and Heidemann, *Vorarbeiten*, vol. 2, pp. 46–47. Achim Dünnwald has even described Veltius as "integrated into the leading councils of the emigree community" ("in die Leitungsgremien der Flüchtlingsgemeinde integriert"). Dünnwald, *Konfessionsstreit und Verfassungskonflikt*, p. 144.
18. Kipp, *Landstädtische Reformation*, p. 193. Johannes Hillmann even called Venraid a minister of the Dutch Reformed Church in Wesel, a post that never existed; and Hillmann, *Evangelische Gemeinde Wesel*, p. 99.
19. August Franzen, "Die Herausbildung des Konfessionsbewußtseins am Niederrhein im 16. Jahrhundert," *Annalen des Historischen Vereins für den Niederrhein* 158 (1956): 185–190; Kessel, "Reformation und Gegenreformation," p. 27; and Johannes Bölitz, *Die evangelischen Pfarrer Wesels* (Wesel, 1978), p. 15. For a discrepancy with the minister Johannes Heidfelt, see Rotscheidt, "Übergang," p. 246; Dünnwald, *Konfessionsstreit und Verfassungskonflikt*, p. 144; and Schilling, "Dortmund." For nearby Berg, see Kurt Wesoly, "Katholisch, Lutherisch, Reformiert, Evangelisch? Zu den Anfängen der Reformation im Bergischen Land," in Burkhard Dietz and Stefan Ehrenpreis, eds., *Drei Konfessionen in einer Region: Beiträge zur Geschichte der Konfessionalisierung im Herzogtum Berg von 16. bis zum 18. Jahrhundert* (Cologne, 1999), pp. 300–301.
20. Ernst Walter Zeeden, for instance, has pointed out the "confessional ambiguities" (*konfessionelle Unklarheiten*) and "confusion in matters of faith" (*Glaubensverwirrung*) of people living in northwest Germany, combined with a strong tradition of "*Naivität und Ignoranz*" among the populace; Zeeden, *Die Entstehung der Konfessionen: Grundlagen und Formen der Konfessionsbildung im Zeitalter der Glaubenskämpfe* (Munich, 1965), pp. 68–78.
21. In March 1564 he wrote, "Natura abhorreo a conviciis et, quum neque Calvini, Bezae, Bullingeri, Lutheri etc. nomen baptizatus sim, sed in nomen filii dei, quid opus es, debacchari in hunc aut illum?" in J.F.G. Goeters, ed., "Zum Weseler Abendmahlstreit von 1561–64," *Monatshefte für Evangelische Kirchengeschichte des Rheinlandes* 2 (1953): 136. The reference is to 1 Corinthians 1:10–17. Similarly, when Heinrich Bommell was accused of calling Reformed Protestants his brothers, he defended himself by proclaiming that all Christians were his brothers, even if they were in error in the matter of the Eucharist. Cited in Rotscheidt, "Übergang," p. 240 and Hillmann, *Evangelische Gemeinde Wesel*, p. 85.
22. Stadtarchiv Wesel (henceforth cited as SAW) A3/56 fol. 119r–v.
23. EKAW Gefach 3,2,31a. The pastors drafted the letter initially for magistrates, who forwarded it to the duke. SAW A3/50 fol. 23r.

24. EKAW Gefach 72,2 fols. 122r, 125r. See Spohnholz, "Multiconfessional Celebration of Communion," p. 724.
25. Scholars studying European colonization have noticed similar problems with framing religious changes in terms of conversion. Jean and John Comaroff reject conversion as an analytical category in *Of Revelation and Revolution: Christianity, Colonialism and Consciousness in South Africa*, vol. 1 (Chicago, 1991), pp. 198–251. Richard Eaton, in contrast, has addressed the problem by redefining conversion as a process of "creative adaptation" in "Comparative History as World History: Religious Conversion in Modern India," *Journal of World History* 8, no. 2 (1997): 243–271. My argument does not deny the relevancy of conversion as a heuristic framework altogether, but rather demands that it be examined alongside other contexts.
26. Wolters, *Reformationsgeschichte der Stadt Wesel*, pp. 314–32; Kessel, "Reformation und Gegenreformation," pp. 38–40; and Hashagen, *Rheinische Protestantismus*, p. 130.
27. J.P. van Dooren, "Der Weseler Konvent 1568. Neue Forschungsergebnisse," *Monatshefte für Evangelische Kirchengeschichte des Rheinlandes* 31 (1982): 41–55.
28. This was Christian Mostaert, who had held a post in Wesel since 1561; SAW A3/56 fols. 16v–17r.
29. For an intellectual history of Calvinism and iconoclasm, see Carlos Eire, *War against the Idols: The Reformation of Worship from Erasmus to Calvin* (Cambridge, 1986). For studies of iconoclasm as demonstration of attitudes toward religious rituals, see Natalie Zemon Davis, "The Rites of Violence," in *Society and Culture in Early Modern France* (Stanford, 1975), pp. 152–187; Lee Palmer Wandel, *Voracious Idols and Violent Hands: Iconoclasm in Reformation Zurich, Strasbourg, and Basel* (Cambridge, 1995); and Peter Arnade, *Beggars, Iconoclasts, and Civic Patriots: The Political Culture of the Dutch Revolt* (Ithaca, 2008).
30. SAW A1/133,1 Mappe 2; A5/79 Missivenbuch 1569 fols. 12r, 90r–91r, 175r. Sammlung von Dorth, in Landesarchiv Nordrhein-Westfalen, Abteilung Rheinland (formerly Hauptstaatsarchiv Düsseldorf), HS N III XIII, fol. 51v. EKAW Gefach 3,1,70 fol. 335r–v; Gefach 65,1,56 fols. 156–158; 57 fols. 159–162; 89 fols. 278–279. See also Kipp, *Landstädtische Reformation*, pp. 163–164, 207, 212, 215–219, 254–255; and Hillmann, *Evangelische Gemeinde Wesel*, pp. 104–106.
31. EKAW Gefach 37,7 fol. 1263.
32. EKAW Gefach 33,5 fol. 24. Into the 1590s the council refurbished and rebuilt altars and retained clerical vestments. See also Niall Oakey, "Fixtures or Fittings: Can Surviving Pre-Reformation Ecclesiastical Material Culture be Used as a Barometer of Contemporary Attitudes to the Reformation in England?," in David Gaimster and Roberta Gilchrist, eds., *The Archaeology of Reformation* (Leeds, 2003), pp. 58–72.
33. EKAW Gefach 72,2 fols. 75v, 98r, 99v, 120v, 134v–135r; Gefach 3,2,28. See also Spohnholz, "Multiconfessional Celebration of the Eucharist," pp. 715–720.
34. Hillmann, *Evangelische Gemeinde Wesel*, pp. 157–80; and Martin Wilhelm Roelen, "Die Altäre und ihre Standorte in den Weseler Pfarrkirchen," in Roelen, ed., *Ecclesia Wesele: Beiträge zur Ortsnamenforschung und Kirchengeschichte* (Wesel, 2005), pp. 185–192. While Lutheran leaders condemned Catholic teaching on the intercessionary roles of saints, many were reluctant to reject them altogether. See Carol Piper Heming, *Protestants and the Cult of the Saints in German-Speaking Europe, 1527–1531* (Kirksville, MO, 2003); and Bridget Heal, *The Cult of the Virgin Mary in Early Modern Germany: Protestant and Catholic Piety, 1500–1648* (Cambridge, 2007).

35. Kipp, *Landstädtische Reformation*, p. 190; and Freeman, "Wesel and the Dutch Revolt," p. 322.

36. EKAW Gefach 72,1 fol. 65r; Gefach 72,2 fol. 17r–v.

37. Attendance rosters for both are both detailed and unambiguous. Herbertz never appears on either; EKAW Gefach 12,5; Gefach 72,1–2. The elders did consult with the city's pastors, however, in writing an attestation for him as he left for Gouda; EKAW Gefach 72,2 fols. 60r, 91r.

38. C.C. Hibben, *Gouda in Revolt: Particularism and Pacifism in the Revolt of the Netherlands, 1572–1588* (Utrecht, 1983), pp. 113–126; J.L. van der Gouw, "Herman Herbertz te Wesel," in P.H.A.M. Abels et al., eds., *In en om de Sint-Jan: Bijdragen tot de Goudse Kerkgeschiedenis. Een-en-twintigst Verzameling: Bijdragen van de Oudheidkundige Kring 'Die Goude'* (Delft, 1989), pp. 66–67; and Benjamin J. Kaplan, *Calvinists and Libertines: Confession and Community in Utrecht, 1578–1620* (Oxford, 1995), pp. 72–73, 230, 299.

39. EKAW Gefach 72,2 fol. 200v. For these claims, see Dünnwald, *Konfessionsstreit und Verfassungskonflikt*, p. 144; Hillmann, *Evangelische Gemeinde Wesel*, pp. 109–110; Stempel, *Reformation in der Stadt Wesel*, p. 58; and Kipp, *Landstädtische Reformation*, pp. 100–103.

40. EKAW Gefach 72,2 fol. 175r. Five times between October 1578 and the last classical meeting, in summer of 1586, either Heidfelt or Havenburg served as chair. Yet the other thirteen times the classis met, a Calvinist refugee chaired; EKAW Gefach 12,5 fols. 33r–87v.

41. When a few of the pastors did start attending, they were consulted about problems facing the local church and asked, for instance, not to baptize infants without parents being present; EKAW Gefach 12,5 fols. 35v, 39v. In April 1581 the classis asked that elders consult with pastors before bringing a matter (in this case, rules about legitimate interest rates) before the body, and to proceed with the case only if they disagreed with the pastors; EKAW Gefach 12,5 fol. 49v.

42. EKAW Gefach 12,5 fol. 69r.

43. Several of Wesel's pastors had been present at the start of the meeting, but the decision to admonish the ministers later in the day suggests that they left soon after the meeting started; EKAW Gefach 12,5 fol. 43r.

44. J.G.J. van Booma and J.L. van der Gouw, eds., *Communio et Mater Fidelium: Acta des Konsistoriums der niederländischen reformierten Flüchtlingsgemeinde in Wesel, 1573–1582* (Cologne, 1991), p. 601.

45. EKAW Gefach 72,2 fol. 52v.

46. EKAW Gefach 72,2 fol. 164r.

47. Elders resolved that they should continue to have tolerance until God brought the pastors a change of heart; EKAW Gefach 72,3 fol. 68. Despite their unwillingness, both ministers later attended classis meetings, further underlining that attendance at these meetings did not imply that the ministers were Calvinist; EKAW Gefach 12,5 fols. 41r–87r.

48. SAW A3/60 fol. 71r. The ministers did not subsequently comply, however.

49. Rotscheidt, "Übergang"; and Freeman, "Those Persistent Lutherans."

50. EKAW Gefach 3,1,63 fol. 293r–v. Bellinckhoven issued complaints about the clergy in March 1575 as well. SAW A3/58 fol. 66r.

51. EKAW Gefach 3,2,20; 3,2,33.

52. EKAW Gefach 72,2 fol. 130v.

53. EKAW Gefach 72,2 fol. 129r.

54. EKAW Gefach 72,2 fol. 139r, 232r; Gefach 72,3 fols. 46–47.

55. The six were Jorien ter Man, Simon Claessen, Jan ter Smytten, Hendryck ter Smitten, Reyner Reynertz, and Maryken, the wife of Adriaen Care; EKAW Gefach 72,3 fols. 139. These names have been cross-referenced with other records.

56. On Jan ten Boom's denial of the immortality of the soul see EKAW Gefach 72,2 fols. 193v–217v, 226v, 235v–237r, 246r, 249r–v. For Peter van Lyre, EKAW Gefach 72,2 fols. 181r, 194r. For Jan le Bruin, see EKAW Gefach 72,2 fol. 243. For Peter van Breda, see EKAW Gefach 72,2 fol. 166r.

57. EKAW Gefach 65,1,12 fols. 31–35; Werner Teschenmacher, *Annales ecclesiastici* (Düsseldorf, 1962), pp. 250–253; Kessel, "Reformation und Gegenreformation"; Dieter Keller, "Herzog Alba und die Wiederherstellung der katholischen Kirche am Rhein," *Preußische Jahrbücher* 48 (1881): 586–606; and Stephan Laux, "Wege und Grenzen der Konfessionalisierung: Der Kölner Erzbischöfe des 16. Jahrhunderts als geistliche Oberhäupter und Dynasten," in Dietz and Ehrenpreis, eds., *Drei Konfessionen in einer Region*, pp. 49–70.

58. For examples, see EKAW Gefach 72,2 fols. 193v, 197r, 217v, and 232v.

59. These numbers come from a prosopography of 7,697 Wesel residents between 1550 and 1600, drawn from civil and ecclesiastical records in the Stadtarchiv Wesel, Evangelisches Kirchenarchiv Wesel, and Landesarchiv Nordrhein-Westfalen, Abteilung Rheinland (formerly Hauptstaatsarchiv Düsseldorf).

60. EKAW Gefach 72,2 fols. 134r, 140v, 141r, 149v, 150v.

61. E.g., "*außlandischen Gemeinde*," "*Nidderlendische Reformierter Gemeinde binnen Nidder Weesell*," "*ghereformerde nederlanse ghemeynte In Wesel*," and "*die Gemeinden der Nidderlendisscher fremden*"; EKAW Gefach 72,3 fols. 17–18, 20–21, 32, and 56.

62. For recent historiographical discussions, see Ute Lotz-Heumann, "The Concept of 'Confessionalization': A Historiographical Paradigm in Dispute," *Memoria y Civilización* 4 (2001): 93–114; Thomas A. Brady, "Confessionalization: The Career of a Concept," in Headley et al., *Confessionalization in Europe*, pp. 1–20; and Luise Schorn-Schütte, "Konfessionalisierung als wissenschaftliches Paradigma?" in Joachim Bahlcke and Arno Strohmeyer, eds., *Konfessionalisierung in Ostmitteleuropa* (Stuttgart, 1999), pp. 61–77. See also Nichole Grochowina, "Confessional Indifference in East Frisia," *Reformation and Renaissance Review* 7 (2005): 111–124.

63. Marc R. Forster, *Counter-Reformation in the Villages: Religion and Reform in the Bishopric of Speyer, 1560–1720* (Ithaca, 1992); Heinrich Richard Schmidt, *Dorf und Religion: Reformierte Sittenzucht in Berner Landgemeinden der Frühen Neuzeit* (Stuttgart, 1995); and Frauke Volkland, *Konfession und Selbstverständnis: Reformierte Ritual in der gemischtkonfessionellen Kleinstadt Bischofszell im 17. Jahrhundert* (Göttingen, 2005).

64. See the essays in Greyerz et al., eds., *Interkonfessionalität – Transkonfesssionalität – binnenkonfessionelle Pluralität*.

65. Keith Luria highlights the adaptability and contingency of confessional boundaries in the face of changing historical conditions; see his *Sacred Boundaries: Religious Coexistence and Conflict in Early-Modern France* (Washington, DC, 2005).

66. In 1582 Archbishop Gebhard Truchseß of Waldburg converted to the Reformed faith and tried to introduce a Protestant church order. According to the Peace of Augsburg, a prince-bishop who converted to Protestantism had to renounce his office. Accordingly, Pope Gregory XIII deposed the Truchseß and the Cathedral chapter appointed Duke Ernst of Bavaria in his place. War broke out early the next year.

67. SAW A1/144,1,4; A1/111,1 fols. 14r–15r; A1/152,1 fols. 209r–211r, 246–247v.
68. Hermannus Ewichius, *Vesalia, Sive Civitatis Vesaliensis Descriptio. Wesel: Oder Beschreibung der Stadt Wesel* (1668; reprint Wesel, 1979), pp. 56–57.
69. *Chronik des Arnold von Anrath*, in Klaus Bambauer and Hermann Kleinholz, eds., *Geusen und Spanier am Niederrhein: Die Ereignisse der Jahre 1580–1632 nach den zeitgenössichen Chroniken der Weseler Bürger Arnold von Anrath und Heinrich von Weseken* (Wesel, 1992), p. 21.
70. SAW A3/62 fol. 33v.
71. SAW A3/62 fol. 6r.
72. SAW A3/62 fol. 34v; EKAW Gefach 42,1; Gefach 33,6 1586–1587; Gefach 37,6 1586–1587.
73. SAW A3/63 fols. 83v–84r.
74. EKAW Gefach 72,3 fols. 16–17.
75. SAW A3/62 fol. 25r; A3/63 fol. 84r.
76. SAW A3/64 fol. 3r. Parma shifted troops from the Lower Rhine to France because the murder of King Henri III in August 1589 intensified the military struggle for control of that country; Geoffrey Parker, *The Dutch Revolt* (New York, 1977), pp. 226–227.
77. *Chronik des Arnold von Anrath*, pp. 26–31.
78. SAW A1/111,1 fol. 85r. The *stadholder* of Gelderland also humbly apologized for the damage his troops did to Wesel. SAW A1/111,1 fols. 60r–v, 86r.
79. Among the Lutherans were Rutger Brecht (*Bürgermeister*), Franciscus Brecht, Wilhelm van Reid, and Henrich van School (council), and Bert van School (judge). Among the Calvinists were Arnt Beyer, Henrich ter Smitten and Hans Boots (judges), Jasper ter Smitten (council), Willem Butting, Victor van Xanten, Peter ter Hornen, Pasque Fontein, Christian Hannis, and Johan Sticker (*Gemeinsfreunde*). Xanten, Fontein, and Hannis had served as Calvinist elders. See SAW A3/64 fol. 1r–v. See also Kipp, *Landstädtische Reformation*, pp. 92–93.
80. EKAW Gefach 72,3 fol. 252.
81. Heinrich Friedrich Jacobson, ed., *Urkunden-Samlung von bisher ungedruckten Gesetzen nebst Uebersichten gedruckter Verordnungen für die evangelische Kirche von Rheinland und Westfalen* (Königsberg, 1844), pp. 75–77.
82. Calvinist elders staged an ineffectual protest against the town's communion services, calling for the removal of the high altar and its replacement with a simple table. Following this, Jodicus Willich, who allied himself with the Reformed, was replaced by the moderate Philippist Lutheran Georg Scheutzlich. See Hillmann, *Evangelische Gemeinde Wesel*, pp. 114–116; and Gerhard Sardemann, "Johannes Brantius, Rektor an den Höhen Schule in Wesel, 1594–1620öhHHh," *Zeitschrift des Bergischen Geschichtsvereins* 4 (1867): 135–139. This situation was briefly interrupted for just over five months in 1598/99, when Spanish troops captured the city and Catholics took over the churches. See Ewichius, *Vesalia, Sive Civitatis*, pp. 58–59; and Jutta Prieur, "Wesels Große Zeit – Das Jahrhundert in den Vereinigten Herzogtümern," in Jutta Prieur, ed., *Geschichte der Stadt Wesel*, 2 vols. (Düsseldorf, 1991), vol. 1, pp. 196–197.
83. Johann Sigismund publicly converted to Calvinism in 1613, although he had apparently secretly converted seven years before; Nischan, *Prince, People and Confession*, pp. 83, 91–98. Wolfgang Wilhelm, who succeeded to the throne in the middle of the crisis, married the sister of Duke Maximilian of Bavaria in late 1613.
84. SAW A3/67 fol. 37v. Margrave Ernst was aided in his efforts by the Calvinist minister Simon Ulrich Pistoris; Nischan, *Prince, People and Confession*, pp. 83–94.

85. Manuela Werner, *'Gott geb, daß dis das letzte sey': Alltag in Wesel um 1600* (Wesel, 2003), pp. 40–41.

86. *Chronik des Heinrich von Weseken*, in Bambauer and Kleinholz, eds., *Geusen und Spanier am Niederrhein*, p. 344; Hillmann, *Evangelische Gemeinde Wesel*, p. 115; and Stempel, *Reformation in der Stadt Wesel*, p. 64. French-speaking Calvinists were also allowed public sermons in St. Willibrord's church at this time.

87. He wrote this in a letter to King Philip II of Spain on 16 December 1614. Quoted in Alison D. Anderson, *On the Verge of War: International Relations and the Jülich-Kleve Succession Crises (1609–1614)* (Boston, 1999), p. 195; and Martens, *Kirchenregiment in Wesel*, pp. 73–74.

88. In the seventeenth-century Franconian parishes studied by Günther Dippold, demographic shifts, war, and political pressures were similarly more important in shifting the confessional profile of villages than were spiritual conversions. Those conversions that he does identify were rarely sincere; Günter Dippold, *Konfessionalisierung am Obermain: Reformation und Gegenreformation in den Pfarrsprengeln von Baunach bis Marktgraitz* (Staffelstein, 1996).

89. A Catholic member of the Sisters of the Common Life, Elizabeth Wolffcoel, submitted to the discipline of the Calvinist consistory in Wesel in 1595; Kipp, *Landstädtische Reformation*, p. 286.

CHAPTER FOUR

The Right to Be Catholic—
The Right to Be Protestant?
Perspectives on Conversion before and after
the Peace of Westphalia

RALF-PETER FUCHS

In the mid eighteenth century, the author of an article on "Conversion" (*Religions-Veränderung*) in Johann Heinrich Zedler's *Universal-Lexicon* claimed that Germany was a country that promised freedom of conscience, where everyone should be permitted to convert from one of the established religions to any of the others—Catholicism, Lutheranism, and Calvinism—and to do so without loss of honor.[1] This writer was sure that conversion was a right available to all. But this position grew out of a long period of conflict. In the sixteenth and seventeenth centuries, when the idea of religious plurality had not yet won widespread acceptance, conversion became a major bone of contention among the three mainstream confessions. Many feared that large-scale conversion would result in bitter enmity between confessions. The diplomats who negotiated the Peace of Westphalia in 1648 believed that the Thirty Years' War had originated from those "quarrels about religion" (*Streitigkeiten wegen der Religion*).[2]

Although these diplomats did not often mention the problem of conversion explicitly, their treaty took it into account. The Peace of Westphalia represented a crucial watershed because it settled divisive tensions. Conversion was a point of contention because the right of rulers to govern religious matters in their territories had, for the most part, been interpreted as a right to bring the subjects to their religion (*ius reformandi*). On the other hand, the question of freedom of conscience had generated demands of shelter from many subjects of the Holy Roman Empire who did not want to convert to their rulers' religion.[3] A solution to this problem was found finally in the so-called "normative year" principle, which stipulated that every territory in the Empire should revert to the confessional status it had in 1624. Under the terms of the treaty signed in Münster and Osnabrück, the normative year would remain valid and effective forever as an "eternal peace" (*pax perpetua*). Johann Jacob Moser, the famous eighteenth-century Protestant commentator on imperial affairs, considered it the very "soul of the Peace of Westphalia."[4]

The following essay sketches the development of this settlement and the impact it had on the politics of religion.[5] I begin with a look at the different political strategies of Catholics and Protestants during the sixteenth and seventeenth centuries, as well as at the norms and concepts that guided them. The essay then shows how the Thirty Years' War encouraged new perspectives on the politics of religion. Finally, the essay looks forward into the eighteenth century and the new conditions that emerged when fears about conversions, now centering upon the reversal of Catholic and Protestant positions, once again appeared in political discourse.

Religious Pluralization and "Freezing"

In the Holy Roman Empire, attitudes toward conversion were bound up with a pan-European development that I characterize as religious pluralization.[6] In his recent survey of the Reformation era, Diarmaid MacCulloch describes the emergence of "multiple reformations," resulting both in the construction of new churches by the various "Protestantisms," as well as transformation of the old church through the Council of Trent and the Catholic Reformation it set in motion.[7] Thus, MacCulloch writes, "Europe's house" divided over the course of the sixteenth century.

The same was no less true of the Holy Roman Empire. For most of the nineteenth century and much of the twentieth, German historians used the term *Kirchenspaltung* ("schism" or "division of the church") to characterize this process. This term has come under criticism, however, because it does not take into account the fact that fundamentally different institutions and ecclesiastical doctrines developed within each confession as pluralization ran its course.[8] Furthermore, it evokes the image of two monolithic systems while also presenting the Protestant movements as mere splinter groups of the Catholic Church.[9] Finally, the term has a negative connotation. The historian Leopold von Ranke, for example, held the *Kirchenspaltung* partly responsible for the political division and weakening of the German nation.[10] Nowadays religious plurality is seen as a nucleus of modern societies, and scholars are focusing on how early modern contemporaries dealt with those forms of plurality.[11] And they increasingly examine the role of religious plurality in everyday life.[12]

Despite the fact that Catholic and Protestant writers of the sixteenth century often discussed the problem of "divided religion" (*spaltige Religion*) and its destructive effects on the Holy Roman Empire, I consider the term "religious pluralization" more appropriate for analyzing the evolution of religious life in early modern Germany.[13] This term has two advantages: first, rather than present each denomination as homogeneous, pluralization accounts for differences within each confession; second, the term emphasizes the evolutionary quality and contextual determinants of differentiation among and within the confessions. Even though a factual plurality of different denominations existed since the first half of the sixteenth century, the process of pluralization did not simply come to a halt in this period. On the contrary, pluralization represented a long-term development that continued throughout the sixteenth century and into the seventeenth. Before the mid seventeenth century, the forms and structures of religious life in the Empire were in a state of continuous flux. This is not to say that there were no efforts to establish unity of doctrine and practice within denominations. But even this process of consolidation of confessions within the territories—normally referred to as "confessionalization"—contributed to the pluralization of religion because it continued to establish differences between Catholics, Lutherans, and Calvinists.[14]

The effects of pluralization extended well beyond the religious sphere. Perhaps the most important of these was legal. One of the most divisive questions in the Empire during the mid sixteenth century centered upon whether or not denominational plurality should be given a legal basis within the imperial constitution. The legal historian Martin Heckel has called this conflict a division or fragmentation of the law (*Spaltung des Rechts*), describing it as the emergence of essentially different ways of interpreting the law.[15] The historian Fritz Dickmann, similarly, has pointed to the fact that over the course of the sixteenth century, the deliberations of the Imperial Diet were gradually reorganized around two denominational political "parties," Catholic and Protestant, which pursued policies that were entirely antagonistic to one another. In Dickmann's view, these parties in the Imperial Diet were the main protagonists in the struggle for domination and the distribution of territory within the Empire.[16]

Taking such areas of conflict into account should not, however, detract from the great range of less militant attitudes and approaches toward religious pluralization. The Empire's princes and free cities dealt with the problem of religious pluralization in many different ways, not all of them militant or repressive, which suggests that pluralization was not always a source of conflict. While historians have often portrayed the Thirty Years' War as inevitable, more recent research has emphasized the variety of strategies the imperial princes employed in order to interpret and manage the political problems caused by religious difference.[17] The Lutheran princes of Electoral Saxony are a good example. At times, their own legates characterized their policy as "popish" (*Bäpstisch*).[18] The historian Moriz Ritter referred to the imperial estates that adopted this policy of rapprochement as the "Saxon party" (*sächsische Partei*), contrasting it with the "party of action" (*Aktionspartei*) or the "Palatine party" (*pfälzische Partei*)— so named for the Calvinist and more militant elector Palatine.[19] The irenicist policies of Emperors Ferdinand I (1556–1564), Maximilian II (1564–1576), and—at times—Rudolf II (1576–1612) also make it clear that to some extent, religious plurality could be integrated within the imperial political system. To be sure, a close connection always persisted between emperorship and Catholicism as well as the Papacy. Nevertheless, the Protestants highly respected these emperors as imperial leaders, perceiving them, rightfully or not, as pursuing a policy of toleration and peace between the religious groups.

In sum, then, the term *Kirchenspaltung* tends to eclipse early modern attempts to develop forms and patterns of coexistence among the denominational parties. But another term that is sometimes used in historical research—*Kirchenpluralismus*, "ecclesiastical pluralism"—exaggerates in the opposite direction.[20] The term pluralism implies a condition of accepted multiplicity that did not represent a fundamental threat to claims of denominational truth; such a notion did not exist—or at least hardly existed—in the early modern period.[21] Fundamental skepticism obscured the process of religious pluralization: Catholics as well as Protestants wanted to establish one "true religion."[22] Few if any endorsed pluralization as a positive good; far louder and more insistent were demands to eradicate it. A particularly corrosive effect of this skepticism was the fear among both Catholics and Protestants that one's own denomination might be outnumbered by its religious opponents, or would soon be overwhelmed. Over the long term, this apprehension led to a weakening of moderate elements and promoted antagonistic postures.

The Holy Roman Empire, then, was capable of integrating plurality as a temporary reality but lacked the normative means to justify plurality as a permanent fixture of political and religious life. The basic problem stemmed from a lack of legal stability.[23] Religious pluralization occurred as an open-ended process; it therefore evoked substantial fears about the future. As we can see in many pamphlets published before the Thirty Years' War, many writers anticipated chaos, confusion, and war;[24] others forecast the possibility of "depluralization" to the disadvantage of their own religion.[25] The political rulers found themselves in a situation in which it seemed necessary to act in order to shape the course of future developments. As in any perceived zero-sum struggle for space and resources, the religious parties, Catholics and Protestants, tried to strengthen their respective positions with regard to a future moment of decision.

This struggle for territory within the Empire in turn stimulated the emergence of two antagonist programs of religious parties, opposing each other at the Imperial Diets and other assemblies of the Empire. The Catholic program came to center upon the concept of "freezing": the attempt to prevent the further spread of Protestantism through the conversion of princes by locking in place the existing confessional status of specific territories and city-states. Catholics were particularly keen to prevent Protestant princes from seizing more temporal possessions of the Catholic Church—the *Kirchengüter*—especially those territories ruled by bishops, abbots, and other prelates as secular overlords.[26]

An example of "freezing" can be seen in a clause in the Peace of Augsburg (1555) that regulated the confessional status of ecclesiastical territories: the so-called "ecclesiastical reservation" (*Geistlicher Vorbehalt*), aimed to secure the Catholics' possession of *Kirchengüter* even if their rulers converted. The ecclesiastical reservation stipulated that prince-bishops and other prelates who converted to Protestantism would be required to resign their offices, including all the authorities and incomes that derived from them. The Catholic party also demanded that the Protestant princes should restore all the *Kirchengüter* they had seized since 1552, the year of the Peace of Passau (a forerunner to the Peace of Augsburg), even if those establishments were subject to the secular authority of a Protestant overlord. Catholics also sought to prevent future seizures by pressing Protestants to renounce all further secularization.

The Protestant party, on the other hand, tried to wrest from the Catholics a formal recognition of their right to exist. By recognizing the "Augsburg Confession" as a lawful religion, the Peace of Augsburg went a long way toward satisfying this demand. The Protestants also fought to be accepted as a denominational group on a par with the Catholics (*Parität*).[27] In many respects this point, too, was conceded during the decades following 1555. But a very important cause of religious conflict before the Thirty Years' War was the Protestants' insistence on the right to spread their religion in a peaceful manner. From their point of view, this included the right to acquire ecclesiastic possessions and the right to convert (*autonomia*). At the Imperial Diets following the Peace of Augsburg, they disclaimed the ecclesiastical reservation and maintained that they never had given their consent to this clause.

One of the most radical opponents of *autonomia* was the Catholic jurist Andreas Erstenberger, whose tract bearing that title appeared in 1586. Erstenberger remained convinced that Protestants were striving to extinguish Catholicism in Germany by converting the subjects of Catholic princes. He described five types of *autonomia*, distinguished by the status of groups that might be affected: first he mentioned the freedom of religion granted to the electoral princes and other imperial estates; next came the *autonomia* of the clergy; then the *autonomia* of nobles; then the *autonomia* of the subjects of ecclesiastical territories; and, finally, that of the whole of mankind. Erstenberger regarded this fifth variety of *autonomia*—the "general concession of religious freedom to all Christians" (*Generalfreystellung aller Christen*)—as absurd and dangerous.[28]

Erstenberger's attempt to expose the Protestant concept of *autonomia* as a "general concession" provoked reactions. Some Protestant writers denied strictly that their aim was unlimited freedom of religion. They tried to delimit the term as an exclusive right of Lutherans to practice their religion and to acquire ecclesiastical benefices.[29] For them, Erstenberger's allegation that *autonomia* meant that anyone had the right to believe whatever he or she wanted was a defamation of Protestant belief. In point of fact, the Protestant program of religious freedom as represented in those polemic papers and in discourses at the Imperial Diets implied only the right for Protestants to avow their own doctrine.

To be sure, the Catholics undermined their own position by deploying Jesuit missionaries and religious confraternities to proselytize among the subjects of Protestant princes; similarly, Protestant princes adopted their opponents' position by denying their own subjects the right to convert to Catholicism. Even so, the main concepts of the two religious parties may be delineated as follows: the Catholics tried to restrict *autonomia* and sought to preserve the confessional status quo by law. It was, in essence, a policy of "freezing." The Protestants, for their part, endorsed the right to convert as a means to encourage the advance of Reformation.

It should therefore be emphasized that the cause of political instability in late sixteenth-century Germany lay not in religious plurality itself but in the tension between these two opposed political programs. After 1555, Catholics defamed Protestants as peace-breakers every time they acquired more ecclesiastical possessions through the conversion of a secular lord, even though the settlement had conferred on them the right to determine the religion of territories subject to their authority. From the Catholics' point of view, the "ecclesiastical reservation," indeed the entire religious peace of 1555, was meant to freeze the confessional status quo. Any advance of Protestantism violated its letter and spirit. On the other hand, the Protestants' party denied that the "ecclesiastical reservation" was a formally valid part of the Peace of Augsburg. The Protestants rather complained that the Catholics tried to force the Empire's estates and subjects in religious matters and prevented them from following their consciences. They also protested that they tried to deprive Protestants of their right to gain property.

Finding the "Normative Year"

After the harrowing first phases of the Thirty Years' War, German Protestants developed their own concept of freezing. The years between 1618 and 1629 (Peace of Lübeck) saw a period of great military success for the armies of Emperor Ferdinand II and the Catholic League. In 1629, just as the tide of Catholic fortunes was cresting, the emperor and his closest allies, the elector of Bavaria and the archbishop-electors of Cologne, Mainz, and Trier, attempted to put the Catholic concept of freezing into practice with the "Edict of Restitution."[30] In essence, the edict decreed the immediate execution of the ecclesiastical reservation as Catholics understood it—to restore all church property secularized since 1552. More than that, the inhabitants of these territories were supposed to revert to Catholicism as well. The edict, in other words, did more than put a stop to Protestant *autonomia*; it attempted to reverse the effects of eighty years of conversions. A wave of mass conversions in formerly Protestant territories ensued throughout the Empire. Imperial commissioners accompanied by troops forced the reversion of monasteries that had been secularized by Protestant rulers. In many locations, Protestant preachers were expelled and replaced by Catholic priests.[31]

Faced with an unprecedented and mortal threat, some Protestant princes put forward a new religious policy proposing years that were more favorable for them than 1552. Their first aim, obviously, was to advance an alternative to the edict. To that end, they began offering fixed dates that would be grounded in consensus between Catholics and Protestants and therefore provide a stable legal basis for religious plurality. Those fixed dates, which were to be binding for Catholics as well as for Protestants, can be defined as "normative years" though analogous terms like *annus normalis* or "Normal-Jahr" were created later, in the eighteenth century.[32]

The first of these proposals was advanced at a convention of the electoral princes in 1630 at Regensburg. Anton Wolff, the chancellor of Hessen-Darmstadt, proposed 1555 as a normative year for nearly all imperial estates and 1621 as an alternative for the highest-ranking Protestant princes, the electors of Saxony and Brandenburg. The year 1555 stood for the Peace of Augsburg, which the Protestants considered as a basic law that guaranteed them the right to exist. The other favored year, 1621, was especially germane for the elector of Saxony, who, as the Emperor's ally in the first years of the war from 1620 to 1622, had obtained Lusatia and in 1621 had gained free practice of their religion for the Protestants in Silesia. But Wolff found no support for his concept.[33] The Catholics were unwilling to withdraw the Edict of Restitution. The electors of Saxony and Brandenburg made clear that they also were disinclined to accept Wolff's proposal. Georg Wilhelm, elector of Brandenburg, saw the true evangelical doctrine in danger.

Then in 1631 at the so-called Frankfurter Kompositionstag, a gathering of imperial princes and diplomats in Frankfurt, the Lutheran Elector of Saxony Johann Georg I, who wanted to assert himself as a peacemaker, offered 1620 as a general normative year, it being the year of the Battle of the White Mountain near Prague, which in the view of many princes marked the beginning of the great war. That same year, 1620, Johann Georg had negotiated a safeguard on behalf of the Protestant territories in northern Germany in return for his own military support of the emperor against the "Bohemian rebellion." Like Anton Wolff's proposal the year before, the elector's proposal found critics among Protestants, many of whom considered him an untrustworthy turncoat. Perhaps Johann Georg saw his proposal as an opportunity to restore his reputation among the Protestant faithful. Be that as it may, he and his diplomats faced a difficult task: the concept of *autonomia* was deeply ingrained in Protestant self-awareness, and any notion of "freezing" seemed to contradict it. But with hard work and persistence, the elector's diplomats eventually persuaded a majority of Protestant princes to accept a peace based on a normative year.[34] Nevertheless, this proposal failed too because the Catholics did not accept it. The Frankfurter Kompositionstag finally ended abruptly because the Catholic diplomats fled the Swedish troops approaching after the Battle of Breitenfeld.

Four years later, in 1635, Elector Johann Georg and the emperor settled on 1627 as a normative year in the Peace of Prague—the first time the two parties were able to agree on a common point for "freezing" the confessional status quo.[35] But the Peace of Prague failed because Sweden had been excluded from the negotiations and France's entry into the war prolonged it for many years. It was the Peace of Westphalia that formally ended the great war in 1648. It pushed the normative year back three years to 1624, simply because it lay halfway between the Protestants' initial proposal in Munster and Osnabruck to select 1618, the year of the Bohemian revolt, and the emperor's choice—1630, when the Swedish King Gustav II Adolph had fallen on the Empire with his troops.[36] This Solomonic compromise reflected a deliberate effort on both sides to generate confidence and equity. As a solution, 1624 simply split the difference; it was the "great deal," the "middle point," the "medium."[37]

For Protestants, negotiations about accepting the normative year implied an important change of attitude. Unquestionably, their own war experience had led toward caution and away from a policy designed to promote the spread of the Reformation. In order to secure guarantees of their own terrain, Protestants had been forced to concede to Catholics the right to hold theirs. Many still insisted that such concessions should not limit *autonomia* and that conversion to the "true" church should remain possible for everybody. Indeed, the Protestants inserted their idea of *autonomia* into the Peace of Westphalia with a clause that allowed anyone to practice his or her own religion within the private, domestic sphere. Despite these exceptions, however, the possessions of each confessional group were fixed by the normative year 1624.

This solution had a profoundly stabilizing effect on religious plurality. For one thing, it meant that the Protestants' struggle for parity in the Empire had been successful: their rights and properties would be secured by imperial law. Yet it also meant that Catholics living as minorities in Protestant regions could make claims demanding parity, too. Finally, all religious dissenters, Catholic or Protestant, were protected from forcible conversion if they could prove that they had practiced their religion in 1624. All parties to the negotiations recognized that the normative year would have a freezing effect. Indeed, the Protestants sometimes interpreted it as a kind of ecclesiastic reservation, now guaranteed for both religions.[38]

The main intention of the normative year was to fix the confessional landscape in order to prevent further quarrels over religion. But one question remained unresolved: should the confessional landscape stay frozen forever? To be sure, the Protestants had insisted on a perpetual peace; from their point of view, the treaty should have no expiration date. By the same token, however, the idea that existing confessional distributions should remain forever fixed struck many Protestants as odd. Their immediate aim in 1648 centered upon recovering territories and possessions lost during the Thirty Years' War; in the years after the Peace of Westphalia from 1648 to 1653 they therefore appealed strongly to the normative year 1624 in order to justify and facilitate restitution.

These years of restitution and the consolidation of peace have attracted a great deal of attention from historians of religious life.[39] But there is a lack of research into the strategies employed to make peace in the Empire's various regions and territories. Almost immediately, conflicts arose when the emperor, at the urging of Swedish field commanders, dispatched bi-confessional commissions to initiate restitutions in the Empire's territories and localities in accordance with the normative year.[40] The normative year was a double-edged sword: on the one hand, it safeguarded the rights of many parishes, but on the other it authorized a new wave of conversions. The first of these struggles erupted in the autumn of 1648, when the Catholic inhabitants of Pfalz-Sulzbach, fearing that they would forfeit the right to practice their religion in public, protested against the restitution of Protestant worship. In this instance, Catholics now began to conduct themselves as advocates of freedom of conscience, declaring that, as a deputy of the prince-bishop of Bamberg formulated it, a well-administered order should not depend solely on the normative year, but also on the subjects' individual will. This of course was the position that Protestants had advanced against the ecclesiastical reservation prior to the Thirty Years' War.

Depending on the circumstances, Protestants also found reason to oppose restitutions based on the normative year. In 1651, Elector of Brandenburg Friedrich Wilhelm protested against such restitutions in the former duchies of Jülich and Berg, which were under the rule of the duke of Pfalz-Neuburg though he himself sustained claims to both territories originating in succession quarrels (*Jülich-Klevischer Erbfolgestreit*). The two princes failed to reach an agreement, and the result was a brief military confrontation known as the "Düsseldorf Cow War" (*Düsseldorfer Kuhkrieg*). Its name traces back to the military seizure of some cows belonging to the palace surroundings of the duchess of Pfalz-Neuburg near Düsseldorf. But it would be more accurate to call it a "War of the Normative Year" because its origin lay definitively in the duke's effort to bring the normative year rule to execution against the elector's objection.

Be that as it may, the point remains that the normative year regulation, though intended to bring religious violence to a halt, had the effect of stimulating new debates and conflicts. The "War of the Normative Year" between the elector of Brandenburg and the duke of Pfalz-Neuburg was stopped with the aid of the Imperial Aulic Court (Reichshofrat) and its deputies as mediators. Only the suspension of the normative year rule could achieve peace. Indeed, the difficulties of implementing the normative year were such that in many regions of the Empire, it could be enforced only with the help of locally negotiated settlements. In many regions, it was simply brushed aside.

The Politics of Conversion after 1648

It comes as no surprise, therefore, that long after 1648, many Protestant estates and subjects still complained that the normative year had not been realized in many territories of the Empire.[41] Indeed, its execution remained a patchwork. But it should be stressed that by bringing the old quarrel between the Empire's religious parties to an end, the normative year had a profoundly pacifying impact. The Gordian knot it severed had made the Peace of Westphalia possible.

The normative year principle continued to spark controversy well into the eighteenth century, but the texture of these debates differed profoundly from those of the sixteenth and early seventeenth centuries. Just as the protests in Pfalz-Sulzbach foretold, the political arguments of Catholics and Protestants were now inverted. After all, in the eighteenth century, Protestants sought to freeze denominational proportions in order to halt the progress of religious change; now it was they who defended "freezing," both as a means to recover territories that had been lost to Catholicism during the Thirty Years' War and in order to conserve their possessions in the long term. The motive for this reversal of position lay in the considerable number of conversions of princes from Protestantism to Catholicism since the second half of the seventeenth century. Protestantism in the Empire weakened after those rulers became Catholics. The normative year thus more and more drew the attention of jurists in Protestant territories.

During the negotiations that led to the Peace of Westphalia, the normative year regulation had had no specific name. The envoys in Münster and Osnabrück had called it simply the "rule" (Regul), the "general rule" (General-Regul), the terminus a quo, or the medium. A specific juridical term entered the legal vocabulary around 1700, when Protestant jurists coined the term annus *decretorius,* the "determinative year."[42] In subsequent years, several Protestant doctoral candidates published dissertations that stressed its importance and described its effects.[43] These dissertations also generated new alternative labels such as *annus regulativus* ("regulatory year"), *annus decisivus* ("decisive year"), and *annus normalis* ("normative year"). Later, from the mid eighteenth century on, German terms as such as the *Entscheid-Jahr* ("decisive year") or *Normaljahr* ("normative year") would become more common.[44]

The reversal of positions between Protestants and Catholics is most apparent in the work of the Swabian jurist Johann Jacob Moser, who in 1773 published a treatise on "territorial sovereignty in ecclesiastical matters" (*Landeshoheit im Geistlichen*). Like many of his fellow Protestants, Moser never tired of emphasizing that the normative year clause created "the permanent and never-ending counterbalance between both religions," Protestant and Catholic.[45] For Moser, one of the most "holy" principles of the Peace of Westphalia was to "conserve forever the status quo of the year 1624."[46]

Moser also underlined the idea of freedom of conscience, drawing upon Protestant traditions. But Moser was nothing if not precise: he defined freedom of conscience as the right of subjects to keep their religion, even if their ruler converted to another religion. According to him, the normative year granted specific rights for subjects, including protections for their manner of public worship and the ownership of churches and ecclesiastical possessions, in perpetuity.[47] These "rights" included access to church revenues, schools, hospitals, and the preservation of liturgical customs, among many other things. A close inspection of Moser's text reveals, in short, that freedom of conscience was defined primarily as a means to conserve property and traditions, not as a right to convert.

Moser was by no means alone in this judgment. Throughout the eighteenth century, the Protestant delegates to the Imperial Diet reaffirmed the everlasting legal force of the normative year, filing protests or petitions in support of Protestant subjects claiming a right to public worship under the normative year clause.[48] In 1720, for example, the Protestant estates presented a writ to Emperor Charles VI, complaining that in their view, the Peace of Westphalia clearly forbade many "mutations" that had occurred in religious matters.[49] In the same year, they objected to the disturbing presence of Catholic priests among the subjects in the county of Leiningen-Westerburg.[50] And they opposed attempts to introduce the Gregorian calendar in territories with mixed Protestant and Catholic populations.[51]

To be sure, the Protestants' high estimation of the normative year still resulted from their ceaseless efforts to guarantee freedom of religion to the Protestant subjects of Catholic princes. But even more it derived from the Protestants' preoccupation with protecting their lands and possessions from Catholic expansion. The forward push of Catholicism fed an obsession with preserving the status quo of 1624. Protestant estates and jurists interpreted the normative year as an instruction to determine the boundaries between both religions forever.[52]

As foretold, Protestant princes who converted to Catholicism posed a great threat to the status quo. One of those rulers was Count Christian August of Pfalz-Sulzbach, who converted to Catholicism in 1655 and then gave his Catholic subjects the right to practice their religion in public.[53] This act violated the normative year clause: in 1624, there had been no public observance of Catholicism. For Moser and like-minded Protestant jurists, the case of Pfalz-Sulzbach represented the origin of a new institution that violated both the spirit and the letter of the normative year clause—*Simultaneum*, a situation in which two religions were observed in public within a single territory, in some cases within a single church.[54]

Moser was prompted to give his account of the controversy in Pfalz-Sulzbach after Catholic subjects demanded the right to celebrate the Mass in the same churches Protestants used. Catholics had argued that the normative year clause, while it had rightfully restored the churches to Protestant congregations, did not necessarily forbid the use of those same buildings by Catholic subjects at other times of day. To the contrary, Protestants argued that *Simultaneum* necessarily infringed on their rights of ownership. They argued that they could not be considered "owners" of religious buildings if they were forced to share them.[55] In contrast to the sixteenth century, the specter of shifting confessional landscapes now haunted Protestants more than Catholics. Protestants' fear of conversion found expression in Moser's judgment that the ultimate cause of the Thirty Years' War had been the princes' "ceaseless reforming and counter-reforming" (*unaufhörliches reformieren und wider reformieren*).[56] Only by halting conversion could peace be guaranteed.

Protestants were further spooked by the fear that *Simultaneum* would expose their coreligionists to Catholic "contamination." To be sure, many Protestants still took the view that freedom of religion and conscience were necessary. This conviction implied a general right to convert—the very position advanced by the aforementioned article on "Conversion" in Johann Heinrich Zedler's *Universal-Lexicon*.[57] Nevertheless, Protestants increasingly approached the question of conversion with skepticism. Conversion at this point was often presented as a threat endangering the Protestants and the Empire's constitution. The author of a different article in Zedler's *Universal-Lexicon* put it this way: "everyday experience has proven sufficiently that the Catholic side wastes no effort to propagate the Roman Catholic religion in every possible way."[58]

The analogy to Catholic assertions made in the sixteenth century is striking; the basic pattern of argumentation is nearly identical. But the effects were not. In the sixteenth century, such assertions had fanned the flames of religious conflict; by the eighteenth century, however, the normative year and the mutual agreement on which it was based had exerted profound psychological impact. In contrast to the sixteenth century, Protestants were now in the position of defending the Empire's status quo of religious constitution, a constitution basically accepted by both sides. Rather than circumvent the law, Protestants brought their grievances before the Imperial Diet or the Empire's sovereign court, the Imperial Chamber Court (*Reichskammergericht*), where they tried to prevent the expansion of *Simultanea* in the region of Franconia.[59] Although Catholic subjects sometimes also asserted the normative year clause, for Protestants it had become the keystone of political discourse in religious matters.[60]

As a tool for blocking conversion, the usefulness of the normative year clause was, to be sure, quite limited. The conversion of princes to Catholicism, in particular, cost the Protestant religious party plenty of terrain after 1648. Still, the very act of formulating and litigating claims under the normative year clause restrained and redirected the Protestants' energies in ways that tended to reinforce peace.

The stability of religious plurality was a most important result of the Peace of Westphalia. The normative year rule was crucial to the establishment of legal parity (*Parität*) between the religions in the Holy Roman Empire.[61] To a certain degree it also helped to release existential fears about conversions. Though it never had the effect of freezing the religious status quo perfectly, it enabled both religious parties to quarrel for "their properties" before the Imperial Diet and the judges. With its calming effects, the normative year principle may also have facilitated the development of the idea that everybody, as mentioned in Zedler's *Universal-Lexicon*, should have a personal right to convert. But its central feature was the agreement of both religious parties to avoid further martial conflict. During the negotiations of Münster and Osnabrück, it was considered the most important *medium*, so to speak, of religious peace. Ultimately, however, it was the near-universal respect and authority accorded to the Peace of Westphalia that distinguished the period after 1648. That respect rested, in large measure, on the normative year.

Notes

1. N.a., "Religions-Veränderung," in Johann Heinrich Zedler, ed., *Grosses vollständiges Universal-Lexicon aller Wissenschaften und Künste*, vol. 34 (Halle and Leipzig, 1742), col. 523.
2. See the introduction to the fifth article of the peace treaty of Osnabrück: "...bello magnam partem gravamina, quae inter utriusque religionis electores, principes et status Imperii vertebantur, causam et occasionem dederint." Antje Oschmann, ed., *Die Friedensverträge mit Frankreich und Schweden*, vol. 1 (Münster, 1998), no. 18, art. V.
3. See, for example, lawsuits brought by subjects against rulers' attempts to force them to emigrate: Stephan Ehrenpreis and Bernhard Ruthmann, "Jus reformandi, jus emigrandi: Reichsrecht, Konfession und Ehre in Religionsstreitigkeiten des späten 16.

Jahrhunderts," in Michael Weinzierl, ed., *Individualisierung, Rationalisierung, Säkularisierung. Neue Wege der Religionsgeschichte* (Vienna, 1997), pp. 67–95.

4. "Seele des Westphälischen Friedens in Religions-Sachen"; Johann Jacob Moser, *Von der Landeshoheit im Geistlichen, nach denen Reichs-Gesetzen und dem Reichs-Herkommen, wie auch aus denen Teutschen Staats-Rechts-Lehrern und eigener Erfahrung...* (Frankfurt and Leipzig, 1773), p. 539.

5. This is the main issue of my book about the invention of the normative-year rule: Ralf-Peter Fuchs, *Ein 'Medium zum Frieden': Die Normaljahrsregel und die Beendigung des Dreißigjährigen Krieges* (Munich, 2010).

6. The term has been adapted in our research group at the Ludwig-Maximilian University in Munich (SFB 573: Pluralisierung und Autorität in der Frühen Neuzeit). For insight into our discussions, see Andreas Höfele et al., eds., *Representing Religious Pluralization in Early Modern Europe* (Münster, 2007).

7. Diarmaid MacCulloch, *Reformation: Europe's House Divided, 1490–1700* (London, 2003), pp. xix, 171–173.

8. Harm Klueting, *Das konfessionelle Zeitalter 1525–1648* (Stuttgart, 1989), p. 23.

9. Catholic scholars in particular believed that the reformed movements were schismatic and therefore responsible for the 'division of the church.' See, for example, Richard van Dülmen, *Religion und Gesellschaft: Beiträge zu einer Religionsgeschichte der Neuzeit* (Frankfurt, 1989), p. 12.

10. Leopold von Ranke, *Deutsche Geschichte im Zeitalter der Reformation*, vol. 2 (Meersburg, 1933), p. 85. See also Winfried Schulze, "Pluralisierung als Bedrohung: Toleranz als Lösung," in Heinz Duchhardt, ed., *Der Westfälische Friede: Diplomatie – politische Zäsur – kulturelles Umfeld – Rezeptionsgeschichte* (Munich, 1998), pp. 115–140, here p. 118. Thomas A. Brady, *German Histories in the Age of Reformations, 1400–1650* (New York, 2009), pp. 417–420.

11. See Winfried Schulze, "Kanon und Pluralisierung," in Aleida Assmann and Jan Assmann, eds., *Kanon und Zensur* (Munich 1987), pp. 317–325, here p. 324. The role of religious pluralization for modern complex societies is also examined in sociological literature. See Peter L. Berger and Thomas Luckmann, "Secularization and Pluralism," *International Yearbook for the Sociology of Religion* 2 (1966): 73–86.

12. See, for example, Etienne François, *Die unsichtbare Grenze. Protestanten und Katholiken in Augsburg 1648–1806* (Sigmaringen, 1991); Frauke Volkland, *Konfession und Selbstverständnis. Reformierte Rituale in der gemischtkonfessionellen Kleinstadt Bischofszell im 17. Jahrhundert* (Göttingen, 2005); C. Scott Dixon et al., eds., *Living With Religious Diversity in Early-Modern Europe* (Farnham, 2009); David M. Luebke, "Customs of Confession: Managing Religious Diversity in Late Sixteenth- and Early Seventeenth-Century Westphalia," in Howard Louthan et al., eds., *Religion and Authority: Rethinking Central Europe from the Middle Ages to the Enlightenment* (New York, 2010).

13. See, for example, the proposal of the legates of Electoral Saxony, which was handed over to the Protestant estates at the Diet of Augsburg in 1566. The legates expressed their hope that the "divided religion" would soon cease to exist: Maximilian Lanzinner and Dietmar Heil, eds., *Deutsche Reichstagsakten: Reichsversammlungen 1556–1662*, vol. 2, *Der Reichstag zu Augsburg 1566* (Munich, 2002), no. 296.

14. See, for example, Wolfgang Reinhard, "Was ist katholische Konfessionalisierung?" in Wolfgang Reinhard and Heinz Schilling, eds., *Die katholische Konfessionalisierung* (Heidelberg, 1995), pp. 419–452; and in the same volume Heinz Schilling, "Die Kon-

fessionalisierung von Kirche, Staat und Gesellschaft—Profil, Leistung, Defizite und Perspektiven eines geschichtswissenschaftlichen Paradigmas," pp. 1–49.

15. Martin Heckel, "Die Religionsprozesse des Reichskammergerichts im konfessionell gespaltenen Kirchenrecht," in Klaus Schlaich, ed., *Martin Heckel: Gesammelte Schriften: Staat – Kirche – Recht – Geschichte*, vol. 3 (Tübingen, 1997), pp. 382–440.

16. Fritz Dickmann, *Friedensrecht und Friedenssicherung. Studien zum Friedensproblem in der neueren Geschichte* (Göttingen, 1971), p. 9.

17. See Schulze, "Pluralisierung."

18. Axel Gotthard, "'Politice seint wir Bäpstisch': Kursachsen und der deutsche Protestantismus im frühen 17. Jahrhundert," *Zeitschrift für historische Forschung* 20 (1993): 275–319.

19. Moriz Ritter, *Deutsche Geschichte im Zeitalter der Gegenreformation und des Dreissigjährigen Krieges (1555–1648)*, vol. 2 (Darmstadt, 1962), pp. 121, 383.

20. See van Dülmen, *Religion*, p. 12. The expression "konfessioneller Pluralismus in Europa" is used by Erwin Iserloh; see his *Geschichte und Theologie der Reformation im Grundriß*, 3rd ed. (Paderborn 1985), p. 161. Christoph Schwöbel considers "denominational pluralism" an outcome of the Reformation; Christoph Schwöbel, "Pluralismus II," in Gerhard Müller, ed., *Theologische Realenzyklopädie*, vol. 26 (Berlin, 1996), pp. 724–739, here p. 725.

21. Armin Kreiner, "Pluralismus (fundamentaltheologisch)," in Walter Kasper, ed., *Lexikon für Theologie und Kirche*, vol. 8 (Freiburg, 1999), p. 362–363.

22. Also Melanchthon and other Protestants claimed unity to preserve order: Schulze, "Kanon und Pluralisierung," pp. 323–324.

23. See Martin Heckel, "Die Krise der Religionsverfassung des Reiches und die Anfänge des Dreißigjährigen Krieges," in Klaus Schlaich, ed., *Martin Heckel: Gesammelte Schriften*, vol. 2 (Tübingen, 1989), pp. 970–998, here p. 976.

24. See, for example: *Kurze doch gründtliche Anzeig und Unterricht woher die Uneinigkeiten so heutigs tags im Römischen Reich schweben, entsprungen, und wem die Zerrüttung desselben zuzumessen sey* (n.p., 1615); and *Lermen, Blasen auch Ursachen und Ausschlag, deß besorgten innerlichen Kriegs zwischen den Catholischen und Calvinisten in Teutschlandt. Das ist: Kurtze und gründtliche anzeig unnd erleuterung, welchem theil der Krieg lieber sey alß der Friedt: was ein jeder für tringende Ursachen zum Krieg hab: und was der ein oder ander für einen Außschlag zugewarten* (n.p., 1616).

25. Andreas Erstenberger [Franciscus Burghardt], *De Avtonomia, Das ist, von Freystellung mehrerlay Religion vnd Glauben: Was vnd wie mancherlay die sey, was derhalben biß daher im Reich Teutscher Nation fürgangen, Vnnd ob dieselb von der Christenlichen Obrigkeit möge bewilliget vnnd gestattet werden*, vol. 3 (Munich, 1586), p. 275.

26. See, for example, Ronald G. Asch, *The Thirty Years War: The Holy Roman Empire and Europe, 1618–1648* (New York, 1997), pp. 12–13. Even before the Treaty of Augsburg the Catholics had claimed restitutions; Thomas Brady, *Zwischen Gott und Mammon: Protestantische Politik und deutsche Reformation* (Berlin, 1996).

27. Martin Heckel, "Parität (I)," in Klaus Schlaich, ed., *Martin Heckel: Gesammelte Schriften*, vol. 1 (Tübingen, 1989), pp. 106–226. See also in the same volume Martin Heckel, "Parität (II)," pp. 227–323.

28. Andreas Erstenberger, *De Avtonomia*, p. 275.

29. See, for example, Jacob Jacobi, *Summarische Relation. Von der Lutherischen Freystellung, derselbigen Hundertjärigen Verlauff, und derentwegen Newlich gehaltenem Jubel*

Jahr, und von Bruder Josemans ernewertem alten Predicanten Latein, von deß Römischen Bischoffs Alter, Lehre, Wandel, Raht und Anschlag. Zu Erleuterung dieser Zeit Streittigkeiten in dem Religionswesen sehr dienstlich und nothwendig, Auß den furnembsten Romanischer und Luterischer Seiten HistoriSchreibern...zusammen getragen (Strasbourg, 1618).

30. Martin Heckel, "Das Restitutionsedikt Kaiser Ferdinands II. vom 6. März 1629—eine verlorene Alternative der Reichskirchenverfassung," in Gerhard Köbler and Hermann Nehlsen, eds., *Wirkungen europäischer Rechtskultur* (Munich 1997), pp. 351–376; Heike Ströler-Bühler, *Das Restitutionsedikt von 1629 im Spannungsfeld zwischen Augsburger Religionsfrieden 1555 und dem Westfälischen Frieden* (Regensburg 1991); and Michael Frisch, *Das Restitutionsedikt Kaiser Ferdinands II. vom 6. März 1629: Eine rechtsgeschichtliche Untersuchung* (Tübingen, 1993).

31. See, for example, Heinrich Günter, *Das Restitutionsedikt von 1629 und die katholische Restauration Altwirtembergs* (Stuttgart, 1901).

32. The term *annus normalis* was frequently used after 1750. See, for example, *Verdrähung des nudi facti possessionis anni normalis 1624: Ungrund der sogenannten Selbst-Hülff. Gesprächs-Weiss zwischen einem Catholischen und zwischen einem Protestanten* (Regensburg, 1758).

33. Wolff's offer would be criticized harshly by Protestant historians; see, for example, Johannes H. Gebauer, *Kurbrandenburg und das Restitutionsedikt von 1629* (Halle, 1899).

34. German historians have held the Frankfurter Kompositionstag and its efforts at peacemaking in low esteem; see Fuchs, *Ein 'Medium' zum Frieden*, pp. 99ff. See also Ralf-Peter Fuchs, "Für die Kirche Gottes und die Posterität—Kursachsen und das Friedensmedium eines Normaljahres auf dem Frankfurter Kompositionstag 1631," *Mitteilungen des Sonderforschungsbereichs 'Pluralisierung und Autorität in der Frühen Neuzeit'* 1 (2007): 19–27, http://www.sfb-frueheneuzeit .uni-muenchen.de/mitteilungen/M1-2007/fuerdiekirche.pdf.

35. Michael Frisch, "Die Normaltagsregelung im Prager Frieden," *Zeitschrift der Savigny-Stiftung für Rechtsgeschichte, Kanonistische Abteilung* 87 (2001): 442–454. See also Kathrin Bierther, ed., *Die Politik Maximilians von Bayern und seiner Verbündeten 1618–1651*, vol. 2, part 10, *Der Prager Frieden von 1635*. Munich and Vienna, 1997.

36. See Fuchs, *Ein 'Medium' zum Frieden*, pp. 159ff. A general overview of the negotiations' results may be found in Konrad Repgen, "Die westfälischen Friedensverhandlungen: Überblick und Hauptprobleme," in Klaus Bußmann and Heinz Schilling, eds., *1648: Krieg und Frieden in Europa*, vol. 1, *Politik, Religion, Recht und Gesellschaft* (Münster, 1998), pp. 355–372.

37. Godofredus Daniel Hoffmannus, *Commentatio Iuris Publici Ecclesiastici de Die Decretorio Kalendis Ianuarii Anni 1624 Omnique ex Pace Westphalica Restitutione* (Ulm 1750), p. 93.

38. Fuchs, *Ein 'Medium' zum Frieden*, p. 194.

39. See Marc R. Forster, *The Counter-Reformation in the Villages: Religion and Reform in the Bishopric of Speyer, 1560–1720* (Ithaca, 1992); Volker Wappmann, *Durchbruch zur Toleranz: Die Religionspolitik des Pfalzgrafen Christian August von Sulzbach 1622–1708* (Neustadt an der Aisch, 1995); Albrecht Ernst, *Die reformierte Kirche der Kurpfalz nach dem Dreißigjährigen Krieg (1649–1685)* (Stuttgart, 1996); Wolfgang Seegrün, "In Münster und Nürnberg: Die Verteilung der Konfessionen im Fürstentum Osnabrück

1648–50," *Blätter für deutsche Landesgeschichte* 134 (1998): 59–93; and Gerd Stein-wascher, "Die konfessionellen Folgen des Westfälischen Friedens für das Fürstbistum Osnabrück," *Niedersächsisches Jahrbuch für Landesgeschichte* 71 (1999): 51–80.

40. See Antje Oschmann, *Der Nürnberger Exekutionstag 1649–1650: Das Ende des Drei-ßigjährigen Krieges in Deutschland* (Münster, 1991); and Fuchs, *Ein 'Medium' zum Frie-den*, pp. 226ff.

41. See examples in Moser, *Von der Landeshoheit im Geistlichen*, pp. 537ff.

42. Henricus Hildebrandus, *Annus decretorius 1624 in Instrumenti Pacis Caesareo-Svecici Articulo V.* (Altorf, 1705).

43. These include Iustus Christopherus Dithmarus, "Dissertatio de Anno Decretorio Exercitii Utriusque Religionis in Germania," in Iustus Christopherus Dithmarus, ed., *Dissertationum Academicarum atque Exercitationum Varii ex Iure Publico, Naturali et Historia Desumti Argumenti* (Leipzig, 1737); Hoffmannus, *Commentatio Iuris Publici Ecclesiastici*; Ioannes Ernestus Floerke, *Programma de eo quod extremum est in Defen-sione Status Evangelicae Religionis qui fuit in Anno decretorio* (Halle, 1755); Franciscus Haus, *De anno decretorio M.DC.XXIIII. Opificum Collega non concernente* (Würzburg, 1771); and Ioannes Carolus von der Becke, *Dissertatio Inauguralis de Die Decretorio Pace Westphalia Posito Maxime ad Paragraphos XXV. et XXVI. Art. V. Instrumenti Osnabrugensis...* (Göttingen, 1776).

44. Moser used the term *Entscheid-Jahr* ("decisive year") and considered 1618 the year of restitution in cases of amnesty (*Amnestiejahr*), as an "*Entscheid-Jahr*," too; see Moser, *Von der Landeshoheit im Geistlichen*, pp. 527–528.

45. "das immerwährende und unaufhörliche Regulativum zwischen beiderseitigen Reli-gionen"; Moser, *Von der Landeshoheit im Geistlichen*, p. 539.

46. "Daß es in Religions-Sachen ... auf ewige Zeiten so verbleiben solle, wie es im Jahr 1624 gehalten worden ist"; Moser, *Von der Landeshoheit im Geistlichen*, p. 557.

47. Moser, *Von der Landeshoheit im Geistlichen*, p. 536.

48. See Eberhard Christian Wilhelm von Schauroth, *Vollständige Sammlung Aller Conclu-sorum, Schreiben und anderer übrigen Verhandlungen des Hochpreißlichen Corporis Evan-gelicorum vom Jahr 1663, biß 1752...*, vol. 3 (Regensburg 1752), pp. 1055, 1065 and 1970.

49. "Das Instrumentum Pacis Westphalicae abhorriret am meisten von allen, vor Errich-tung desselben, vorgegangenen so vielfältigen Veränderungen in Religions-Sachen, und hat man daher so mühsam einen Zustand des...1624sten Jahrs ausgefunden"; *Fortsetzung des Abdrucks einiger Acten-Stücke, die von Ihro, des regierenden Herrn Marg-grafen zu Brandenburg-Onolzbach Hoch-Fürstl. Durchl. als dermahligem ausschreibendem Fürsten des Fränckischen Crayses, auf Requisition eines Hochlöblichen Corporis Evangelico-rum, übernommene Restitutions- u. Executions-Commission betreffend in Causa des Grä-flich-Hohenlohischen Hauses, Neuensteinischer Linie, contra die Herren Fürsten v. Hohen-lohe-Waldenburg* (n.p., 1750), pp. 24–25.

50. "Ferner werden von dem bey dem Herrn von Romberg wohnenden Catholischen Prie-ster die Evangelische in ihrem Gottes-Dienst sehr beunruhiget, da doch vormahlen weder anno 1624. noch bis auf des Herrn von Romberg Ankunfft in Wachenheim ein Catholischer Geistlicher gewohnet"; *Fortsetzung des Abdrucks einiger Acten-Stücke*, annex E.

51. "Catholische Landes-Herren sind nicht berechtiget, ihren Evangelischen Unter-thanen ratione des Calenders etwas aufzudringen, und würde den Catholischen auch

nicht gefallen, wann die Evangelische ihren Catholischen Unterthanen auferlegten, den Gregorianischen Kalender zu verlassen"; Schauroth, *Vollständige Sammlung*, vol. 1, p. 130.

52. "…die Gräntzen zwischen beyden Religions-Seiten auf ewig dermassen gezogen werden"; Schauroth, *Vollständige Sammlung*, vol. 1, p. 866.

53. Wappmann, *Durchbruch zur Toleranz*.

54. Moser, *Von der Landeshoheit im Geistlichen*, p. 614.

55. "Es würde sich auch keiner bereden lassen, der ein Haus hätte, daß dasselbe Haus sein ganz verbleibe, wann ein anderer ihm die Helffte davon nähme, oder wider seinen Willen sich in Gemeinschaft zu ihm eindrünge"; Moser, *Von der Landeshoheit im Geistlichen*, p. 615.

56. Moser, *Von der Landeshoheit im Geistlichen*, p. 603. See also *Allerunterthänigstes Vorstellungs-Schreiben, Welches an Ihre Käyserliche Majestät, Auf Dero über die Religions-Gravamina der Augspurgischen Confessions-Verwandten den 12. Aprilis 1720. erfolgte Commissions-Decret Das Corpus Evangelicorum unterm 16. Novembr. erstbesagten Jahrs allergehorsamst abgelassen* (n.p., 1721), Lit. E: "Bericht über das Simultaneum in der Grafschaft Leiningen-Westerburg (zuwider 1624)": "Ferner werden von dem bey dem Herrn von Romberg wohnenden Catholischen Priester die Evangelische in ihrem Gottes-Dienst sehr beunruhiget, da doch vormahlen weder anno 1624. noch bis auf des Herrn von Romberg Ankunfft in Wachenheim ein Catholischer Geistlicher gewohnet."

57. N.a., "Religions-Veränderung."

58. "…die tägliche Erfahrung aber zur Gnüge zeiget, das man Catholischer Seits niemahln ruhet, sondern auf alle Art und Weise die Römisch-Catholische Religion fortzupflanzen drohet"; n.a., "Recht zu reformieren oder Reformations-Recht," in Zedler, *Grosses vollständiges Universal-Lexicon*, vol. 30 (Halle and Leipzig, 1742), cols. 1418–1422, here col. 1422.

59. Edith Koller, "Die Rolle des Normaljahrs in Konfessionsprozessen des späten 17. Jahrhunderts vor dem Reichskammergericht," in *Zeitenblicke* 3 (2004), http://deposit.ddb.de/ep/netpub/43/37/61/976613743/_data_stat/koller/index.html.

60. See *Allerunterthänigste Repraesentatio Gravaminum Religionis der Römisch-Catholischen im Herzogthumb Cleve, Auch Graffschafft Marck und Ravensberg, Cum Justificationibus, Erstattet Von Ihro Churfürstl. Durchl. zu Pfaltz, Jülich- und Bergischer Regierung* (Düsseldorf, 1723).

61. Fritz Dickmann, *Der Westfälische Frieden*, 7th ed. (Münster, 1998), pp. 349–350.

CHAPTER FIVE

Conversion and Diplomacy in Absolutist Northern Europe

DANIEL RICHES

In 1690 a diplomatic scandal damaged relations between Sweden and Brandenburg, leaving both sides embittered and frustrated at a moment when they agreed that getting along would have served their respective foreign policy interests. The core of the scandal did not concern traditional international relations issues, but rather centered on the religious identity of the wife of the Brandenburg ambassador to Stockholm, a native-born Swede who had converted to Calvinism upon marrying her German Reformed husband. News of her conversion caused an uproar at the Swedish court and precipitated a mutually unwelcome showdown between the king of Sweden and the elector of Brandenburg, in which each believed that his honor and image as a sovereign lord were at stake. As the diplomatic situation deteriorated, the two rulers were handcuffed by the logic of their own absolutist self-understanding, which limited their ability to lessen tensions through compromise. The end result was a diplomatic rupture that neither prince wanted, which took several years to heal. This essay focuses on certain elements of the absolutist system—namely the role of religion in the justification of absolutist rule, a paternalistic understanding of the relationship between ruler and subject, and the performative aspects of monarchical image projection—to provide an explanation for how a diplomat's wife's conversion could have such unexpectedly broad consequences.

Scholars writing on the intersections of conversion and diplomacy in early modern Europe frequently focus on those dramatic instances of princely or dynastic conversion that sent shockwaves throughout the courts of Europe and sometimes brought with them notable shifts in foreign policy, or on the equally colorful moments when individual diplomats, their chaplains, and their embassies acted as agents for conversion or as the guardians of converts—often at significant personal risk—while serving in a land that was confessionally different from that of their principal.[1] Instances of the diplomatic and jurisdictional struggle that could ensue over singular acts of conversion by individuals of mixed, unclear, or contested "state" membership have received far less attention. This essay contends that such cases reveal structural vulnerabilities in the absolutist system and suggests that the combination of conversion and diplomacy could be a particularly potent threat to the absolutist rulers of early modern northern Europe. That the incident studied here involved a diplomat's own wife allows it to shed even sharper light on the complex nexus of relationships between religious identity, the prerogatives of sovereignty, and the performative elements of princely rule that characterized the European diplomatic arena in the age of absolutism.

The term "absolutism" itself has long been the object of considerable controversy. As decades' worth of scholarship has effectively shown, the European princes we call absolutist faced severe limitations on their ability to rule in the manner they may have wished. This was due to the relatively underdeveloped institutions of government they had at their disposal and the successful strategies of noncompliance or outright resistance they faced from various sectors of society. Absolutist princes were forced by necessity to operate through consultation and compromise with other power structures, much as European monarchs had been doing for centuries. In other words, the self-image and expectations of absolutists always outstripped their capacity, with the actual power at their disposal being far from 'absolute' according to any current sense of the word. This has led some modern historians to consider the entire concept of absolutism to be an unhelpful and distracting myth that stands in our way of understanding what actually went on in the seventeenth and eighteenth centuries.[2] Even scholars who accept the utility of the term are quick to point out that "[t]he image of the absolute monarch did not correspond to the reality," and that it was indeed "a myth of power."[3] In the context of central Europe, however, Peter H. Wilson has recently shown that absolutism remains a viable and indeed useful framework for understanding various aspects of early modern princely rule, even if it may mean something less monolithic and imposing than has often been assumed.[4] In this essay, the term "absolutism" will refer to the specific manner in which certain late seventeenth-century central and northern European princes conceived of their authority, presented it to others, and encouraged their subjects to acquiesce to its exercise. The gray areas between this absolutist image and the realities of early modern princely power are precisely where the most revealing interactions between diplomacy, conversion, and absolutism play out.

The diplomatic confrontation between Sweden and Brandenburg illustrates these connections. In May 1690, Ambassador Alexander von Dohna, accompanied by his wife Emilie, arrived in Stockholm as Elector Friedrich III of Brandenburg's representative to the Swedish court.[5] For Alexander, a scion of the famous East Prussian noble family that played such an important role in Brandenburg-Prussian history, the mission to Stockholm returned him to a country he was already somewhat familiar with from earlier travels in the 1680s.[6] For Emilie, however, going to Stockholm was a true homecoming. She was Alexander's first cousin, the daughter of Christoff Delficus von Dohna, who had entered Swedish service in the 1650s and established a Swedish branch of the von Dohna family that became influential in Swedish society and politics.[7] Although Christoff Delficus was a Calvinist and remained so his entire life, his Swedish wife Anna—who happened to be the sister of Sweden's Chancery President (and de facto foreign minister) Bengt Oxenstierna—saw to it that the couple's children were raised in conformity with the Swedish Lutheran Church. Emilie was therefore a native-born Swede, connected to the leading circles of Swedish society, who was raised, like virtually all Swedish children, as a Lutheran.

By all appearances, Alexander's marriage to such a well-connected Swedish wife seemed an important asset for his delicate mission. The particular circumstances of the mission, in fact, made it more important than usual that Brandenburg's ambassador be seen as personally agreeable to Sweden's King Karl XI. Connections between religion and diplomacy had much to do with this. Von Dohna's predecessor as Brandenburg's ambassador to Stockholm, the Huguenot refugee Pierre de Falaiseau, had recently been recalled from Sweden, at Karl's request, following a series of confessionally tinged controversies that arose out of Falaiseau's activism on behalf of Sweden's small Calvinist minority—incendiary activity in a country that was uncompromisingly and almost uniformly Lutheran.[8] At the same time, Alexander's embassy marked a rare moment of consensus in relations between Brandenburg and Sweden, which for decades had been poisoned by territorial disputes. Both governments now stood in sincere agreement on the need to get along, in this case to defend an endangered Protestantism from the menace of Louis XIV's France.[9] To top it off, Alexander and Emilie arrived in Stockholm during a heightened phase in the construction of Swedish absolutism known as the *reduktion*, in which the Crown confiscated much of the property and revoked some of the special financial privileges that earlier monarchs had granted to the Swedish nobility, alienating large segments of the nobility in the process and moving the king to lean more heavily on his relationship with Sweden's strongly anti-Calvinist orthodox Lutheran clergy for support.[10] In short, Alexander was asked to soothe the confessional wounds opened by Falaiseau and to work for broad Protestant cooperation against France at a time when Karl's own dogmatic Lutheranism was coupled with a heightened sense of obligation to his clergy to show no fondness toward Calvinists.[11] It was to be a mission as much of personal charm as of the pursuit of specific policy objectives.

At the outset of the mission, things seemed to be working perfectly. The couple instantly became regular participants in the social life of the Swedish court. Emilie on one occasion sent her daughter to spend the day with Queen Ulrike Eleonora, and the young girl returned that evening with expensive gifts for Emilie from the queen. When the von Dohnas' son fell ill, Queen Mother Hedvig Eleonora personally sent them medicine.[12] This rosy picture quickly darkened, however, and the reasons for this bring us back to the theme of conversion. Emilie, unbeknownst to her Swedish friends and relatives, had quietly converted to Calvinism after her marriage to Alexander. News of Emilie's conversion became public shortly after the von Dohnas arrived in Stockholm when someone, most likely a domestic servant, observed Emilie taking part in Calvinist services at the ambassadorial residence. News of this incident was passed along to Emilie's mother, who confronted her daughter and pleaded with her to return to the Lutheran fold. Emilie replied calmly but firmly that her conversion was genuine and its reversal out of the question. It is unclear whether Anna herself or someone else took the issue to the king, but within days the news of Emilie's conversion was the talk of the Swedish court, where this turning away from the established Lutheran faith by someone of such prominent lineage was seen as nothing short of scandalous. Noble marriages across confessional lines with one partner converting may have been common elsewhere in Europe, but in Sweden they were extremely rare. As Karl later wrote to his diplomats at various posts on the continent, the news of Emilie's conversion had "given rise in these parts to no small scandal in which our religion has been not lightly defamed."[13] Since Emilie had been born and raised in Sweden, the king considered her a Swedish subject and her conversion a violation of Swedish religious law. He subsequently banned her from appearing at the Swedish court unless she renounced her conversion.[14]

Friedrich III's response upon hearing of Emilie's ban from court was to declare it an open attack against all of Calvinism and a particular affront to his own dignity to have his ambassador's family treated in such shabby fashion.[15] The offense given by the ban was "so enormous, and Our subsequent resentment held by the entire reasonable world to be so justified," that only a complete reversal of Karl's decision could prevent von Dohna from being withdrawn.[16] But Karl refused to bend, Friedrich angrily recalled von Dohna, and high-level diplomatic relations between Brandenburg and Sweden at this critical juncture were broken off for the following three and a half years.

So how—despite the fact that both Brandenburg and Sweden wanted to cooperate at this moment—did things get to this point? More importantly, what larger issues might this single incident suggest? A first angle to consider is the central role of religion in absolutist self-understanding and in the justification of absolutism to others. That absolutist theorists considered royal power to be sacral in nature and derived from divine right does little to distinguish absolutism from other images of monarchy prevalent throughout the Western tradition. Indeed, as scholars such as Edward Shils and Clifford Geertz have shown, belief in the "inherent sacredness of sovereign power" transcends not only absolutism, but also the apparent divisions between East and West, "primitive" and "advanced."[17] Absolutist princes certainly embraced the roles of guardian of the faith and embodiment of divine order, but in this they demonstrated their solidarity with, rather than distinction from, monarchs across the expanses of human time and space. What made the situation in early modern Europe during the formative years of absolutism distinctive was the sudden appearance of viable, mass religious alternatives, accessible to broad swaths of the population, where there been none for centuries, and the impact this had on the function and representation of princely rule.

On the one hand, the prospect of religious disunity within a polity posed what one scholar has described as "a frontal assault on the essentially religious nature of monarchy itself," shaking not only the theoretical underpinnings of monarchical rule but also the grip that certain dynasties had on their thrones.[18] At the same time, however, the threat of religious division provided a distinct opportunity to extend princely power on which many ruling houses capitalized. Recent work has shown that following the onset of the Protestant Reformation, rising popular concerns over a newly pluralistic religious landscape allowed absolutizing monarchs to present themselves as uniquely capable of securing the ascendancy of dominant religious groups against threats from below, moving these same dominant groups to acquiesce to the implementation of the absolutist system in ways they may not have otherwise.[19] Whether motivated by fear or by opportunism, monarchs were encouraged by the very definition of their office to react to religious disunity amongst their subjects with a firm hand.

In Sweden, Karl XI's image as the guarantor of Lutheran orthodoxy and unity was an especially important justification for a style of rule that differed markedly from that of his more constitutionally bounded predecessors.[20] Anthony F. Upton has noted that Sweden "came as close to the ideal of total religious unity as any post-Reformation European society ever could."[21] Although a close reading of Swedish history reveals that this did not equate to the complete disappearance of religious controversy or dissent, it is fair to say that Sweden enjoyed one of the highest levels of religious consensus in all of Europe.[22] Both Karl and the bulk of his subjects believed that religious unity was the cornerstone of Swedish society and state, and the king viewed its maintenance as a mandate given to him by God. Karl readily employed stern church laws aimed at uniformity of practice and sent soldiers to patrol the streets on Sundays to ensure church attendance in order to fulfill his divinely ordained obligation.[23]

The religious aspects of Swedish absolutism become more relevant to understanding the von Dohna case when viewed in conjunction with another element of Karl's rule: its overweening paternalism. The most famous of all European apologists for absolutism, Bossuet, was careful to state that absolutist power was paternal as well as sacral, and the intimate links between these two characteristics are where the complications of the von Dohna case begin to become apparent.[24] As awe-inspiring father figures, absolutist rulers treated their subjects as their children and held themselves responsible for not only their physical well-being but their moral and spiritual health as well. The *Landesvater* was the particular central European iteration of this image of monarchy, defending the true faith, shielding his subjects from the seductions of heresy, and pulling them back—by force if necessary—from the abyss of apostasy.[25] The extent to which Karl XI's Sweden embraced this image of king-as-father is captured in a speech delivered by the powerful Swedish noble and leading intellectual Erik Lindschöld at the *Riksdag* of 1686:

> To be called a king, that is a great title, a glorious title, but *Pater patriae*, father of the country is a living title, the best title there can ever be.... A king's nature is to attend to his power, his authority, his supremacy ... but a father's duty is to attend to his childrens' well being, to protect them, to help them, to seek their progress, further their hopes, add to their bounties.... This fatherly heart means that all your Majesty's subjects, the meanest as well as the greatest, can approach your Majesty's lofty throne, and come before your Majesty's mild countenance to lament his need, present his condition and beg help and support, with the same confidence and the same freedom as a child with a tender father.[26]

A letter from Queen Ulrike Eleonora to Electress Sophie Charlotte written during the height of the von Dohna controversy makes use of precisely this idiom, stating that "since [Emilie] was born here in this country, the King must act as Father and custodian in a matter where [Emilie] could harm herself.... His Majesty will treat Emilie no differently than he would his own children in the same situation, [doing] everything for her best."[27]

It is no coincidence that this explicit discussion of Karl's attitude toward Emilie was not expressed in direct correspondence between the two rulers themselves, but rather between their wives. This reflects the atmosphere of heightened tensions growing around the von Dohna affair and the challenges of finding appropriately diplomatic language for princely correspondence when issues of mutual honor were seen to be at stake. On a deeper level, however, the decision to express these arguments through the medium of female conversation represents an effort to locate the von Dohna incident within the domestic sphere, where Karl's rights as paternal figure would be undisputed and any broader international implications of his actions muted. The role of gender becomes even sharper when considering that Emilie was not merely a subject, but rather a *female* subject, believed by prevailing gender theories to be, by her very feminine nature, prone to the kind of childlike behavior described in the queen's letter as needing correction from a strong male figure able to look out for her best interests. Karl's actions toward Emilie were therefore not only a defense of his royal honor, but also of his male honor.[28]

Conflict arose from the fact that Friedrich III could and did make recourse to the same paternalistic rhetoric: Emilie, in marrying Alexander, had become a member of his household, and thus by extension of the elector's own. On one level Karl's efforts to discipline Emilie flew in the face of the theory of exterritoriality, according to which diplomats and their accompanying personnel legally never leave the symbolic territory of their principal, wherever they might be stationed.[29] More significantly, though, Karl's justification for disciplining Emilie was based on a claim that is still reflected in modern international law, namely that the privileges and immunities usually accorded to diplomats' family members do not apply when the diplomat serves in a state in which the family member is a citizen or subject.[30] Karl's stance toward Emilie centered on a claim of jurisdiction—that she was, in the language of absolutism, his child rather than Friedrich's. The rage Friedrich felt over the way Emilie was being treated therefore derived not only from his belief that Karl was committing a serious violation of diplomatic protocol, but also that the king's actions created a tangible injury, an intrusion onto Friedrich's own paternal turf. The paternalistic rhetoric of absolutism contained no conceptual space for an individual being subject to more than one father figure, and Friedrich and Karl were engaged in what amounted to a custody battle to see who the real father was. At a loss for acceptable mechanisms to settle the matter, the logic of absolutism left the contestants with no other recourse than dramatic and unwelcome diplomatic steps, in this case the breaking off of relations at an inopportune moment.

This image of dueling father figures competing for the attachment of a child resonates with scholarship on the psychology of modern religious conversions. In language that would have been familiar to readers of late-seventeenth-century political tracts, one scholar writes that modern converts' descriptions of their conversion experiences often hinge upon a "figure … perceived as an omnipotent father who supplied order and protection," adding that "[i]n many cases, conversion centers on an intense attachment to a figure perceived as a perfect father."[31] Although one must use great caution in drawing parallels between the conversions of twentieth-century Americans and those that took place in the very different circumstances of early modern Europe, one common element—the emphasis on perception—is relevant to the von Dohna affair. The projection of an image of absolute power and the appropriate outward performance of the princely role formed crucial aspects of the métier of an absolute monarch, and indeed these symbolic actions cannot be cleanly separated from the essence of absolute rule itself. To draw once more from Geertz, the lines between the "symbolics of power" and its actual nature can be blurry at best. Absolute princes may have felt an especially acute need to establish a relationship "between the trappings of rule and its substance," due to the gap between their expansive theoretical pretensions and their much more limited practical capacities.[32] Efforts taken to maintain the image of absolutism were therefore crucial to the legitimation of the entire system, and indeed were constitutive elements of the system. As Wilson describes, "[t]he image conveyed by absolutism was a myth of power, but the process of projecting and sustaining this myth constituted a tangible reality and helped shape the practice of political authority."[33]

Early modern Europe provided fertile ground for those fabricating and managing the image of absolute monarchy. J.H. Elliott has written that the seventeenth century "possessed an unusually acute awareness of the complex relationship of image and reality," and that "[t]he application of the arts of the theater to political life, and especially to the projection of kingship, is one of the principal characteristics of seventeenth-century monarchies."[34] At the center of absolutist image creation stood the princely court itself, where the monarch performed the role of absolute ruler and sent out a shining signal of his power to both domestic and foreign audiences.[35]

Of all European princes, Karl XI may have been amongst the least-suited to carry out this performative task. The great historian of Sweden Michael Roberts wrote that Karl was "ill-equipped for the representative side of royalty: personally unprepossessing, invincibly shy, and of no general conversation."[36] He had neither the natural gifts nor the creativity to cut much of a courtly figure, with intellectual horizons set so firmly within the restrictive confines of orthodox Swedish Lutheranism that he struggled to interact with those who did not share his worldview. Upton has written, for instance, that "[a]part from the Bible and works of piety, he seems to have read nothing"—hardly a favorable situation for one expected to engage and impress an array of foreign dignitaries.[37] Karl's lack of intellectual and cultural interests and commitment to a somber piety were mirrored in his court, which was marked by austerity and seriousness of purpose with little sign of the flashy pomp and circumstance so common elsewhere.[38] The king was aware of and perhaps somewhat embarrassed by his intellectual shortcomings and lack of social grace and subsequently avoided conversation when he could with those whom he considered more cultured, including foreign diplomats.[39] The ironic upshot of this situation, however, was that when Karl did interact with others he was especially sensitive to any perceived slights to his dignity and majesty and prone to violent outbursts of temper and intractable insistence on getting his way.[40] He refused above all to compromise in matters of religion, where practical concerns over the consequences of his actions counted little in the face of carrying out the God-given duties of his office and representing to others that these duties were his and his alone.[41] Karl's court therefore may have been somewhat unique, but performative elements representing his right to absolute rule still held a central position, indeed in a manner that could hardly have been less opportune for a case like Emilie von Dohna's.

The successful performance of absolutism depended not only on the ruler playing his or her part, but also on all observers of the performance fulfilling their assigned roles as well.[42] Complications arose, however, when those in the audience being fed the image of absolutism did not play along, or when, worse still, they disrupted the performance with one of their own that provided a persuasive argument for reconfiguring the audience's relationship to the authority of the sovereign. In the early modern world, an act of conversion had the potential to serve as one such counter-performance. Recent work on the literary analysis of conversion narratives stresses that the transformed identity that emerges from the conversion experience serves itself as a persuasive rhetorical strategy, as constitutive discourse capable of transforming those exposed to it and compelling them to act in accordance with the convert's convictions.[43] Studies in the anthropology of conversion add that conversions also highlight the tensions between individuals and the structural demands placed upon them by the systems to which they belong, which can in turn produce important effects on the group or system the convert leaves behind.[44] It should come as no surprise, then, that early modern texts often linked conversion rhetorically to treason.[45] In this light, Emilie's conversion was not only the self-damaging act of a wayward and disobedient child, flouting the religious supremacy of the paternal sovereign and the conformity and uniformity that his unique sovereign power was supposed to secure. It was also—even if Emilie did not intend this—an act of stealing the stage upon which the king was performing his role and subverting others to question the performance running before their eyes.[46] Her conversion was, in this sense, a profound challenge to the very cornerstones of Karl's authority, to which he was obligated to respond firmly.

With this in mind, the nature of the action taken by Karl against Emilie becomes understandable. The king never suggested that she be expelled from Sweden, that she be imprisoned or fined, or even that she be subjected to a concerted effort to persuade her of the superiority of Lutheran doctrine. Even less did Karl desire to have Alexander's promising embassy withdrawn in those internationally dangerous times. He in fact went out of his way to assure Alexander that he continued to hold him personally in the highest regard and that he hoped the incident involving Emilie would not damage his government's friendship with Brandenburg. Rather, the full extent of Karl's action was to ban Emilie from physically appearing before the king's person at his court until she returned to the role of an obedient Lutheran subject. The international diplomatic consequences entailed by this decision were sincerely unwelcome collateral damage.

We have every reason to believe that Friedrich III viewed his withdrawal of von Dohna as an equally unwelcome decision that he nevertheless felt obligated to carry out. The reasons for this derive once more from the representative aspects of absolute monarchy. Diplomacy was one of the grandest stages of princely display and performance, and ruling houses counted the drive to have their honor and dignity internationally recognized amongst their highest priorities.[47] Early modern diplomatic theory stressed that a diplomat was an extension of the principal's own person and was due the same honor and respect that would be accorded the monarch him- or herself.[48] Any mistreatment or insult suffered by an ambassador was therefore an egregious affront to the dignity of his prince and needed to be responded to as such. As Montell Ogdon has written, early modern diplomatic theorists argued that a "prince who was not sensible to the injuries to his ambassador or minister was said not to deserve the name of prince; if he permitted his minister to be abused he was indifferent to his own reputation." Ogdon looked in particular to the work of Abraham de Wicquefort, a diplomat in Brandenburg's service, who "concluded that it must be believed that Princes, who ought to consider their ministers as their own image, ought to employ all the courage and strength they have to revenge the injury which is done them in the person of their minister."[49]

As we have seen, an absolutist prince could not afford the luxury of indifference to reputation if he intended to maintain his system, and Friedrich's actions in the von Dohna affair are consistent with this belief. The disrespect shown to the household of his minister equated to disrespect shown to his own sovereign majesty, and Karl's claims to a form of jurisdiction over Emilie amounted to an insufferable intrusion upon Friedrich's own sovereign rights. These actions demanded a vigorous response that included not only Alexander's recall but also an international public relations campaign in which Friedrich ordered his diplomats at other allied courts to spread the word of Karl's shameful conduct and firmly assert the elector's rights.[50] Friedrich also fought back with the symbolic weapons at his disposal, instructing von Dohna to refuse to accept the traditional gifts Karl was offering on his departure. This action scandalized many at the Swedish court and further disrupted the symbolic political order.[51] Emilie's religious identity may have mattered less to Friedrich than it did to Karl, but his own absolutist understanding demanded that he respond aggressively to her treatment at the hands of a different lord, even if this response would fly in the face of his own foreign policy objectives.[52]

What we see, then, is that Emilie's conversion and its aftermath locked both Sweden and Brandenburg into courses of conduct that neither side liked and that resulted, to their mutual dismay, in a diplomatic mess. What are we to learn from this? First, it bears considering whether the demands of absolutist self-definition and the necessity of projecting and protecting the image of absolutist power could run directly counter to other important imperatives of rule, such as the ability to conduct foreign policy in a manner of the sovereign's choice. Absolutism may have been an elaborate façade of coverings designed to mask the deficiencies of what lay underneath, but the coverings themselves were of a particular nature, and the work of maintaining them created specific stresses and strains and conditioned specific behaviors that could harm the health of the system just as easily as they could help it. Was the projection of the image of absolutism, which scholarship rightly points to as so integral to its reality, therefore also a fundamental limitation on the ability of the system to function as those creating the image would hope?[53]

The huge wrench that Emilie's conversion threw into relations between Brandenburg and Sweden also makes one wonder whether absolutism as a system was structurally incapable of dealing well with the conversions of individuals whose identity lacked the clarity that the absolutist system craved. Since the performative elements of absolutism played out on the fields of religion and foreign relations, those moments where conversion, identity, and diplomacy intersected seem to have struck at an Achilles' heel in the diplomatic world of absolutist Europe and were almost bound to end in mutual dissatisfaction.

Finally, the fact that Emilie's complex identity following her marriage and conversion was able to pose such a challenge for both a king and an elector suggests that, rather than being robust and self-assured as often assumed, absolutism itself was something quite fragile, acutely vulnerable to challenge from below when quietly persistent subjects made their own decisions and refused to fit into the roles and categories carved out for them. One almost feels sympathy for the poor, insecure absolutist prince, caged in by a system of his own creation.

Notes

1. Scholars interested in the development of theories of exterritoriality and diplomatic immunity have taken special interest in what such cases can tell us about the evolving international legal standards surrounding diplomats and their activities. See, for example, E.R. Adair, *The Exterritoriality of Ambassadors in the Sixteenth and Seventeenth Centuries* (London, New York, and Toronto, 1929).

2. The most prominent proponent of this theory is Nicholas Henshall, *The Myth of Absolutism: Change and Continuity in Early Modern European Monarchy* (London and New York, 1992).

3. David Parker, *The Making of French Absolutism* (London, 1983), p. 136; Peter H. Wilson, *Absolutism in Central Europe* (London and New York, 2000), p. 122.

4. This is Wilson's central argument in *Absolutism in Central Europe*.

5. An account of von Dohna's embassy and the scandal caused by his wife's conversion is given in chapter 5 of my doctoral dissertation, "The Culture of Diplomacy in Brandenburg-Swedish Relations, 1575–1697" (Ph.D. diss., University of Chicago, 2007). An edited version of that chapter appeared as "The Rise of Confessional Tension in Brandenburg's Relations with Sweden in the Late Seventeenth Century," *Central European History* 37, no. 4 (2004): 568–592. The discussion in this essay follows these earlier versions closely.

6. For biographical information on Alexander von Dohna, see the entry "Alexander Burggraf und Graf zu Dohna-Schlobitten" by Lothar Graf zu Dohna in *Neue Deutsche Biographie*, vol. 4 (Berlin, 1971), pp. 52–53. On the von Dohna family as a whole, see Volker Press, "Das Haus Dohna in der europäischen Adelsgesellschaft des 16. und 17. Jahrhunderts," in Andreas Mehl and Wolfgang Christian Schneider, eds., *Reformatio*

et Reformationes. Festschrift für Lothar Graf zu Dohna zum 65. Geburtstag (Darmstadt, 1989), pp. 371–402.

7. For biographical information on Christoff Delficus von Dohna, see the entries for him by G. Jacobson and Bengt Hildebrand in the *Svenskt Biografiskt Lexikon*, vol. 11 (Stockholm, 1945), pp. 328–333; and by Lothar Graf zu Dohna in *Neue Deutsche Biographie*, vol. 4 (Berlin, 1971), pp. 48–49.

8. On Falaiseau and his embassy, see the material cited in n. 5 above.

9. Driven largely by a mutual fear of France, Brandenburg and Sweden entered into a defensive alliance with one another in 1686. This occurred after the two had fought three wars in the previous decades, the most recent of which had come to an end only in 1679. For the 1686 alliance, see Theodor von Moerner, *Kurbrandenburgs Staatsverträge von 1601 bis 1700* (Berlin, 1867), pp. 478–481. On Brandenburg-Swedish relations in the preceding decades, see Riches, "Culture of Diplomacy."

10. On the *reduktion*, see K. Ågren, "The *reduktion*," in Michael Roberts, ed., *Sweden's Age of Greatness, 1632–1718* (London, 1973), pp. 237–264; Göran Rystad, *Karl XI: en biografi* (Lund, 2003), esp. pp. 181–203; and Anthony F. Upton, *Charles XI and Swedish Absolutism* (Cambridge, 1998), esp. pp. 51–70.

11. On the dominance of orthodox Lutheranism in Karl XI's worldview, see Upton, *Charles XI*; and his chapter "Sweden," in John Miller, ed., *Absolutism in Seventeenth-Century Europe* (Basingstoke, 1990), pp. 99–121.

12. Alexander von Dohna to Friedrich III, Stockholm, 8 October 1690, Geheimes Staatsarchiv-Preußischer Kulturbesitz [hereafter: GStA-PK], I. HA: Nr. 247I Schweden, Rep. fasc. 47; and Alexander von Dohna to Friedrich III, Stockholm, 25 October 1690, GStA-PK, I. HA, Rep. 11, Nr. 247I Schweden, fasc. 46.

13. Karl XI to Friedrich Wilhelm Horn, Justus Heinrich Storren and Dörfler, Stockholm, 13 December 1690, Riksarkivet [hereafter: RA], Utrikesexpeditionens registratur, 1690-II, 599r–601r.

14. See Alexander von Dohna to Friedrich III, Stockholm, 8 October 1690, GStA-PK, I. HA, Rep. 11, Nr. 247I Schweden, fasc. 47.

15. Friedrich III to Alexander von Dohna, Cleves, 28 October/8 November 1690, GStA-PK, I. HA, Rep. 11, Nr. 247I Schweden, fasc. 47.

16. "… so finden Wir doch auch gantz keine Uhrsach, warumb Ihr die wegen Eures Abschids Euch *eventualiter* ertheilte *ordre disimulis* solte … daß man Uns in d[er] Sache thue so *enorm*, und unser desfals tragendes *resentiment* von der gantzn *raisonnable* Welt vor so gerecht gehelt und; daß Wir beständig … bestehen, man Ewre Gemalin der Zutrit bey Hofe eben so frey wie Sie ihn Vorhin gehabbt nicht wider Verstatte werden solte, als dan Ihr so fort Euch Von dort wieder zuruck … sollt"; Friedrich III to Alexander von Dohna, Cöln/Spree, 12/22 December 1690, GStA-PK, I. HA, Rep. 11, Nr. 247I Schweden, fasc. 47.

17. See Clifford Geertz, "Centers, Kings and Charisma: Reflections on the Symbolics of Power," in Sean Wilentz, ed., *Rites of Power: Symbolism, Ritual, and Politics since the Middle Ages* (Philadelphia, 1985), pp. 13–38, here pp. 14–15.

18. Parker, *The Making of French Absolutism*, p. 42.

19. See Patricia Behre Miskimin, *One King, One Law, Three Faiths: Religion and the Rise of Absolutism in Seventeenth-Century Metz* (Westport, 2002). Parker similarly links the French monarchical resurgence of the seventeenth century to its leadership of a broadly popular program of religious repression; Parker, *The Making of French Absolutism*, pp. 56–59.

20. The leading scholar on Karl XI's absolutism is Anthony F. Upton. See his works cited in n. 11 above. See also Rystad, *Karl XI*. For works on Swedish church history that stress the deep connections between the church reforms of Karl's reign and the consolidation of his absolutist system, see Hilding Pleijel, *Karolinsk Kyrkofromhet, Pietism och Herrnhutism 1680–1772*, vol. 5, *Svenska Kyrkans Historia* (Stockholm, 1935), pp. 7–61; and part 3 of Lars Anton Anjou's *Svenska Kyrkans Historia ifrån Upsala Möte år 1593 till Slutet af Sjuttonde Århundradet* (Stockholm, 1866).

21. Upton, "Sweden," p. 100.

22. Upton's later work, in stating that Sweden was "without *significant* religious dissent" (*Charles XI*, p. 170 [emphasis added]), is more accurate than his earlier claim that Sweden was "free of religious dissent" ("Sweden," p. 100).

23. Upton, "Sweden," p. 100; idem, *Charles XI*, pp. 21–22, 111.

24. See J.H. Burns, "The Idea of Absolutism," in Miller, ed., *Absolutism in Seventeenth-Century Europe*, pp. 21–42, here p. 22.

25. See Wilson, *Absolutism*, p. 57; Burns, "Idea," pp. 31–32; and Charles H. O'Brien, "Ideas of Religious Toleration at the Time of Joseph II: A Study of the Enlightenment among Catholics in Austria," *Transactions of the American Philosophical Society*, new series, 59 pt. 7 (1969): 1–80, here p. 12.

26. Cited in Upton, *Charles XI*, p. 256.

27. "Ich habe aber nachdem vom Könige selber erfahren, daß Sr. Mtt. nichts geschehen laßen alß was der Grafin E. Ihm fraw Mutter selber gethan, umb Ihre *indignation* zu *marquiren* und daß der König, weill die Gräfin E. hier in Lande gebohren, sich als Vater und Vormundt in einer sachen worin die Gräfin sich selbsten an schädlichen wehre vorstellen müsten, wo Ihre Mt. nicht von einer *blasmablen indifference soupçonniret seyn* wolten. der König hat dabey Versicherten daß I. Mayt. die Gräfin E. nicht anders, als dero eigene Kinder in gleichen fall wolten begegnen laßen, und weill alles zu Ihren besten angesehen"; Ulrike Eleonora to Sophie Charlotte, 8 October 1690, GStA-PK, I. HA, Rep. 11, Nr. 247I Schweden, fasc. 47.

28. The literature on gender in early modern Europe is rich and growing. The best introduction remains Merry E. Wiesner-Hanks, *Women and Gender in Early Modern Europe*, 3rd ed. (Cambridge, 2008).

29. On exterritoriality, see Adair, *Exterritoriality of Ambassadors*; Montell Ogdon, *Juridical Bases of Diplomatic Immunity: A Study of the Origin, Growth and Purpose of the Law* (Washington, DC, 1936); and Grant V. McClanahan, *Diplomatic Immunity: Principles, Practices, Problems* (New York, 1989), pp. 30–32.

30. Article 37 of the Vienna Convention on Diplomatic Relations (which came into force on 24 April 1964) begins: "The members of the family of a diplomatic agent forming part of his household shall, if they are not nationals of the receiving State, enjoy the privileges and immunities specified in Articles 29 to 36." The full text of the convention is printed as Appendix A in McClanahan, *Diplomatic Immunity*, pp. 187–199, here p. 195.

31. Chana Ullman, *The Transformed Self: The Psychology of Religious Conversion* (New York and London, 1989), pp. xvii, 29–30.

32. Geertz, "Centers, Kings, and Charisma," p. 15.

33. Wilson, *Absolutism*, p. 122.

34. J.H. Elliott, "Power and Propaganda in the Spain of Philip IV," in Wilentz, ed., *Rites of Power*, pp. 145–173, here pp. 146–147.

35. See Wilson, *Absolutism*, pp. 63ff.

36. Michael Roberts, "Charles XI," in *Essays in Swedish History* (Minneapolis, 1967), pp. 226–268, here p. 226.

37. Upton, *Charles XI*, p. 152.

38. On Karl's court, see Upton, *Charles XI*, chapter 8.

39. See Roberts, "Charles XI," p. 259.

40. Roberts wrote that "his violent temper, so easily aroused, as well as his obstinacy and honesty, made him a difficult man to handle: easy to antagonize, impossible to drive. He was quick to resent anything like an affront.... And though his ideas might be few and elementary, he knew what he believed, and also what he wanted; and on these things he would not compromise"; Roberts "Charles XI," p. 257.

41. See Upton, *Charles XI*, p. 217.

42. Wilson writes that "princes still depended on everyone else playing their part. Those courtiers who did not know the rules—which varied from court to court—or made mistakes were liable to destroy the whole performance." Wilson's context of courtiers and court ceremony may be different from the example under discussion here, but the fundamental point remains; Wilson, *Absolutism*, pp. 76–77.

43. See Dana Anderson, *Identity's Strategy: Rhetorical Selves in Conversion* (Columbia SC, 2007). David K. O'Rourke argues that converts can exude a "marketable euphoria" that has the potential to "prove a liability both for the convert and his community"; see his "The Experience of Conversion," in Francis A. Eigo, ed., *The Human Experience of Conversion: Persons and Structures in Transformation* (Villanova, 1987), pp. 1–30, here pp. 11–12.

44. See Andrew Buckser and Stephen D. Glazier, "Preface," in Buckser and Glazier, eds., *The Anthropology of Religious Conversion* (Lanham, MD, 2003), pp. xi–xviii.

45. Massimo Leone, *Religious Conversion and Identity: The Semiotic Analysis of Texts* (London and New York, 2004), pp. 53–78.

46. Leone interestingly notes that conversion is often presented to the mind of the convert in a theatrical idiom as a kind of one-man play; *Religious Conversion*, pp. 66–67.

47. This theme is stressed by those who claim that foreign policy concerns were the driving force behind the creation of absolutism; see Wilson, *Absolutism*, p. 18.

48. This theory stretches back at least into the early medieval period; see Donald E. Queller, *The Office of Ambassador in the Middle Ages* (Princeton, 1967).

49. Ogdon, *Juridical Bases*, pp. 106, 113.

50. See GStA-PK, I. HA, Rep. 11, Nr. 247I Schweden, fasc. 47.

51. Alexander von Dohna to Friedrich III, Stockholm, 7 February 1691, GStA-PK, I. HA, Rep. 11, No. 247I Schweden, fasc. 47.

52. For a variety of pragmatic reasons, the rulers of Brandenburg-Prussia did not place the same premium on the religious uniformity of their subjects as Swedish rulers did, in part because they were a Calvinist dynasty ruling over an overwhelmingly Lutheran population. For other practical concerns, including the desire to attract immigrants, see H.W. Koch, "Brandenburg-Prussia," in Miller, ed., *Absolutism in Seventeenth-Century Europe*, pp. 123–155, here p. 148.

53. In discussing the political fictions that "operate as the unchallenged first principles of a political order," Sean Wilentz wisely points out that these political symbol systems can be double-edged—that they can "either legitimize a political order or hasten its disintegration." The von Dohna case suggests that the political fictions of absolutism may have served both functions simultaneously; see Sean Wilentz, "Introduction: Teufelsdröckh's Dilemma: On Symbolism, Politics, and History," in Wilentz, ed., *Rites of Power*, pp. 1–10, here pp. 3–4.

CHAPTER SIX

Irenicism and
the Challenges of Conversion
in the Early Eighteenth Century

ALEXANDER SCHUNKA

Introduction

In 1710, the English politician Robert Harley (1661–1724) received news from Germany that "Duke Antonie of Wolfinbutle had given one of his [grand]daughters to a Papist, the other he was to give to a Barbarian, and if the Devil wo[ul]d ask the third, he believed he wo[ul]d give him her."[1] As this bit of gossip suggests, the dynastic marriage policies of Duke Anton Ulrich of Braunschweig-Wolfenbüttel were closely observed across Europe.[2] Of the three marriages, the one that generated most attention was that of Elisabeth Christine (1691–1750), who in 1708 married the future Habsburg emperor Charles (VI.). This alliance required Elisabeth Christine to convert from Lutheranism to the Roman Catholic faith, which in turn caused a major uproar in Protestant Europe.[3]

Elisabeth Christine's conversion, and the controversy it stirred, allows us to see mechanisms of theological networking, scholarly honor, and the divergent perceptions of confessional affiliation in England and continental Europe. More broadly, the episode illuminates the relationship between dynastic politics and religion in the early eighteenth century. The very fact that Duke Anton Ulrich could contemplate marrying his granddaughter into a Catholic house, no matter how lofty, registers the changing importance of confession in dynastic decision-making. However, the conversion did not mark a secular turn in politics. If anything, the controversy exposed the complexity of interconfessional relations on the eve of the Enlightenment.

Ironically, the Wolfenbüttel conversion also seemed to distort the efforts of (mainly Protestant) theologians to unite the confessions. "Irenicism," understood as the quest for religious peace among the different Christian denominations, was a major topic among European Protestants throughout the early modern era.[4] Advocates of irenicism wanted to merge the Christian confessions and move beyond the mere toleration of different faiths. Irenicism also differed from conversion in that irenicists did not advocate defection from one faith to another.[5] Promoting neither toleration nor conversion, irenicists offered a third strategy for dealing with confessional differences. But as the conversion of Elisabeth Christine showed, irenicists were anything but agreed on the form unification should take, particularly in regard to Roman Catholicism. Moreover, the conversion had consequences for international relations that, in the end, overpowered the irenicist movement. Ultimately, confessional commitments remained too strong for irenicism to prevail. The episode thus represents an important milestone in the evolution of European Protestantism and of confessional relations in general.

Protestant Irenicism in Central Europe

The duchy of Braunschweig-Wolfenbüttel was a small territory sandwiched between the Empire's two most energetic climbers. To the east lay the Electorate of Brandenburg-Prussia, and to the west was Braunschweig-Lüneburg (i.e., Hanover), whose ruler would soon ascend the British throne. Considering the traditional dynastic links between Berlin and the Hanoverians, the Lutheran duke Anton Ulrich of Braunschweig-Wolfenbüttel (1633–1714), although a member of the Hanoverian Guelph family and a close relative of the electors of Hanover, struggled to protect his duchy from his more powerful neighbors.[6] In a political sense, the duke's marriage plans for his granddaughters were therefore quite clever, since they connected his family and territory with some major powers of Europe: the Russian tsar and the Holy Roman emperor. But many European Protestants found them abhorrent as the source of both political rancor and confessional troubles.

Considering the religious traditions of Braunschweig-Wolfenbüttel and its ruling dynasty, the Catholic marriage of Elisabeth Christine was not completely surprising. The theological faculty of the University of Helmstedt included prominent advocates of confessional irenicism and interconfessional dialogue. One of them, Georg Calixt (1586–1656), had sparked the so-called Syncretism Controversy (*Synkretismusstreit*) when he tried to overcome confessional differences with the help of a system of fundamental truths that all denominations could agree upon. The Lutheran professor of theology, Johann Fabricius (1644–1729), had studied at Helmstedt during the Syncretism Controversy and worked with Gottfried Wilhelm Leibniz on an agreement between Protestantism and Roman Catholicism. These two proponents of confessional reconciliation also lent their support to Duke Anton Ulrich in his decision to marry Elisabeth Christine into the Catholic house of Habsburg.

But whereas Leibniz and Fabricius participated in talks about an inner Protestant union only as a starting point for a confessional unity that would include Roman Catholics, Prussian irenicists such as Daniel Ernst Jablonski (1660–1741) aimed at unifying Lutherans and Calvinists in order to strengthen Protestantism against the threat of Popery. Many Protestant polemicists believed that in 1700, the Reformation's achievements were in acute danger. The political situation in Saxony and Poland, the Habsburg crown lands, and the Palatinate all seemed to favor Roman Catholicism. This was taken as proof that Protestants lacked the strength and the high degree of organization the Roman Catholic Church possessed. Jablonski and the Prussian irenicists sharply opposed reunion with Roman Catholics not only on theological grounds, but also for fear that Protestant-Catholic dialogue would result in forced conversions to Popery.[7] The relationship between irenicists in Berlin and Wolfenbüttel was complicated for personal reasons as well. Jablonski considered Duke Anton Ulrich too old and weak politically to be of use to his irenicist scheme, and it seems likely that the marriage of his granddaughter to a Habsburg simply confirmed Jablonski's low opinion of Anton Ulrich.[8]

While Protestant irenicists could not agree on the question of the inclusion of Catholicism within a unified Christianity, they did survey the European landscape for solutions to the problem of confessional difference and sometimes came to similar results. As a model for confessional unification, the Church of England played a major role for theologians in Wolfenbüttel and in Berlin, either as part of a general Christian reconciliation or as an instrument to merge the Protestant denominations against Roman Catholicism. From the viewpoint of Prussian Calvinists such as Jablonski, the Church of England emerged as the "middle way" to unite European Protestants under the umbrella of Anglicanism.[9] Jablonski and other Prussian theologians also knew that Duke Anton Ulrich highly valued the idea of introducing Anglicanism in his territories as a primary step toward reunion. In 1705 the British traveler Robert Hales even reported from Wolfenbüttel that Anton Ulrich was about to use the German translation of the Book of Common Prayer in his private chapel.[10]

Protestant irenical ideas and networks, spanning from Britain to Hanover, Wolfenbüttel, and Brandenburg-Prussia, shaped the context of the conversion controversy. Its leading figures were Fabricius (Wolfenbüttel), Leibniz (Hanover), and Jablonski (Berlin), along with some fellow theologians and high-ranking Anglican clergy. After promising efforts to stimulate interconfessional dialogue, a number of closely connected events in 1706 worsened the atmosphere within these communication networks. These circumstances are important to keep in mind in order to explain why Duchess Elisabeth Christine's conversion sparked off such wide-ranging disputes.

Early in 1706, it seemed that Prussian irenicists were finally succeeding in their efforts at Protestant unification. In April, the celebration of the 200th anniversary of the University of Frankfurt an der Oder was staged as a festival of Reformed irenicism. The anniversary was considered so important that the University of Cambridge sent representatives, and the University of Oxford even arranged a special celebration at home. More promising still was the wedding of Prussia's Prince Frederick William, a Calvinist, to the Lutheran princess Sophie Dorothea of Hanover, scheduled for autumn. Initially, theologians viewed this marriage as an opportunity to advertise the benefits of Protestant unification. But these hopes were soon dashed when Leibniz proposed that neither of the partners should convert but both should stick to their faiths and practice an "occasional conformity" of worship inspired by British practice. This proposal proved much too delicate for both courts involved, once politicians realized the international implications and the political and confessional dangers of dynastic irenicism.[11] Instead, the courts of both Prussia and Hanover immediately abandoned the irenicist project. Fabricius of the University of Helmstedt was denied further contacts to other irenicist theologians and even a trip to Berlin.[12] Leibniz's initiative also ended the long friendship between him and Jablonski.

The breakup of irenicist correspondence in the summer of 1706 was followed by an event that added to the discord between theologians of the Guelph territories and Berlin. A slanderous pasquil from Helmstedt appeared whose aim was to interfere with the marriage between the Hanoverian princess Sophie Dorothea and Prince Frederick William of Prussia. Masked as a congratulatory piece, the anonymous pamphlet *Delicatissimum Solomoneum epithalamium* (Most Delicate Wedding Song of Solomon) drew upon analogies between Prince Frederick William and King Solomon of the Old Testament. It offered a reinterpretation of Psalm 45, portraying a rather worldly Solomon who was attracted to heathen women. This implied that while Solomon had married an Egyptian pharaoh's daughter, Frederick William might as well marry the Lutheran princess Sophie Dorothea of Hanover. The author was almost certainly a member of Fabricius's circle—one of his students or his colleague, perhaps the eccentric Hermann von der Hardt.[13]

By the time of Elisabeth Christine's betrothal, these controversies had already severely damaged the reputations of Wolfenbüttel theologians in general and Fabricius in particular. In Germany, the conversion issue of the duke's granddaughter fit well into the numerous theological quarrels on the dangers of irenicism.[14] Within international Protestantism, and especially in Great Britain, it soon raised serious questions about the reliability of continental Lutherans because the conversion seemed to blur the differences between Lutheranism and the Catholic faith.

The Conversion Issue and its International Implications

The conversion of Duchess Elisabeth Christine of Wolfenbüttel from the Lutheran to the Roman Catholic faith turned out to be one of the biggest threats to international Protestant collaboration in the early eighteenth century, linking dynastic politics with theological controversy and public debate. As far as questions of gender are concerned, this conversion seemingly reiterates the early modern picture of a male-headed (royal) household where the wife had to surrender to the decisions of her husband. The present case as well as other contemporary examples, however, reveal that a princely conversion was more connected to dynastic rank and power than to gender hierarchies. Frederick I of Hesse-Kassel, for instance, converted from the Reformed to the Lutheran faith because his Swedish wife was Lutheran and his conversion enabled him to succeed to the throne of Sweden in 1720. Further, conversion was not the only solution to the problem of mixed royal marriages. The cases of Prussia and Great Britain prove that a nonruling spouse could at times keep his or her original faith. Still, early modern rulership was largely male-dominated. This is true even for Elisabeth Christine's daughter Maria Theresia, who did not become Holy Roman Empress, but "king" (Rex) of Bohemia and Hungary.[15]

Elisabeth Christine's marriage was preceded by sixteen commentaries from major Protestant scholars such as Leibniz and Christian Thomasius. Only the one written by the Helmstedt theologian, Fabricius, was published. What followed was a pamphlet war that developed alongside a confessional and political crisis between Britain and the continent. The conversion, in other words, sparked an international debate on the future and meaning of Protestant unification. The public debate surrounding Fabricius's commentary entered British ecclesiastical politics at the threshold of the Hanoverian succession. It was fueled by Protestant quarrels on the continent, and it relied upon the infrastructure of irenicist communication.

The idea that several renowned scholars should give their written opinion on the conversion came from Leibniz, who had been involved in the marriage preparations.[16] The sixteen intellectuals, mostly theologians, had to deal with two separate yet connected queries. The first was whether Catholics as well as Protestants held equal opportunities to gain eternal salvation if only they centered their belief on Jesus Christ. The second, more concrete question was whether a Lutheran princess could still be eligible for salvation even if she converted to Catholicism for the sake of marriage. The replies were not supposed to be published, which also underlines that this was a delicate issue. Nine of sixteen replies consented to the conversion of the duchess, including the one by Johann Fabricius.[17]

Fabricius's published commentary on these questions bore the telling title *Erörterte Frage…, daß zwischen der Augspurgischen Confession und Catholischen Religion kein sonderlicher unterscheid seye* (Consideration on the Lack of Difference between the Augsburg Confession and the Catholic Faith).[18] He argued that Lutherans and Catholics agreed in their catechetic essentials, and he avoided the usual points of Catholic/Lutheran disagreement such as the infallibility of the Pope or the sacraments. The circumstances of the treatise's publication are somewhat dubious, but it seems that it was first published against its author's will by Roman Catholics. The fact that it was published not in Latin but in German suggests that it aimed at a wide audience, which it indeed quickly received. Readers could easily attribute it to the theological faculty of Helmstedt, but perhaps only the theological insiders ascribed it directly to Fabricius, who initially denied his authorship although he never objected to the contents.[19]

Fabricius's opinion on the conversion of a Lutheran princess to Catholicism was translated into major European languages and caused a storm of protest among Protestants in the Empire and beyond.[20] When news about the opinion crossed the English Channel in 1708, it quickly became a matter of high politics. It seemed as if German Lutherans mingled Lutheranism with Catholicism, and that Lutherans were much closer to Roman Catholic doctrines than Britons could bear. What weighed even more heavily were perceptions that the whole marriage issue came at the initiative of Duke Anton Ulrich, who was a close relative of the expected Hanoverian successor to Queen Anne on the British throne. The neglect of "Protestant Interest" quickly added to the prevalent anti-Catholic fears in Britain and made the Wolfenbüttel conversion a matter of public debate. It soon became clear that the contents of Fabricius's document were far less important than the overall reactions it elicited.

The marriage plans of Elisabeth Christine had not been kept secret from the British public, but initially they caused no major public reactions. British foreign policy around 1700, although officially anti-French as well as anti-Catholic, depended on a number of continental allies who hardly identified with a "Protestant Cause," such as the Habsburg emperor, Joseph I. Despite his Roman Catholic persuasion, the emperor was a major British ally during the War of the Spanish Succession. Thus British readers could easily learn about the intention of Joseph's nephew Charles, the designated king of Spain, to marry a Lutheran princess.[21] The marriage was an almost constant topic in London newspapers from 1706 on, long before news about the Helmstedt treatise reached the British Isles. At first, the faith of the bride and the confessional consequences of her conversion were little remarked on, apart from one succinct statement that the princess "had some difficulties at first to renounce her religion, but those difficulties were soon overcome."[22] Even a travel diary of the future "Queen of Spain" was published in the *Daily Courant* in June 1708.[23]

Negative attitudes toward the Wolfenbüttel marriage first emerged in England in the summer of 1708, when journalist Abel Boyer published details of Fabricius's theological opinion in the *Post Boy*.[24] So shocking was Fabricius's opinion that some British readers initially assumed it was a forgery.[25] It is not known whether Boyer undertook the English publication of the Helmstedt commentary single-handedly, but its general critique on the trustworthiness of Lutheranism, the faith of the next ruling dynasty, certainly suited the Tories' anti-Hanoverian attitudes. The *Post Boy* publication also endangered the efforts of British ecclesiastics who had attempted a dialogue with continental Protestants. Meant to support Protestantism in Europe with the aid of the Anglican Church in order to withstand a presumed Roman Catholic threat, this dialogue was thus strongly connected to continental irenicism. Anglican involvement on the continent also aimed to strengthen the Church of England at home in order to achieve comprehension of dissenting groups under an Anglican communion and episcopal hierarchy. The fact that continental Protestants did not share certain peculiarities of Anglican ecclesiology and administration had made the international dialogue with continental Protestants difficult from the start.

The *Post Boy* article was clearly targeted at discrediting continental Protestants and at thwarting the Hanoverian succession, which is the main reason why Fabricius's commentary caused considerable concern among British as well as German ecclesiastics. Anti-Hanoverian propaganda was abundant and originated mainly from the Tories.[26] British observers of continental Protestantism around 1706–1708 were also highly alarmed because only recently a few newspapers had published reports about the king of Prussia's efforts to unite the Lutheran and the Reformed denominations.[27] The news about the Helmstedt opinion reached Britain at a time when the Lutheran faith had become increasingly acceptable to British observers within the broader framework of a "Protestant Interest"—not only because of the imminent succession of the Lutheran prince-elector of Hanover to the British throne, but also because Britain championed Protestantism and interconfessional harmony in the Holy Roman Empire, especially in Silesia, in the Palatine Electorate, and in the imperial city of Hamburg.[28] What most Anglicans and a number of continental supporters of Protestant unity had in common was their aversion to Popery and the politics of Catholic states. In the wake of the Helmstedt opinion, which seemed to imply that Lutheranism resembled Roman Catholicism, the very essentials of the "Protestant Cause" seemed to be at stake.

Now important British observers made use of the irenicist correspondence networks that joined Britain, the Hanoverian lands, and Brandenburg-Prussia in order to understand better the context of Fabricius's text and the validity of the *Post Boy* exposé. Archbishop Thomas Tenison of Canterbury, a supporter of the Hanoverian succession with a number of continental Protestant contacts, immediately started to inquire in Helmstedt and at the Protestant courts of the empire whether the Helmstedt opinion was common among Lutherans.[29] In trying to locate the root of the problem, Tenison's aim was to support the Hanoverian succession and to avert any more unnecessary damage to the future king's faith. Tenison also asked William Ayerst, chaplain of the British envoy at Berlin, to get information from Jablonski about the background of the *Post Boy* article. Jablonski reactivated his contacts with Leibniz, which he had given up after the failure of the 1706 irenicist effort. In his letter to Leibniz, Jablonski quoted at length from the *Post Boy* article and immediately suspected not the whole theological faculty of Helmstedt but Fabricius in particular to be responsible for the commentary.[30]

Among the theologians who approached Jablonski in this matter was Andrew Snape, who had been one of the deputies of the University of Cambridge at the irenical anniversary celebration of the University of Frankfurt an der Oder in 1706. Jablonski enclosed Snape's letter to Fabricius in his own letter to Leibniz.[31] The fact that British ecclesiastics relied upon Jablonski's information and contacts underlines his reputation as an important Anglo-German middleman. The Prussian court preacher was immediately aware of the political and religious dangers of the published Fabricius commentary in Britain, but his aim was to "save Mr. Fabricius as much as possible."[32]

These networks worked in the opposite direction as well, which once again illustrates the importance of irenicist contacts for Anglo-German communication but also highlights the international scope of the problem. Fabricius himself tried to get in touch with British clerical circles with the help of Jablonski's friend in Oxford, the native Prussian John Ernest Grabe. Fabricius ended up publishing an apology *ad eruditos Britannos*. This treatise appeared in Helmstedt, with the help of Leibniz, and it apparently received a wide audience.[33] In another of Fabricius's writings, addressed personally to "A. S. doctorem Anglicanum" (Andrew Snape), he conceded some errors in Popery but still maintained his own innocence in the scandal.[34]

Under the influence of Elector Georg Ludwig of Hanover and in response to rising international pressure, the theological faculty of Helmstedt officially dismissed the original opinion on 7 September 1708. A new statement signed by the members of the faculty, including Fabricius, maintained that the University of Helmstedt would never encourage anyone to convert to the Roman Catholic faith.[35] However, the damage Fabricius had done to his position was beyond repair. Owing to the political influence of Georg Ludwig of Hanover, he eventually quit his position and was relocated to a more distant post.[36]

The new Helmstedt declaration quickly circulated in Anglo-German correspondence networks originating in Hanover and Berlin.[37] It made its way to the press as well. In October 1708, the *Post Boy*'s rival, the *Post Man*, not only published the faculty's official counter-declaration in both Latin and English but also mentioned that it had already been sent out to the Hanoverian envoy in London, who was supposed to hand it over to the archbishop. The introductory text clearly attributed the scandal to Roman Catholic propaganda.[38] It is obvious that Hanoverian Whig circles in church and state tried hard to neutralize the problem as quickly as possible, and by using the same means of communication as their opponents.

Britain and Continental Protestantism after the Conversion

Perhaps the most remarkable reaction to the conflict fought in England over his granddaughter's marriage and conversion came from Duke Anton Ulrich himself. There is some evidence that the duke blamed himself for the end of Fabricius's career at Helmstedt.[39] Yet more importantly, Anton Ulrich sharply objected to the international reaction to a seemingly domestic affair. In a letter to a Hanoverian diplomat, he regarded the British archbishop's intervention at the Protestant courts of Germany and particularly in Hanover as an intrusion into his territorial and dynastic rights and as a personal insult that he believed was far from appropriate, coming from a prelate and an Englishman. English history, he wrote, was full of "rebellious spirits" such as this. The duke demanded that one should inquire about the religious principles of the archbishop, who he believed belonged to the sphere of darkness rather than being an enlightened spirit. Considering the disputed validity of Lutheran orders and sacraments, the duke asked how other territorial princes would be expected to react upon questioning of, for instance, the validity of their baptism. Other issues raised by the duke were whether an intrusion such as this would not fit better with the doctrines of Satan than with those of Christian charity. If the archbishop's piety was that great, the duke mused, why did he not confine himself to religious matters?[40]

From this letter it becomes evident that the duke felt his honor was at stake. What is also clear is that the conflict touched upon different notions of governance and princely rule—a fine example of cultural (mis)translations between Germany and Britain—and that Anton Ulrich was forced into making the whole issue a personal affair. The duke's polemic illustrates the characteristic differences between, on the one hand, the self-image of the Church of England as a political actor in its own right within and outside Britain, and on the other, the Lutheran *Kirchenregiment* of a German territorial prince that connected religious decisions strongly to the ruler's politics.

It is important to note that Tenison wanted to secure the Hanoverian succession but did not advocate Protestant union. In a political sense, the unity of European Protestants (in order to secure Anglicanism at home) was perhaps more a project of the Tories and High Church Episcopalians, while Tenison was closer to Latitudinarian Whigs.[41] By increasing Anglican influence on the continent, the High Church expected to gain in popularity at home. However, as the peace negotiations with France at Utrecht revealed in 1712/13, even Tory support for international Protestantism had its limits.[42]

For Tenison, the Helmstedt opinion came at the right moment. It impeded any more unnecessary involvement with confessional unity. Tenison's disinterest in irenicism was something that particularly bothered ecclesiastics and politicians in Brandenburg-Prussia. The archbishop's suspicion of continental Lutherans led him to turn a blind eye to both Anglican involvement on the continent and reconciliatory efforts between Lutherans, Calvinists, and Anglicans. Even if Jablonski tried to prevent any more damage,[43] the Prussian court was so offended by Tenison's coolness that Prussian interest in the Anglican Church diminished in 1708, only two years after domestic efforts at unification had suffered a major setback in combination with Prince Frederick William's wedding.[44] However, the Helmstedt affair served Tenison with a convenient excuse for his reservations. When the British chaplain Ayerst inquired about Tenison's reluctance in 1708, the archbishop replied that it was Helmstedt that would "for ever be an Obstacle to our meddling w[i]th any thing of Religion in Germany."[45] The Helmstedt affair added significantly to Tenison's aversion toward an Anglican approach to continental Protestantism because it "was such a Reflection on All ye Protestant Churches of Germany, that it was sufficient at that time to hinder his Corresponding with Any of them."[46]

In England, efforts to calm down the whole Wolfenbüttel affair were mainly the work of Tenison and his pro-Hanoverian friends in politics.[47] They were quite successful. Elisabeth Christine's conversion and the Helmstedt opinion seem to have been soon forgotten. In the end, the affair of Fabricius did not put the Hanoverian succession at general risk, although concerns about continental Lutheranism remained, not only in printed polemics but also in a conflict between Halle Pietist missionaries and Anglicans around 1712.[48]

Lutherans in England often had to face particular pressure when it came to proving that their faith did not resemble Roman Catholicism. When Elector Georg Ludwig of Hanover eventually took over as King George I in 1714, he decided to play the part of a staunch Anglican, meanwhile employing the German Lutheran Anthony William Boehm as a court preacher in London and at least occasionally participating in Lutheran services when he visited his native territories.[49] By that time, the elderly Duke of Wolfenbüttel had already died. Only one year after the British succession, Archbishop Tenison passed away. He was replaced by William Wake, a strong proponent of unity with continental Protestants.[50] At any rate, Tenison's reaction to the Helmstedt opinion reflected his overall disgust with Lutheranism. It contributed to the halt of Anglo-Prussian talks on ecclesiastical unification, and it revealed how much irenicism was not only a religious but also a political affair. The connection between the Wolfenbüttel conversion and Protestant irenicism illustrates how sensitive religious matters could be, even in the "enlightened" eighteenth century.

British reactions to the conversion issue had repercussions for Protestants throughout the Holy Roman Empire. Generally, the greatest polemicists and confessional troublemakers were located in the city of Hamburg, usually seen as a place of ecclesiopolitical toleration whose Lutheran orthodox pastors still aroused numerous complaints from all over Germany for their sharp and regular polemics against moderate Lutherans, Pietists, Calvinists, and irenicists.[51] Thus it was not very surprising that the Hamburg pastor Sebastian Edzard[us] attacked Fabricius and Helmstedt for their publications.[52] Even less surprising was that the Lutheran orthodox *Unschuldige Nachrichten* (Impartial News), edited by the Saxon Valentin Ernst Löscher—one of the first and most enduring German theological journals—treated the Helmstedt controversy at length. A reviewer of Fabricius's *Beantwortung der Frage* (Response to the Question) sharply objected to conversions from Lutheranism to the Roman Catholic faith and concluded with the prayer that "God [may] convert the author, wherever possible, and prevent this damnable offence for Christ's sake."[53] Further reviews commented on refutations of the treatise, on the duke's dismissal and expulsion of two ecclesiastics, and on the uproar a translation of the expertise had caused in France.[54]

What is remarkable is that the *Unschuldige Nachrichten* saw the intrinsic connection between the Wolfenbüttel conversion and Protestant irenicism.[55] Their coverage of the affair offers a contemporary synopsis of international polemics, as their writers also reported on the repercussions of the whole affair in Britain. In 1709 the *Nachrichten* reviewed two short treatises dealing with British reactions. One was Fabricius's printed letter *ad pios et eruditos Britannos*. What found more support and sympathy from the editors was a refutation written by Johann Frick, a Lutheran orthodox pastor from Ulm who had previously attacked Fabricius under the pseudonym of Johann Warnefried.[56] Now Frick published his *Britannia rectius de Lutheranis edocta* (Britain Properly Informed about Lutherans), where he not only disassociated himself from Fabricius's interpretation of Lutheranism but even blamed some Anglican theologians like George Bull and John Ernest Grabe for certain affections for Popish doctrines.[57]

Not even Halle Pietists, perhaps the Lutheran group in Germany with the most profound interest in the British situation, remained unaffected by the Helmstedt affair.[58] August Hermann Francke and others kept an eye on the issue of Elisabeth Christine's conversion not just because Pietists enjoyed close relations with Helmstedt theologians.[59] They did not seem unhappy to learn of the British ill humor after Helmstedt. Francke received news from London via his local German correspondents, who construed British reactions as a sign of how much the spiritual world was in motion. The Helmstedt affair seemed to anticipate the beginning of the kingdom of Christ on Earth by challenging outward confessional denominations.[60]

Halle pietists propagated a union of hearts and spirits rooted in the Lutheran faith. They disapproved of anything they considered worldly efforts, such as a modification of liturgy or ecclesiastical administration.[61] The fact that Helmstedt had contributed to the failure of Protestant irenicism affirmed their conviction that it was not the unification of confessional systems but a spiritual unity of believers toward which Protestants had to struggle.

Conclusion

Ironically, only few years after the affair, Duke Anton Ulrich himself converted to Catholicism, which deprived him of what was left of his reputation among Protestants.[62] In the meantime, his granddaughter Elisabeth Christine had become empress of the Holy Roman Empire. The rabble-rouser Fabricius was relocated to the countryside, but he still participated in theological discussions, as did the Prussian court preacher Jablonski, for whom irenicism and the Anglo-German dialogue was a life mission. Archbishop Tenison lived just long enough to see the Hanoverian succession take place in 1714, by which time he had become old and gouty.

The Helmstedt affair and its repercussions on Protestant irenicism illustrate the importance of theological networks and the different perceptions of confessional groups in England and on the continent. The affair underscores the fact that while most European Protestants would agree upon the dangers of Roman Catholicism, some British ecclesiastics considered Popery merely a continental phenomenon. Continental Protestants such as Lutherans could easily be suspected of being close to Catholicism whenever there seemed to be a good reason for it. Considering the support Protestant irenicism had traditionally received from Helmstedt and Wolfenbüttel, it could not have been Duke Anton Ulrich's intention to sabotage the Prussian irenical rapprochement with the Church of England. However, dynastic considerations won out over irenical negotiations. And this was perhaps the greatest danger to confessional unification: Protestant unity as well as the project of a Protestant-Catholic reunion largely depended on political circumstances and on the support particular theologians could receive from certain rulers and politicians.

One of the remaining questions is whether Protestant irenicism could have succeeded at all. The usual, and sometimes justified, accusation against irenicists was that they did not aim at creating one faith out of two on equal terms but that they either aimed at the foundation of an additional sect or, more importantly, expected one group to join another and submit to the doctrines of its opponents. In this respect, unificationist attempts could be decried as forced mass conversions to the wrong faith, and Lutheran reactions to Prussian church reforms in the 1730s went exactly into that direction.[63] This ran counter to the attempts of many irenicists, in whose opinion all Christians, or at least all Protestants, shared the same doctrinal or ecclesiological essentials.[64] Supporters of irenicism would usually propagate perspectives toward unification that originated from the different denominations and would lead to a single Protestant or even universal Christian church. Only in certain cases did dedicated irenicists recommend conversion, knowing that the ideal of complete confessional unity could not be achieved in the near future.

The whole issue of Elisabeth Christine's conversion and Fabricius's role in it has usually been interpreted as a result of an exaggerated confessional relativism deriving from Georg Calixt and the "Syncretism Controversy."[65] But this is only one part of the story. The Wolfenbüttel conversion jeopardized not only Anglican attitudes to continental Protestants but also endangered irenicism in general. An extreme relativism, such as Fabricius's idea of the possibility of salvation in *any* of the Christian churches, would seem to refute the plausibility of irenical negotiations at all. And it would also deprive international and dynastic politics around 1700 of an important bargaining point.

It is anachronistic to see the conversion issue as symptomatic of the separation of religion from dynastic politics. In the eighteenth century it was essential to stick to confessional differences as a means of group coherence—even for dynastic reasons. Acknowledging, vilifying, or even fighting a confessional "other" served as an important means of confessional integration, as can be seen not only in Britain but also in the international politics of the time. In other words, the whole controversy illustrates the ongoing durability of confessional boundaries well into the eighteenth century. Confessional polemics continued, although they changed their outlook and the means of communication. Polemics and irenicism were much more connected than opposed to one another, and both became more political than in earlier decades, when they had been perhaps more restricted to the sphere of scholarly dispute. At any rate, it cannot be ignored that confessional transgressions—individual conversions as well as dynastic and political alliances—were an important part of the framework of religion and politics in the eighteenth century. If the irenicists had succeeded, and if this had resulted in the dissolution of confessional barriers, some contemporaries would have lost important political capital.

Differences of faith increasingly became the subject of political negotiations and as such were immensely useful tools in order to achieve political goals. This adds a very pragmatic dimension to confessional conflict as well as to irenicism and conversion. Even if religion and secular power slowly grew apart, this development did not immediately lead to a general decline of religion or to the beginning of a secular age in the early eighteenth century. It did, however, result in a greater complexity and a new confessional pluralism, something most contemporaries would have decried as dangerous and disturbing.

Notes

1. British Library London, Add. Mss. 70026, fols. 96r–97v, Cunigham [?] to Harley, 16 August 1710. I would like to thank Dr. Kelly Whitmer for most valuable discussions and corrections.

2. The "barbarian" spouse was Prince Alexey Petrovich of Russia (1690–1718), the son of Tsar Peter the Great; cf. [Ferdinand] Spehr, "Charlotte Christine Sophie, Kronprinzessin von Rußland," *Allgemeine deutsche Biographie* 4 (1876): 103–105.

3. F[erdinand] Spehr, "Elisabeth Christine", *Allgemeine Deutsche Biographie* 6 (1877): 11–12.

4. Howard Hotson, "Irenicism in the Confessional Age: The Holy Roman Empire, 1563–1648," in Howard P. Louthan and Randall C. Zachman, eds., *Conciliation and Confession: The Struggle for Unity in the Age of Reform, 1415–1648* (Notre Dame, 2004), pp. 228–285.

5. On the relationship between irenicism and conversion see Heinz Duchhardt and Gerhard May, eds., *Union – Konversion – Toleranz. Dimensionen der Annäherung zwischen den christlichen Konfessionen im 17. und 18. Jahrhundert* (Mainz, 2000).

6. Research is scarce; see Willi Flemming, "Anton Ulrich, Herzog von Braunschweig-Wolfenbüttel, Dichter," *Neue deutsche Biographie* 1 (1953): 315–316. [Ferdinand] Spehr, "Anton Ulrich, Herzog von Braunschweig-Wolfenbüttel," *Allgemeine deutsche Biographie* 1 (1875): 487–490. Only his cultural interests have been analyzed more recently: Jean-Marie Valentin, ed., '*Monarchus poeta*'. *Studien zum Leben und Werk Anton Ulrichs von Braunschweig-Lüneburg* (Amsterdam, 1985).

7. See, for instance, Staatsbibliothek Berlin preussischer Kulturbesitz, Handschriften, Nachlass A. H. Francke, 11,2/13, No. 11: Jablonski to Goetze, 17 March 1700 and 11,2/12, No. 12: Jablonski to Fabricius, 4 July 1699. Leibniz's irenicist plans are addressed in Franz Xaver Kiefl, *Der Friedensplan des Leibniz zur Wiedervereinigung der getrennten christlichen Kirchen* (Paderborn, 1903); Paul Eisenkopf, *Leibniz und die Einigung der Christenheit. Überlegungen zur Reunion der evangelischen und katholischen Kirche* (Munich, 1975).

8. Staatsbibliothek Berlin preussischer Kulturbesitz, Handschriften, Nachlass A. H. Francke 11,2/14, No. 15: Jablonski to Fabricius, 17 September 1701 and No. 57: Jablonski to Hales, 20 May 1704; ibid., 11,2/15, No. 10: Jablonski to Hales, 21 March 1705 and No. 38: Jablonski to Fabricius, 25 September 1705.

9. Jablonski to Leibniz, 15/25 October 1698. Gottfried Wilhelm Leibniz, *Allgemeiner politischer und historischer Briefwechsel*, vol. 16 (Berlin, 2000), No. 133. See the preface of Jablonski's German translation of the Book of Common Prayer: *Die Englische Liturgie, Oder, Das allgemeine Gebeth-Buch...* (Frankfurt an der Oder, 1704), 3. On the Anglican *via media* see Paul Avis, *Anglicanism and the Christian Church: Theological Resources in Historical Perspective* (Edinburgh, 2002); Diarmaid MacCulloch, *The Later Reformation in England, 1547–1603* (Basingstoke, 1990).

10. British Library London, Add. Mss. 70022, Hales to [?], 5 May 1705, fol. 144r. Staatsbibliothek Berlin preussischer Kulturbesitz, Handschriften, Nachlass A. H. Francke,

11,2/14, No. 56: Jablonski to Fabricius, 16 May 1704; ibid. 11,2/15, No. 38: Jablonski to Fabricius, 25 September 1705. Bodleian Library Oxford, Ms. Grabe 23, No. 23: Fabricius to Grabe, 12 March 1705.

11. Alexander Schunka, "Brüderliche Korrespondenz, unanständige Korrespondenz. Konfession und Politik zwischen Brandenburg–Preußen, Hannover und England im Wendejahr 1706," in Joachim Bahlcke and Werner Korthaase, eds., *Daniel Ernst Jablonski. Religion, Wissenschaft und Politik um 1700* (Wiesbaden, 2008), pp. 123–150.

12. Hauptstaatsarchiv Hannover, CalBr 21/3976, Fabricius to Elector Georg Ludwig of Hanover, 27 March 1706, fol. 4v.

13. N.a., *Delicatissimum solomoneum epithalamium...* (n.p., [1706]). Refutations were: Polycarp Leyser, *Ad Virum Illustrem...* (Hanover, 1707); Johannes Christophilus [Friedrich Kind], *Höchstnöthige Warnung, Für der recht Socinianischen ... Ubersetzung ... Des XLV. Psalms Davids, Durch einen Studiosum zu Helmstädt* (Wittenberg and Leipzig, 1708). On the debate see *Unschuldige Nachrichten* (1707), pp. 265–70.

14. On the contemporary controversies see Walter Delius, "Berliner kirchliche Unionsversuche im 17. und 18. Jahrhundert," *Jahrbuch für Berlin-Brandenburgische Kirchengeschichte* 45 (1970): 7–121, here pp. 41–52.

15. I refer to the relevant articles of the *Allgemeine Deutsche Biographie*. On the gender dimensions of religion in the early modern era see Ruth Albrecht et al., eds., *Glaube und Geschlecht. Fromme Frauen – spirituelle Erfahrungen – Religiöse Traditionen* (Cologne, 2008). I intend to do more research on confessionally mixed courts in the near future.

16. It even seems that he was the éminence grise behind the defenses of Helmstedt and Fabricius. See Kiefl, *Friedensplan des Leibniz*, pp. lxxi–lxxx; Heinz Weidemann, *Gerard Wolter Molanus Abt zu Loccum. Eine Biographie*, vol. 2 (Göttingen, 1929), p. 129.

17. Details in Ines Peper, *Konversionen im Umkreis des Wiener Hofes um 1700* (unpublished Ph.D. diss., Graz, 2003), pp. 150–151, 196–233. Now published as Ines Peper, *Konversionen im Umkreis des Wiener Hofes um 1700* (Vienna, 2010). I have used the unpublished dissertation for the present article.

18. Johann Fabricius, *Erörterte Frage, Herrn Fabricii,... Daß zwischen der Augspurgischen Confession und Catholischen Religion kein sonderlicher Unterschied seye...* (n.p., 1706). Later editions appeared in 1707 and 1708.

19. Cf. Martin Ohst, "Späte Helmstedter Irenik zwischen Politik und Theologie," *Jahrbuch der Gesellschaft für Niedersächsische Kirchengeschichte* 92 (1994): 139–170, here 161–163; Peper, *Konversionen*, pp. 201–208.

20. On the frequency of editions and translations into French, Dutch, and English see Peper, *Konversionen*, pp. 201–202 and bibliography.

21. See *Post Boy*, 5 April 1707; *Daily Courant*, 29 May 1707 and 13 April 1708; *English Post with News Foreign and Domestick*, 9 February 1708; *Post Man and the Historical Account*, 30 July 1706 and 7 January 1707.

22. *Post Man and the Historical Account*, 6 March 1707.

23. *Daily Courant*, 4 June 1708.

24. Unfortunately, the original issue under consideration here, i.e., the *Post Boy* of 1 July 1708, is missing in the Burney Collection of the British Library London and could not be traced elsewhere. It is, however, quoted at length in the correspondence. See, among others, Leibniz- Bibliothek Hannover, Leibniz-Nachlass, LBr 251, Jablonski to Leibniz, fols. 247–248, 24 September 1708. On Boyer being the author of the article see British Library, Stowe Mss. 223, la Mothe to Robethon, fols. 167–168, 2 August 1708.

25. British Library London, Mss. Stowe 223, fols. 161r–2, report on the affair by Claude Groteste de la Mothe, 15 July 1708.

26. Eveline Cruickshanks, "Religion and Royal Succession: The Rage of Party," in Clyve Jones, ed., *Britain in the First Age of Party 1680–1750: Essays Presented to Geoffrey Holmes* (London, 1987), pp. 19–43.

27. See, among others, *London Gazette*, 29 December 1707; *Post Man and the Historical Account*, 5 June 1707.

28. Press coverage on the Lutherans in Silesia was impressive, see *Daily Courant*, 23 April 1708, and many other articles from 1707 to 1708.

29. Lambeth Palace Library London, Mss. Gibson 941, fols. 20–21, 131; Edward Carpenter, *Thomas Tenison, Archbishop of Canterbury: His Life and Times* (London, 1948), pp. 342–344.

30. Leibniz-Bibliothek Hannover, Leibniz-Nachlass, LBr 251, fols. 247–248, Jablonski to Leibniz, 24 September 1708.

31. On Snape see Thompson Cooper and William Gibson, "Snape, Andrew (1675–1742)," *Oxford Dictionary of National Biography* 51 (2004): 478–479. See Andrew Snape, *A Sermon Preach'd before the Princess Sophia at Hannover, the 13/24th of May, 1706* (Cambridge, 1706).

32. Leibniz-Bibliothek Hannover, Leibniz-Nachlass, LBr 251, fols. 247–248, Jablonski to Leibniz, 24 September 1708.

33. Johann Fabricius, *Epistola Ad Pios Et Ervditos Britannos: Qua Famam suam contra falsas & ininquas relationes tuetur* (Helmstedt, 1708). The German National Library Catalogue (KVK) lists around fifteen copies in German libraries. A few copies even made it to Britain. On Leibniz's assistance see Ohst, "Irenik," p. 163. On the relationship to Grabe see Bodleian Library Oxford, Ms. Grabe 23, Nos. 22–26. On Grabe see Nicholas Keene, "John Ernest Grabe, Biblical Learning and Religious Controversy in Early Eighteenth-Century England," *Journal of Ecclesiastical History* 58 (2007): 656–674.

34. Johann Fabricius, *Ioannis Fabricii … ad … A. S. doctorem Anglicanvm epistola qva falsas relationes et impvtationes a se depellit* (n.p., 1708). See *Unschuldige Nachrichten* (1709), pp. 44–46.

35. Hauptstaatsarchiv Hannover, CalBr 21/4217 (1708).

36. Georg Schnath, *Geschichte Hannovers im Zeitalter der neunten Kur und der englischen Sukzession 1674–1714*, vol. 4 (Hildesheim, 1982), pp. 194–196; Wilhelm Hoeck, *Anton Ulrich und Elisabeth Christine von Braunschweig-Lüneburg-Wolfenbüttel. Eine durch archivalische Dokumente begründete Darstellung ihres Übertritts zur römischen Kirche* (Wolfenbüttel, 1845), pp. 133–136; Ohst, "Irenik," pp. 162–163.

37. The Helmstedt declaration reached British ecclesiastical circles at least via Jean de Robethon (British Library London, Mss. Stowe 119, fol. 59, no date) and William Ayerst (Bodleian Library Oxford, Mss. Ballard 27, No. 23, Ayerst to Charlett, 3 November 1708).

38. *Post Man and the Historical Account*, 14 October 1708.

39. Peper, *Konversionen*, p. 202 footnote 19; Hoeck, *Anton Ulrich*, p. 134, footnote.

40. British Library London, Mss. Stowe 223, fols. 178r–179v, Anton Ulrich to [la Mothe?], 17 November 1708. The letter is also mentioned in Schnath, *Geschichte Hannovers*, vol. 4, pp. 195–196.

41. George Every, *The High Church Party, 1688–1718* (London, 1956), pp. 114–124. A[rthur] Tindal Hart, *The Life and Times of John Sharp, Archbishop of York* (London, 1949), pp. 261–277.

42. See Tony Claydon, *Europe and the Making of England 1660–1760* (Cambridge, 2007), pp. 192–193, 208–209, 275–276.
43. Lambeth Palace Library London, Gibson Mss. 935, No. 32: Jablonski to Tenison, 27 October 1708.
44. See Jablonski's reflections in York Minster Library, Coll. 1891/1, A 17, Jablonski to Sharp, 23 May 1711; The National Archives London, State Papers Prussia 90/5, fol. 568v, Marquard Ludwig von Printzen to John Raby, 17 February 1711.
45. C. E. Doble, ed., "Letters of the Rev. William Ayerst, 1706–1721 (Continued)," *English Historical Review*, 4, no. 13 (1889): 131–143, here 142–143, No. 23: Ayerst to Charlett, 28 July 1708.
46. British Library London, Add. Mss. 70104, no folio, Daniel Ernst Jablonski, "The State of This Affair" (1708). The text had been translated by Ayerst and sent to John Sharp. On the context see York Minster Library, Coll. 1891/1, B2, Ayerst to Granville Sharp, 18 January 1730/31.
47. See, among others, [Claude Groteste de La Mothe], *Memoires sur la pretendue declaration de l'Université de Helmstad Touchant le changement de Religion de la Reine d'Espagne* (Rotterdam, 1710).
48. Daniel L. Brunner, *Halle Pietists in England: Anthony William Boehm and the Society for Promoting Christian Knowledge* (Göttingen, 1993), p. 107; Hans Cnattingius, *Bishops and Societies: A Study in Anglican Colonial and Missionary Expansion, 1698–1850* (London, 1952), p. 47. See Anton Wilhelm Boehme's letters between c. 1710 and 1715, Archiv der Franckeschen Stiftungen Halle, Hauptarchiv, C 229.
49. Graham C. Gibbs, "Union Hanover/England. Accession to the Throne and Change of Rulers: Determining Factors in the Establishment and Continuation of the Personal Union," in Rex Rexheuser, ed., *Die Personalunionen von Sachsen–Polen 1697–1763 und Hannover-England 1714–1837. Ein Vergleich* (Wiesbaden, 2005), pp. 241–274. On the confessional problems during George's summer visits see, for instance, the correspondence between Lancelot Blackburne and William Wake: Christ Church Library Oxford, Wake Letters 20, passim.
50. See Norman Sykes, *William Wake Archbishop of Canterbury 1657–1737*, 2 vols. (Cambridge, 1957), esp. vol. 2, pp. 65–80.
51. Joachim Whaley, *Religious Toleration and Social Change in Hamburg, 1529–1819* (Cambridge, 1985), pp. 129–144; Eberhard Christian Wilhelm von Schauroth, ed., *Vollständige Sammlung aller Conclusorum, Schreiben Und anderer übrigen Verhandlungen des Hochpreißlichen Corporis Evangelici...*, vol. 2 (Regensburg, 1751), pp. 482–492.
52. Hauptstaatsarchiv Hannover, CalBr 21/4216 (1704–1706). See Sebastian Edzardi, *Vindiciae adversus Jo. Fabricii Theologi Helmstadiensis defensionem* (n.p., 1707). On the author see Johann Friedrich Mutzenbecher, "Sebastian Edzardi," *Zeitschrift des Vereins für Hamburgische Geschichte* 5 (1866): 210–223.
53. See *Unschuldige Nachrichten* (1706), p. 51.
54. Review of Johann Warnefried, *M. B. H. Reiffere Erörterung der Frage ob zwischen der Augspurgischen Confession, und Römisch–Catholischen Religion kein sonderbahrer Unterschied seye...* (n.p., 1707), in *Unschuldige Nachrichten* (1707), pp. 335–336; "D. Jo. Fabricii Defensio, Helmst. 1707," in *Unschuldige Nachrichten* (1708), pp. 115–127; "Nachricht wegen eines grossen Syncretistischen Aergernüsses," in *ibid.*, pp. 344–346; "Nachricht von der Controversie wegen der dimittirten W. Hoff–Prediger," ibid., pp. 706–710.
55. *Unschuldige Nachrichten* (1709), "Kirchenhistorie," p. 35.

56. Review of *Epistola ad Britannos*, in *Unschuldige Nachrichten* (1709), pp. 44–46, Review of *Epistola ad Britannos*; Gustav Moritz Redslob, "Frick, Johann," *Allgemeine deutsche Biographie* 7 (1878): 379–380. See Warnefried, *Reiffere Erörterung der Frage....* The reply was Johann Fabricius, *Send-Schreiben an einen guten Freund über die so genannte reiffere Erörterung Hr. Johann Warnefrieds* (Helmstedt, 1707). What followed was Johann Frick, *Grund Der Wahrheit, Von grossem Haupt–Unterschied der Evangelischen, und Römisch-Catholischen Religionen...* (n.p., 1707).

57. Johann Frick, *Britannia Rectius De Lutheranis Edocta...* (Ulm, 1709). See *Unschuldige Nachrichten* (1709), pp. 46–47.

58. Archiv der Franckeschen Stiftungen Halle, Hauptarchiv, C 638. Ibid., D 64, fols. 285–299. See Alexander Schunka, "Zwischen Kontingenz und Providenz. Frühe England-kontakte der halleschen Pietisten und protestantische Irenik um 1700," *Pietismus und Neuzeit* 34 (2008): 82–114.

59. See, for instance, Joachim Lange's correspondence with Fabricius, Archiv der Franckeschen Stiftungen Halle, Hauptarchiv, A 188a.

60. Archiv der Franckeschen Stiftungen Halle, Hauptarchiv, A 112, fols. 141–144, Ludolf to Francke, 11 August 1708; ibid., C 144a, No. 10: Ludolf to his brother, 12 August 1708; ibid., D 71, fol. 145, Ludolf to Francke, 9 November 1708.

61. See Alexander Schunka, "Daniel Ernst Jablonski, Pietism, and Ecclesiastical Union," in Fred van Lieburg and Daniel Lindmark, eds., *Pietism, Revivalism and Modernity. 1650–1850* (Newcastle, 2008), pp. 23–41.

62. Instructive reports on the duke's conversion can be found in: Archiv der Franckeschen Stiftungen Halle, Hauptarchiv, A 144, fols. 143–150. Both anonymous, apparently Pietist writers blame the conversion on not only the duke's age and stubbornness, but mainly the influence of Fabricius and Helmstedt irenicism.

63. On the background see Thomas Klingebiel, "Pietismus und Orthodoxie. Die Landes-kirche unter den Kurfürsten und Königen Friedrich I. und Friedrich Wilhelm I. (1688 bis 1740), in Gerd Heinrich, ed., *Tausend Jahre Kirche in Berlin–Brandenburg* (Berlin, 1999), pp. 293–324. See the numerous reactions by Prussian pastors in the theological journal *Acta Historico–Ecclesiastica* of the years 1737 and 1738.

64. This is particularly evident in the work of Georg Calixt. See Christoph Böttigheimer, *Zwischen Polemik und Irenik. Die Theologie der einen Kirche bei Georg Calixt* (Münster, 1995), pp. 197–230.

65. Böttigheimer, *Polemik*, pp. 236–237; Hermann Schüssler, "Fabricius, Johann," *Neue deutsche Biographie* 4 (1959): 735–736.

CHAPTER SEVEN

Mish-Mash with the Enemy
Identity, Politics, Power, and the Threat of Forced Conversion in Frederick William I's Prussia

BENJAMIN MARSCHKE

Introduction

"Conversion" is typically understood in the context of the "confessionalization" thesis. "Confessionalization" in early modern Europe emphasized the differences and boundaries between confessions and is generally portrayed as having been a top-down phenomenon in which central authorities starkly differentiated between their own confessions and others and imposed orthodoxy in religious doctrine and conformity in religious practices.[1] In this context, "conversion" reinforced "confessionalization" in that a meaningful "crossing over" from one confession to another emphasized the boundary between them.[2]

The following essay challenges this aspect of the confessionalization thesis by exploring a specific example of irenicism and the attendant threat of forced conversion: the attempt by King Frederick William I of Prussia (1713–1740) to form a confessional union between Lutherans and Calvinists despite the resistance of Halle Pietists.[3] Rather than imposing confessional conformity, the king of Prussia tried to impose confessional flexibility; rather than emphasizing confessional boundaries, he sought to deny their validity.

King Frederick William I of Prussia and the Halle Pietists have long been assumed to have worked together harmoniously. Their relationship has been described as being based on their ideological compatibility and pragmatic collaboration with each other. Their supposed "alliance" has been understood to have resulted in the "bloom" of Lutheran Pietism in the early eighteenth century and to have instilled "Prussian virtues" in the population, which contributed to the near simultaneous "rise of Prussia."[4] The evidence demonstrates, however, that the relationship between *Preußentum* and *Pietismus* was never so rosy.[5] On the contrary, many conflicts touched on a variety of issues. One major bone of contention between the Calvinist Hohenzollerns and the Lutheran Pietists was the monarchy's irenicism and the Pietists' resistance to any steps toward a confessional union. This conflict came to a head during the reign of Frederick William.

In this chapter, I focus both on Frederick William's attempts to achieve confessional union and on Pietist opposition to the king's irenicist agenda. The differences and compatibilities between Lutheranism and Calvinism came up again and again in Frederick William's conversations with the Pietists during the "flowering" of their relationship; indeed, the only religious issue that seemed to interest him more was his own salvation. These conversations are well recorded in the Pietists' reports, diaries, and letters, so it is possible to reconstruct the content and tone of their discussions. It is also possible to record the Pietists' reactions among each other to the imposition of the union by Frederick William. The Pietists, for their part, were in a ticklish position. They had to avoid alienating the Prussian monarchy, on whose tolerance and support they were quite dependent. However, for ideological and political reasons they also wanted to block any kind of union with the Calvinists. To make a long and complicated story short: the Pietists claimed to be cooperating on the union project while also underhandedly sabotaging it.[6]

Frederick William's Irenicism

The Hohenzollerns had already pushed Lutherans and Calvinists in Prussia to combine into one Protestant confession under King Frederick William I's predecessors, "The Great Elector" Frederick William (1640–1688) and Elector/ King Frederick III/I (1688–1713). The rulers of Prussia had many motives for wanting a Protestant union.[7] In the late seventeenth century, it seemed not only desirable but also quite urgent that the Protestant confessions join forces against the apparent resurgence of Catholicism. Moreover, after the conversion of the elector of Saxony from Lutheranism to Catholicism in 1697, Prussia stood as the most important Protestant power in the Holy Roman Empire. As Calvinists, however, they were ineligible to direct the Corpus Evangelicorum in the Empire. The Hohenzollerns sought to overcome this obstacle by bridging the distance between the two Protestant confessions.[8] Finally, by deemphasizing the differences between the confessions—or ideally, combining them—the Hohenzollerns sought to negate the lopsided confessional disparity within their own territories, where Lutherans represented 90 percent and Calvinists only 3 percent of the population.[9]

The Hohenzollern monarchy promoted union and suppressed confessional conflict in three ways. Beginning in the 1660s, the Hohenzollerns repeatedly brought together Lutheran and Calvinist clergymen to discuss a combination of the two confessions.[10] The project was ultimately conceived as a Protestant confessional union not only within Prussia, but also within the Holy Roman Empire (through the Diet of Regensburg) and with other Protestant powers, especially England.[11] Second, Frederick William's predecessors marginalized Lutheran clergymen and expanded and empowered the network of Calvinist court preachers in Prussia. Lutheran preachers were replaced with Calvinists, and Calvinist theologians were given positions of authority over Lutherans regarding censorship and patronage, but never the reverse.[12] Third, the monarchy repeatedly prohibited sectarian strife. Under the guise of "tolerance," the censorship of religious tracts and bans on preaching polemical sermons made it impossible for Lutherans in Prussia to argue publicly against a confessional union or to complain openly about the monarchy's favoritism toward Calvinists and marginalization of Lutherans.[13] In this sense, "religious tolerance" became a euphemism for "confessional oppression" in Prussia.[14]

Unlike his predecessors, Frederick William seems to have been not only genuinely religiously tolerant, but also earnestly irenicist. His wife, Sophie Dorothea of Hanover, was Lutheran, and the Prussian royal court was traditionally bi-confessional. Indeed, Frederick William's own mother had remained Lutheran, and he had been raised by Calvinist and Lutheran governors, as were his children.

Although we can easily imagine that the Hohenzollern monarchy still had political reasons for pushing the union and imposing some kind of confessional uniformity, these concerns seem to have been heavily outweighed by Frederick William's understanding that the difference between Lutheranism and Calvinism, perhaps even Catholicism, was merely *Pfaffengezänk*, the bickering of preachers—he repeated various versions of this irenicist (and anticlerical) statement throughout his reign.[15] Frederick William attended the services of both Lutherans and Calvinists, and he repeatedly advised his successor, in the strongest possible terms, to treat both Protestant confessions equally:

> I recommend to him both Protestant religions, Calvinist and Lutheran, and I give him my curse, if he oppresses the Lutheran religion. Instead he should keep it as I do and not make any difference, because it [Lutheranism] is the same as the Calvinism, and God curse him if he does not do it so. [Note to secretary] von Ilgen, make as strong an expression here as you can write with the pen.[16]

In fact, the only matter that interested the "Soldier King" as much as the equal treatment of Protestant confessions was the preservation of the Prussian army, and he later threatened to curse the entire dynasty and its territories if either proviso were violated.[17] This was a marked departure from the policies of his predecessors, Elector Frederick William I and Elector/King Frederick III/I, who openly favored Calvinists over Lutherans.[18]

In addition to insisting repeatedly that Lutheran and Calvinist clergy discuss a potential union, the Prussian king also took concrete steps toward a union. Frederick William insisted upon building *Simultan-Kirchen*, in which Calvinist and Lutheran services were held alternately in the same space.[19] This bricks-and-mortar unification of the confessions in constructed spaces fit well with the irenicist strategy of first unifying liturgies, regardless of continuing theological disputes.[20] The other religious edifices that Frederick William built, such as the Great Military Orphanage (Große Militärwaisenhaus) in Potsdam, were similarly nondenominational. The orphanage was open to children of all denominations, even Roman Catholics. To cater to the Soldier King's collection of tall troops from all over the world, the Potsdam orphanage included an Eastern Orthodox chapel and even a room that doubled as a mosque.

At the same time, Frederick William also upheld and expanded the prohibitions on confessional controversy.[21] Not only did he ban Lutherans and Calvinists from arguing with each other over religion in Prussia, but Frederick William also eagerly intervened in confessional conflicts in other territories. Frederick William is well known as a champion of Protestants in the face of Catholic oppression.[22] However, he also threatened to intervene in Protestant Hamburg when its Lutheran majority rioted against its Calvinist minority. He even insisted that they ban confessional controversy as Prussia had done, and he pointedly suggested that they silence one specific rabble-rousing Lutheran preacher.[23]

Indeed, Frederick William's *Unionpolitik* was part of a larger international movement. Negotiations with London regarding combining Anglicanism and Calvinism had already come to naught during the reign of his predecessor, and they never regained momentum during his reign.[24] Nevertheless, Prussia's representatives at the Imperial Diet in Regensburg were part of an empire-wide union program during the late 1710s and early 1720s.[25] The union question, then, was posed on a scale far grander than Prussia. Although the initiative ultimately failed, it did energize both the irenicist and anti-union movements throughout the Empire, bringing the controversy far more public attention than it would otherwise have received.

Frederick William, the Pietists, and the Union

It would be wrong to think that Frederick William did not recognize any confessional differences. From his conversations with the Pietists, it is clear that he had at least a rudimentary understanding of the theological issues involved. The Pietists who spoke with the king about religion and about the union project, moreover, were sufficiently aware of his religious ideas to form their arguments to suit their king. For example, when August Hermann Francke, leader of Halle Pietism, traveled to Wusterhausen to visit the king in 1719, he carefully recorded nearly every aspect of his visit. Frederick William asked him directly for his opinion of the union project, and Francke, who was clearly aware of the king's aversion to the doctrine of predestination, responded that the Calvinists' continued adherence to it would make a confessional union impossible. The confessions should remain separate, Francke argued, "because otherwise it would necessarily make a great confusion, when it is supposed to be a union, but soon one preaches that Christ had died for all men, and soon another, that he had *not* died for all men."[26] Frederick William admitted that Francke and the Lutherans were right on this point, but then pressed him on the difference between Lutheran and Calvinist understandings of the Eucharist. Francke, with the support of several military officers who were present, carefully explained the issue, which, according to Francke's own account of the meeting, seemed to satisfy the king.[27]

Nonetheless, Frederick William was relentless. Thwarted regarding predestination and the Eucharist, the king pointed out that these were the only two problems, and that if they could be resolved, then nothing would stand in the way of union.[28] Francke insisted that there were other conflicts, such as the two confessions' views of human nature. At least in his own telling, Francke was thereby able to distract the king from the union project with the question of whether God held rulers to the same standards as everybody else. Francke told the king that though no one disputed that it was more difficult for a ruler than for a private person to be a good Christian, he must do so nonetheless.[29] Francke left the meeting satisfied that he had deflected the king's union agenda.

He was mistaken. Years later, in March 1727, the union question surfaced again when Heinrich Schubert, a Pietist preacher in Potsdam, faced almost exactly the same questions as had Francke.[30] He wrote to Francke that he and a Calvinist court preacher had been summoned to the king, who asked them: "Now I'm asking you, before God, tell me, what is the difference between the Calvinists and the Lutherans? Before God, tell me!"[31] Frederick William told Schubert that he and most reasonable Calvinists did not believe in predestination. The king then turned to the Eucharist, as he had before with Francke. According to his own account of the exchange, Schubert then patiently explained the Lutheran doctrine of the Eucharist and its justification in Scripture. Fortunately for Schubert, Frederick William then turned to discussing his own salvation, as he had done with Francke. This ultimately resulted in the king breaking down in tears. Schubert also mentioned in the same letter that his intimacy with the king resulted in the Calvinists becoming more and more bitter toward him.[32]

The union issue remained high on Frederick William's agenda. The king raised the issue once again in September 1727, this time with Francke's successor and son-in-law, Johann Anastasius Freylinghausen. Like Francke, Freylinghausen kept a careful record of what happened and what was said.[33] The king also bluntly asked Freylinghausen if he thought that there was a difference between Lutheranism and Calvinism.[34] Freylinghausen, like Francke and Schubert before him, proceeded to raise the predestination issue again.[35] Frederick William, for his part, could do no better than point out that he was raising his children (who were ostensibly Calvinist) according to Lutheran teachings, and he had Freylinghausen examine Crown Prince Frederick to prove his point.[36] The king seemed resigned to failure. He assured Freylinghausen that although he was a Calvinist (and would remain so), he loved the Lutherans just as much; indeed, he preferred their church services. He told Freylinghausen: "You will not be able to say that I have done anything to harm you, however, you must not quarrel with one another and call each other heretics, but rather live together in harmony. And though I would give a lot that you could be properly unified, that is still not going to happen now, but you have got to get along with each other."[37] Freylinghausen reassured the king that the Lutherans and the Calvinists tolerated each other as well as could be wished. In his notes on his visit to the king, Freylinghausen also wrote that while he was invited to sit in a place of honor at the royal table, the Calvinist court preacher was relegated to eating with the chambermaids.[38]

Frederick William asked the same questions and presented the same arguments regarding the union to different Pietists at different times over a long period.[39] It is possible that the king was a slow study and really did need to have this explained again and again. It is more likely, however, that the king was trying either to catch various Pietist Lutherans contradicting each other regarding their differences with the Calvinists, or to discover who among the Pietists was open to collaborating with the Calvinists.

Pietists against the Union

In their dealings with the king, Pietists may have seemed amenable to confessional union. However, the tone of their private correspondence was much less conciliatory and cooperative. On the front line of the struggle against a union with the Calvinists was Lampertus Gedicke, head of the army chaplaincy. In 1722, Gedicke drew attention to himself by publishing an anti-Calvinist sermon that purported to explain Lutheran doctrine regarding the Eucharist.[40] Not coincidentally, Gedicke's sermon was published at the same time that the public debate in the Empire was heating up over the union negotiations in Regensburg.[41] Ironically, Gedicke's sermon and its publication came at the same time that Frederick William reissued the royal edicts that prohibited clergy from engaging in confessional controversy from the pulpit and banned any writings that might lead to confessional conflict.[42]

The sermon, which the Calvinists saw as "a stick in the eye," made Gedicke an anti-union celebrity in Germany and unleashed a flurry of pamphlets for and against his position.[43] Frederick William gave Gedicke permission to respond "moderately" to the Calvinist criticism of his sermon. Gedicke, while afraid of "appearing to abuse royal favor," had no intention of responding "moderately."[44] He managed to stay out of trouble with Frederick William, but only because the king read Gedicke's response before it was published and found nothing objectionable in it.[45]

Gedicke was convinced that his involvement in the debate would prevent union. As he wrote to his confidants, "His Royal Majesty is convinced of our veracity, [and] the union proposals, I hope and believe, will not come to pass, and rather will leave an *effectum contrarium* among both parties."[46] Instead, Gedicke was convinced, the king would see the impossibility of a union and the necessity of mutual tolerance. "His Royal Majesty," Gedicke speculated, "may well wish for such, but sees well the difficulties, yes, the moral impossibility of it, and intends only a *mutuam tolerantiam*, which [is] also in our land good and necessary."[47]

However, the threat of a confessional union was far from past. Almost immediately a new pro-union pamphlet appeared, and Frederick William asked Gedicke and several other prominent Pietist clergymen for their opinions.[48] Gedicke's response actually blamed the Calvinists for the union's failure to date. Rather than genuinely seeking a union, Gedicke charged, the Calvinists were instead preparing a "persecution" of Lutherans.[49] In private correspondence with Francke, Gedicke referred to the Calvinists as "*der Feind*" [the enemy] and to a potential union with them as a "*Misch-Masch*."[50] At the same time, Gedicke told Francke that he was assuring the king that "All honest Lutherans hope for the union as I do."[51]

Meanwhile Frederick William was taking concrete steps toward unifying the Protestant confessions in Prussia. One of these steps was to establish the aforementioned orphanage for soldiers' children in Potsdam, which became a kind of pilot project for the confessional union. Calvinist and Lutheran teachers and clergy staffed the orphanage together, and the orphanage became a site of confessional controversy. The supervisor of the orphanage on the Lutheran side was Gedicke—who, of course, was dead set against the union project and did everything in his power to stop it.[52] When presented with the idea that Lutheran and Calvinist teachers would teach children of each other's confession, Gedicke protested vehemently.

In a series of confidential letters to Halle, Gedicke repeatedly voiced three objections to the orphanage. No replies survive, but Gedicke's reiterations imply that his audience agreed with his objections, and so does the fact that Gedicke's objections were included in correspondence between Halle and the Pietist chaplain of the orphanage in Potsdam.[53] The first objection was that the

Calvinist teachers were incompetent and lazy, and they only wanted Lutheran teachers teaching their pupils so that their children could keep up with the Lutheran pupils. Second, Gedicke was concerned about patronage. Gedicke and the other Pietists had gone to great lengths to create an extensive patronage system in Prussia, and controlling the orphanage in Potsdam (and the teachers' positions there) was one of the most valuable (and contested) means of aiding their clients' careers.[54] Gedicke suspected that the Calvinists wanted to edge out Lutheran teachers, replace them with Calvinist teachers, and ultimately swallow up Pietism: "once they have taken this action," he wrote, "then they will not rest until they have little by little nibbled up all of our preceptors, and swallowed us up entirely."[55] Gedicke repeatedly claimed this was part of their enemies' larger plan to gobble up Francke's institutions and then root out the Pietists, step by step.[56] Third, Gedicke warned that the Calvinists wanted to teach Lutheran children in order to make a *"Misch-Masch in der Religion."* Gedicke secretly wrote: "I regard this as a highly dangerous attempt by the enemy to bring the whole work [of Pietism] into the utmost confusion."[57] Nonetheless, Gedicke also included in his letters to Halle the different versions of his objections that he sent to the Calvinist clergy and submitted to the king, all carefully composed in rhetoric calculated to appeal to, or at least not to offend, the king.

By this point it should be obvious from Gedicke's repeated references to the Calvinists as *"der Feind"* and the other Pietists' schadenfreude at the discomforts and defeats of the Calvinists at court that much of what it meant to be part of the "Pietist" network in Prussia in the 1720s was wrapped up with confessional identity. Pietists, in short, were Lutherans, and as such opposed to a union with Calvinists.[58] This is even more apparent if we briefly examine examples of Lutheran clergymen who *did* cooperate with Calvinists.

One of them was Andreas Schmidt, a Lutheran preacher and Gedicke's principal rival in Berlin. Schmidt stood in Gedicke's way, especially regarding patronage, but the latter succeeded in uniting other Pietists against Schmidt and having him demoted to a pastorate in the hinterland.[59] Gedicke reported to Halle that among Schmidt's many faults was his willingness to collaborate with the Calvinists: "Schmidt constantly played along with the Calvinists and was in bed with them.... The Calvinists are still at this hour mostly taking his side, and even now [they] want to use him for the union project."[60] This was especially important, as it turned out, because Schmidt had been slated to become the Lutheran supervisor of the military orphanage in Potsdam. With Schmidt out of the way, it was Gedicke who became the Lutheran supervisor.

The case of Johann Willhelm Mess, a Lutheran teacher at the military orphanage, also illustrates how the Pietists regarded the Calvinists and any of their own who would work with them. Mess ran afoul of the Lutheran chaplain at the orphanage, Johann Christian Schinmeyer. According to Schinmeyer,

Mess spent too much time with the Calvinists and told them what went on at the Pietist teachers' meetings. Schinmeyer reported:

> He colludes with Calvinists and in fact he is more Calvinist than Lutheran, which one can see in all his behavior. In the orphanage and in the city he goes more to the Calvinist than the Lutheran churches. If one says something about the Calvinists in our conference (which one often cannot avoid, because they are here among us, and we are here among them), then they learn about everything, which, one can easily imagine, leads to no good.[61]

This Pietist chaplain in Potsdam repeatedly referred to this teacher who was too friendly with the Calvinists as a *"proditor,"* ("traitor") and requested that he be recalled to Halle.[62] The cases of Schmidt and Mess make clear the extent to which the Pietists in Berlin and Potsdam identified themselves in contrast (and in opposition) to the Calvinists.

By the 1730s Frederick William had soured on the Pietists, and they were no longer able to sabotage or delay the royal union project.[63] Pressure from the king would no longer come in the form of requests that they discuss the issue, but rather increasingly took the form of royal decrees banning or mandating specific religious practices.[64] By the mid 1730s, royal servants entered Lutheran churches in Berlin and seized candlesticks and choir robes, the use of which had been forbidden by royal decree.[65] The Pietists were essentially powerless to resist, and many began to consider abandoning their positions and leaving Prussia.

Conclusion

Frederick William's idea of irenicism was that a confessional union between Lutherans and Calvinists would grow out of the monarchy's policies of religious tolerance. Tolerating both Protestant confessions and insisting that they tolerate each other was a step toward pushing them together. Forcing the confessions into close proximity—at *Simultan-Kirchen* and the Potsdam orphanage, for example—might also bring them closer to union.

Frederick William understood himself as supra-confessional. Not only was he uninterested in enforcing confessional orthodoxy, he even denied its validity.

> "My predecessors introduced [Calvinism] here," Frederick William said to a Catholic priest in 1739, "but I do not believe everything that the Calvinists believe, for example, about predestination; I also believe much of what the Lutherans believe, and much of what the Catholics believe. Namely, what I find credible based on the Holy Scripture and on common sense, that's what I believe."[66]

As a kind of "cafeteria Calvinist," Frederick William took what he liked and found credible, and rejected what he disliked or did not understand. Similarly, he took what he liked from Lutheranism, and even Roman Catholicism. Frederick William felt free to pick, choose, and combine ideas from across confessional lines, whose legitimacy he refused to accept. From his point of view, therefore, conversion from one confession to another was not only unnecessary, but pointless.

Among Pietists, there was a clear sense that Frederick William's irenicism was not about tolerance. On the contrary, being forced to lower confessional boundaries and move toward a confessional union would have been the opposite of religious tolerance: at best it would have meant a *Misch-Masch*, and at worst it would have meant a "persecution" in the form of some kind of forced conversion. Of course, their resistance to the union was hardly based solely on the theological issues that they cited again and again. The Pietists' clandestine correspondence makes it clear that their resistance to any step toward a union with the Calvinists was largely based on the defense of their own patronage system and powerbase in the Lutheran establishment and their clear identification of themselves and "*der Feind*" along confessional lines. As they saw things, their opponents at court, the unionist Calvinists, sought to edge them out of their own institutions. A confessional union, they believed, would mean that Lutheran Pietism would be swallowed up or rooted out by Calvinism.

Notes

1. For a summary of the confessionalization thesis, see Heinz Schilling, "Confessionalization: Historical and Scholarly Perspectives of a Cooperative and Interdisciplinary Paradigm," in John M. Headley et al., eds., *Confessionalization in Europe, 1555–1700: Essays in Honor and Memory of Bodo Nischan* (Aldershot, 2004), pp. 21–35.
2. Kim Siebenhüner, "Glaubenswechsel in der Frühen Neuzeit: Chancen und Tendenzen einer historischen Konversionsforschung," *Zeitschrift für Historische Forschung* 34, no. 2 (2007): 243–272. See also the conceptual contribution by Eric-Oliver Mader to this volume.
3. Irenicism was the notion that all Christian churches could (and should) be recombined into one church. See Alexander Schunka, "Zwischen Kontingenz und Providenz: Frühe Englandkontakte der Halleschen Pietisten und protestantische Irenik um 1700," *Pietismus und Neuzeit* 34 (2008): 82–114; Schunka, "Daniel Ernst Jablonski, Pietism, and Ecclesiastical Union," in Fred A. van Lieburg and Daniel Lindmark, eds., *Pietism, Revivalism, and Modernity, 1650–1850* (Newcastle, 2008), pp. 23–41; and Schunka's contribution to this volume.
4. See the foundational works on the subject by Klaus Deppermann and Carl Hinrichs. Deppermann, *Der hallesche Pietismus und der preußische Staat unter Friedrich III. (I.)* (Göttingen, 1961). Hinrichs's articles are collected in Carl Hinrichs, *Preußentum und Pietismus: Der Pietismus in Brandenburg-Preußen als religiös-soziale Reformbewegung* (Göttingen, 1971).
5. See Benjamin Marschke, "Halle Pietism and the Prussian State: Infiltration, Dissent, and Subversion," in Jonathan Strom et al., eds., *Pietism in Germany and North America, 1680–1820* (Aldershot, 2009), pp. 217–228.

6. Martin Brecht's focus on the Pietists' public rejection of confessional polemic is misguided, and his conclusion that the Pietists contributed to irenicism is invalid; Martin Brecht, "Pietismus und Irenik," in Harm Klueting, ed., *Irenik und Antikonfessionalismus im 17. und 18. Jahrhundert* (Hildesheim, 2003), pp. 211–222. Regarding the aforementioned book, see Martin Gierl's review in *Zeitschrift für Historische Forschung* 34, no. 3 (2007): 554–556.

   Though the Pietists generally refrained from publishing polemical tracts, they used polemical rhetoric among themselves regarding their opponents, and they worked in less public ways against their enemies; see Benjamin Marschke, "'Wir Halenser': The Understanding of Insiders and Outsiders among Halle Pietists in Prussia under Frederick William I (1713–1740)," in Jonathan Strom, ed., *Pietism and Community in Europe and North America: 1650–1850* (Leiden, 2010), pp. 81–93.

7. Schunka, "Zwischen Kontingenz und Providenz," here p. 85.

8. The Corpus Evangelicorum was the Protestant caucus at the imperial diet. See Andreas Kalipke, "The *Corpus Evangelicorum*: A Culturalist Perspective on Its Procedure in the Eighteenth-Century Holy Roman Empire," in Jason Philip Coy et al., eds., *The Holy Roman Empire, Reconsidered* (New York, 2010); and Jürgen Luh, *Unheiliges Römisches Reich. Der konfessionelle Gegensatz 1648–1806* (Potsdam, 1995).

9. Statistics from Jürgen Luh, "Zur Konfessionspolitik der Kurfürsten von Brandenburg und Könige in Preußen 1640 bis 1740," in Horst Lademacher et al., eds., *Ablehnung – Duldung – Anerkennung: Toleranz in den Niederlanden und in Deutschland. Ein historischer und aktueller Vergleich* (Münster, 2004), pp. 306–324, here p. 306.

10. Klaus Wappler, "Kurfürst Friedrich Wilhelm von Brandenburg, das Berliner Religionsgespräch von 1662–63 und das Streitverbot von 1664," in Klueting et al., *Irenik und Antikonfessionalismus*, pp. 141–151.

11. See Schunka, "Zwischen Kontingenz und Providenz"; Wolf-Friedrich Schäuffele, "Erzbischof William Wake von Canterbury (1657–1737) und die Einigung der europäischen Christenheit," in Heinz Duchhardt and Gerhard May, eds., *Union – Konversion – Toleranz: Dimensionen der Annäherung zwischen den christlichen Konfessionen im 17. und 18. Jahrhundert* (Mainz, 2000), pp. 301–314; and Walter Delius, "Berliner Kirchliche Unionsversuche im 17. und 18. Jahrhundert," *Jahrbuch für Berlin-Brandenburgische Kirchengeschichte* 45 (1970): 7–121.

12. Luh, "Zur Konfessionspolitik," passim; and Wappler, "Kurfürst Friedrich Wilhelm," p. 143.

13. Luh, "Zur Konfessionspolitik," pp. 307–308; and Wappler, "Kurfürst Friedrich Wilhelm," p. 147.

14. Luh, "Zur Konfessionspolitik," pp. 306, 315; and Wappler, "Kurfürst Friedrich Wilhelm," pp. 144, 148–149.

15. In his instructions to his successor, written in 1722, Frederick William explained that the difference between Lutheranism and Calvinism was only based on "Prediger Zenkkereien"; "Instruktion Friedrich Wilhelms I.," in Richard Dietrich, ed., *Die politische Testamente der Hohenzollern* (Cologne and Vienna, 1986), pp. 221–243, here p. 234. In 1726, Frederick William similarly answered complaints of a Pietist Lutheran consistory member in Berlin about the introduction of alternating Calvinist and Lutheran church services in the same spaces: "Der unterschied zwischen unser beiden evangelischen Religionen ist wahrlich ein Pfaffengezänk"; Friedrich Christoph Förster, *Friedrich Wilhelm I., König von Preussen*, 3 vols. (Potsdam, 1834–1835), vol. 2 (1835), p. 339. Moreover, in a 1738 letter to the Calvinist clergy regarding the possible appoint-

ment of a Lutheran as head of their consistory, Frederick William asserted that "der ganze Unterschied zwischen beiden Religionen in nichts anders, als einem eingeführten Wortgezänk"; Wilhelm Stolze, ed., "Aktenstücke zur evangelischen Kirchenpolitik Friedrich Wilhelms I.," *Jahrbuch für Brandenburgische Kirchengeschichte* 1 (1904): 264–290, here p. 289.

There is at least anecdotal evidence that by the end of his reign Frederick William even understood the differences with Roman Catholicism in the same way. A Catholic priest recorded this statement by the Prussian king in 1739: "Ich glaube aber, daß alle Christen, welcher Confession sie auch angehören, selig werden können; denn wenn sie auch in einzelnen Nebendingen verschiedener Ansicht sind, so stimmen sie doch Alle in den Hauptsachen überein"; […] Beyer, "König Friedrich Wilhelm I. und der katholischen Pfarrer Pater Bruns," *Mittheilungen des Vereins für die Geschichte Potsdams* 6 (1864): 1–8, here p. 6.

16. "Ich recomendiere Ihm die beide Evangelische Reformi- und Lutteri: Reli: und gehbe Ihm mein pfuch [Pfluch], wo ferne er die Luttersche Religion untertrücken wierdt sonder soll sie so halten wie ich es tue und kein unterseit machen den es eins ist mit der Reformirte und Gott Ihme verfluche wo er es nit so mache[.] von Ilgen so starcke expression als er mit der feder schreiben kan."; Wilhelm Stolze, ed., "Die Testamente Friedrich Wilhelms I.," *Forschungen zur Brandenburgischen und Preußiscen Geschichte* 17 (1904): 221–234, here p. 229. In his instructions of 1722, Frederick William had already advised his successor to treat Lutherans and Calvinists equally, because God would bless him and because both religions would both love him if he did so; "Instruktion Friedrich Wilhelms I.," p. 234.

17. Frederick William concluded the same 1727 draft of instructions: "wegen der Lutterische Religion und beybehaltung der armee auf itzigem fuhs [Fuß] das sollen sie es stercker aufsetzen und hinten daran wo ferne mein sohn das nit tuht ich mein fluch gehbe auf kind und kindes kindt und das sein korn verwelcke und der verdorre wie eine Matte und so starck als es Mögl. ein pfluch aufzusetzen ist mein vernunftiger wohll bedachtsahmer wille"; Stolze, ed., "Testamente," p. 231.

Frederick William's readiness to curse his successor probably had as much to do with his poor relationship with the crown prince in the late 1720s as it did with his eagerness to treat Lutheranism and Calvinism equally; see Benjamin Marschke, "The Crown Prince's Brothers and Sisters: Succession and Inheritance Problems and Solutions among the Hohenzollerns, From the Great Elector to Frederick the Great," in Christopher H. Johnson and David Warren Sabean, eds., *Sibling Relations and the Transformations of European Kinship, 1300–1900* (New York, 2011), pp. 111–44.

18. Luh, "Zur Konfessionspolitik," p. 318.

19. *Simultan-Kirchen* had already been established under his predecessor; Iselin Gundermann, "Verordnete Eintracht: Lutheraner und Reformierte in Berlin-Brandenburg, 1613–1740," *Herbergen der Christenheit: Jahrbuch für deutsche Kirchengeschichte* 28/29 (2004/05): 141–155, here p. 150. In 1722 Frederick William ordered that all new and newly refurbished churches should be established as *Simultan-Kirchen*; Delius, "Berliner Kirchliche Unionsversuche," p. 93.

20. This was the strategy of Daniel Ernst Jablonski, the Calvinist court preacher in Berlin and the driving force for a confessional union in Prussia; see especially Schunka, "Daniel Ernst Jablonski," p. 29; and Delius, "Berliner Kirchliche Unionsversuche," pp. 69–70.

21. For example, Christian Otto Mylius, ed., *Corpus constitutionum marchicarum: oder, Königl. Preussis. und Churfürstl. Brandenburgische in der Chur- und Marck Branden-*

burg, auch incorporirten Landen publicirte und ergangene Ordnungen, Edicta, Mandata, Rescripta, etc. (Berlin, 1737–1751), vol. 1, cols. 511–512 "Verordnung, denen wegen zuerhaltender Einigkeit zwischen beyden Evangelischen Religions-Verwandten vorhin publicirten Edictis genau nachzukomme," 31 July 1714; ibid., vol. 1, cols. 533–536; "Verordnung, daß die Prediger beyder Evangelischen Religionen nicht wieder einander predigen sollen," 10 May 1719; ibid., vol. 1, cols. 543–545; "Verordnung an die Inspectores, wegen derer zu haltenden Catechismus=Predigten, und was dabey zu beobachten, insonderheit wegen derer zwischen beyden Evangelischen Religionen streitigen Puncten," 13 November 1720; ibid., vol. 1, cols. 547–548, and "Verordnung, daß weder von dem Evanglischen Lutherischen noch Evangelischen Reformirten-Predigern der Disput von der Gnaden-Wahl auff die Cantzel gebracht werden soll," 21 April 1722.

22. On Frederick William's spectacular intervention on behalf of the Protestants expelled from Salzburg, see Mack Walker, *The Salzburg Transaction: Expulsion and Redemption in Eighteenth-Century Germany* (Ithaca, 1992). The Salzburg "transaction" was only one episode of Frederick William's very active and very public role as *the* Protestant champion in the empire—see, for example, his intervention on behalf of Protestants in the Palatinate and in Poland, as evidenced by countless contemporary pamphlets and reports. Regarding the Palatinate, see *Die Europaische Fama, Welche den gegenwärtigen Zustand der vornehmsten Höfe entdecket* 188 (1716): 646; *Die Europaische Fama* 226 (1719): 533–535. Regarding Poland, see Stefan Hartmann, "Die Polenpolitik König Friedrich Wilhelms I. von Preussen zur Zeit des 'Thorner Blutgerichts' (1724–1725)," *Forschungen zur Brandenburgischen und Preussischen Geschichte* 5 (1995): 31–58.

23. *Die Europaische Fama* 226 (1719): 568–570.

24. Schunka, "Daniel Ernst Jablonski," passim; and Delius, "Berliner Kirchliche Unionsversuche," pp. 74–80.

25. See Delius, "Berliner Kirchliche Unionsversuche," pp. 81–85; and Wolf-Friedrich Schäuffele, *Christoph Matthäus Pfaff und die Kirchenunionsbestrebungen des Corpus Evangelicorum 1717–1726* (Mainz, 1998), passim.

26. Underlining in original: "weil es sonst nothwendig eine grosse Verwirrung machen wurde wenn es eine einigkeit heißen solte und bald predige einer, Christus wäre für alle menschen gestorben, bald ein anderer, er wäre nicht für alle Mensche gestorben"; August Hermann Francke, "Aufzeichnungen über seinen Besuch i. Wusterhausen bei Friedrich Wilhelm I. i. Spätsommer 1719" (manuscript), Archiv der Franckeschen Stiftungen zu Halle, Hauptarchiv (cited hereafter as AFSt/H), A 173: 54, p. 9.

27. Francke, "Aufzeichnungen über seinen Besuch," p. 9

28. August Hermann Francke, "Diarum Wusterhausen. Die Reise das Hn Prof. A. Herm. Franckens nach Berlin in ao. 1719 worin sich eine Relation von den Gespräch mit Sn. Königl. Majest. Friedrich Wilhelm..." Sept. 1719, (manuscript), AFSt/H, A 173: 80, p. 3. Indeed, these were the same two theological problems that Jablonski had identified. See Schunka, "Daniel Ernst Jablonski," p. 30: "...d. König mit *attention* angehöret, u. gesagt, nun daß wäre auch die beyden *puncten* sonst wäre nichts. Ich antwortete: es wäre noch manche andere. *Rex*: welche denn."

29. Francke, "Diarum Wusterhausen," p. 4–5.

30. On Schubert, see Marschke, "'Lutheran Jesuits': Halle Pietist Communication Networks at the Court of Friedrich Wilhelm I of Prussia," *Covenant Quarterly* 65, no. 4 (November 2006): 19–38.

31. "Nun, ich frage ihn, vor Gott auf sein Gewißen, sage er mir, was iß für ein Unterschied zwischen den *Reformirte & Lutheranen*? vor Gott, sage er mirs!" (italics in original);

Letter from Heinrich Schubert, Potsdam, to August Hermann Francke, Halle, 20 March 1727, AFSt/H, C 632: 26.

32. Letter from Schubert to Francke, 20 March 1727, AFSt/H, C 632: 26.

33. Freylinghausen visited the king at Wusterhausen for a week in September 1727. Johann Anastasius Freylinghausen, "Das Reisetagebuch des Johann Anastasius Freylinghausen," in Jochen Klepper, *Der König und die Stillen im Lande. Begegnungen Friedrich Wilhelms I. mit August Hermann Francke, Gotthilf August Francke, Johann Anastasius Freylinghausen, Nikolaus Ludwig Graf von Zinzindorf* (Witten and Berlin, 1962), pp. 40–87, here p. 60.

34. Freylinghausen, "Reisetagebuch," p. 60.

35. Freylinghausen, "Reisetagebuch," p. 60.

36. Freylinghausen, "Reisetagebuch," pp. 60–61.

37. "Sie werden auch nicht sagen können, daß ich ihnen was zu leide täte; aber sie müssen sich nicht untereinander verketzern und disputieren, sondern einig leben; und wollte ich viel darum geben, daß sie recht könnten vereinigt werden, aber das will nun noch nicht sein, sie müssen sich aber vertragen"; Freylinghausen, "Reisetagebuch," p. 80.

38. Freylinghausen, "Reisetagebuch," p. 82.

39. Several years later, Frederick William asked the same questions again. When the son of August Hermann Francke, Gotthilf August Francke, and an enlightened Pietist provost from Berlin, Johann Gustav Reinbeck, visited Wusterhausen in September 1733, the subject of the difference between Lutheranism and Calvinism was raised again. For whatever reason, in the younger Francke's version of events this conversation is barely mentioned. Gotthilf August Francke, "d. 24. Sept.," in "Acta, Correspondenz und Diarium des Herrn Professoris Franckens Reise und Aufenthalt in Berlin und Wusterhausen, Septbr. et Octobr. 1733," AFSt, Wirtschafts- und Verwaltungsarchiv (AFSt/W), II/-/21.

40. Lampertus Gedicke, *Kurtze Erklärung Der Lutherischen Lehre von der wahren Gegenwart des Leibes und Blutes Christi im heiligen Abendmahl* (Berlin, 1722). The sermon was so popular that it sold out, and a second edition was published in 1724.

41. Schäuffele, "Die Regensburger Unionsbestrebungen 1722–1726," in *Christoph Matthäus Pfaff*, pp. 253–289.

42. Gedicke's sermon was held in Berlin on Holy Thursday (2 April), 1722. Frederick William had repeatedly renewed the bans on confessional controversies and polemics, the latest reiteration of which appeared only weeks after Gedicke's sermon (*Corpus constitutionum marchicarum*, volume 1, section I, number CXI, cols. 547–548, "Verordnung, daß weder von dem Evanglischen Lutherischen noch Evangelischen Reformirten-Predigern der Disput von der Gnaden-Wahl auff die Cantzel gebracht werden soll," 21 April 1722).

At about the same time, in his instructions to his successor, drafted in January 1722, Frederick William emphasized the same point: "An alle Consistorien in euere Prowincen müßet Ihr scharf anbefehlen, das die Reformirte und Lutterahner auf den Kancellen keine Contrawersen tracktieren und absonderlich von der genadenwahl nichts davon tuchiren und sonsten auf den Kancellen nur blohs das reine wohrt Gottes Predigen und Keine Zenckereyen anfangen, sondern müßet Ihr ummer zu einigkeit der beyden Religionen zu bearbeiten trachten." "Instruktion Friedrich Wilhelms I.," pp. 234–235.

43. "ein Stachel in den Augen"; Lampertus Gedicke, *Kurtze Erklärung Der Lutherischen Lehre von der wahren Gegenwart des Leibes und Blutes Christi im heiligen Abendmahl*.

Nach Anleitung der Worte der Einsetzung am Grünen-Donnerstag in einer Predigt Der Guarnison-Gemeine in Berlin vorgetragen Und auf Begehren zum Druck übergeben (Berlin, 1722). See Benjamin Marschke, *Absolutely Pietist: Patronage, Factionalism, and State-Building in the Early Eighteenth-Century Prussian Army Chaplaincy* (Tübingen, 2005), pp. 144–145.

44. See Marschke, *Absolutely Pietist*, p. 145.

45. Letter from Lampertus Gedicke, Berlin, to August Hermann Francke, Halle, 1 September 1724, AFSt/H C 42: 58; and letter from Lampertus Gedicke, Berlin, to Ernst Salomo Cyprian, Gotha, 30 September 1724, Universitäts- und Forschungsbibliothek (cited hereafter as FLB) Gotha, A 430: 19. See Marschke, *Absolutely Pietist*, p. 145. Cyprian was a court chaplain and a member of the consistory in Gotha. He was an important orthodox Lutheran and an outspoken opponent of a confessional union. See Ernst Koch and Johannes Wallmann, eds., *Ernst Salomon Cyprian (1673–1745) zwischen Orthodoxie, Pietismus und Frühaufklärung. Vorträge des Internationalen Kolloquiums vom 14. bis 16. September 1995 in der Forschungs- und Landesbibliothek Gotha Schloß Friedenstein* (Gotha, 1996).

46. "Sr. Konigl. Mag. sind von dieser unser Warheit völlig überzeuget, die *Unions* Vorschläge werd, wie ich glaube und hoffe, nicht zum Stande komm, und vielmehr *effectum contrarium* bey beyd Partheyn hinterlaßen"; Letter from Gedicke, Berlin, to Ernst Salomo Cyprian, Gotha, 12 June 1725, FLB Gotha, A 430: 22.

47. "Sr. Konigl. Mag. unser allergn. Herr möchte dieselbe wohl wünsch, sehe aber wohl die Schwierigkeit, ja moralische *inpossibilitaet* davon, und intendier nur *mutuam tolerantiam*, die in unserm Lande auch gut und nöhtig." Letter from Gedicke to Cyprian, Gotha, 12 June 1725.

48. This was Johann Christian Klemm's anonymously authored *Christian Fratelli Unpartheyisches Liebes-Schreiben An einen guten Freund Wegen Veriningung Derer beyden Protestirenden Religionen. Nemlich, der Evangelisch-Lutherischen und Evangelisch-Reformirten* (Regensburg, 1725). See Marschke, *Absolutely Pietist*, p. 147; and Delius, "Berliner Kirchliche Unionsversuche," p. 91.

49. Lampertus Gedicke, Berlin, copy of memorandum to Friedrich Wilhelm, 27 December 1725, FLB Gotha A 430: 28. Letter from Gedicke, Berlin, to Ernst Salomo Cyprian, Gotha, 9 January 1726, FLB Gotha, A 430: 25.

50. Letters from Gedicke, Berlin, to August Hermann Francke, Halle, 16 February 1726 and 13 July 1726, AFSt/H, C 42: 71, C 42: 72.

51. "Die Union wünschen mit mir alle redliche Lutheraner." Copy of memorandum from Gedicke, Berlin, to Friedrich Wilhelm, sent to Cyprian, 27 December 1725, FLB Gotha A 430: 28.

52. The Calvinist supervisor was the pro-union court chaplain, Jablonski.

53. See the letters of Joachim Wäger, who was a teacher and then the chaplain at the orphanage in Potsdam, 1725–1727, AFSt/H, C 468: 1–58; and C 822: 26–28.

54. Regarding Pietist patronage and clientalism, especially involving the military chaplaincy and the Potsdam orphanage, see Marschke, "Patrons, Brokers, and Chaplains," in *Absolutely Pietist*, pp. 158–184.

55. "haben Sie … solche Eingriff gethan, so werd Sie nicht ruhen, biß Sie unserer praeceptores nach und nach aus gebißen, und uns gantz verschlungen." Letter from Gedicke, Berlin, to August Hermann Francke, Halle, 16 February 1726, AFSt/H, C 42: 71.

56. Letter from Gedicke, Berlin, to August Hermann Francke, Halle, 13 July 1726, AFSt/H, C 42: 72.

57. "Wie ich es aber für eine höchst gefährlichen Griff des Feindes achte, das gantze Werck in aüßerste *Confusion* zu bringen"; Letter from Gedicke to Francke, 16 February 1726.
58. Marschke, "Halle Pietism and the Prussian State," pp. 224–226; and Marschke, "Wir Halenser."
59. Marschke, *Absolutely Pietist*, pp. 129–136.
60. "der alte H Schmidt hat beständig den Reformiert[en] geheuchelt und mit under der Decke geleg[en] … Die Reformiert[en] nehm[en] sich noch diese Stunde seiner an meist[en] an, und haben ihn eb[en] zum Unionswerk mit gebrauch[en] woll[en]." Letter from Gedicke, Berlin, to Cyprian, Gotha, February 1726, FB Gotha A 430: 26.
61. "Auch *colludiret* er mit *reformatis*, und ist in der *Etat* mehr *reformirt*, als *Lutherisch*, welches man aus seinen gantzen Betragen sehen kan. Er gehet auf dem Waysenhause und in der Stadt mehr in die *reformirten* als *Lutherischen* Kirchen. Redet man in denen *Conferentz* etwas von *Reformatis*, welches man oft keinen Umgang haben kan, weil wir unter ihnen, und sie unter uns sind, so erfahren sie alles wieder, welches, wie leicht zu erachten, nichts gutes stifften kan." Letter from Schinmeyer, Potsdam, to Gotthilf August Francke, Halle, 27 January 1730, AFSt/H, C 439: 1.
62. Letter from Schinmeyer to Francke, 27 January 1730.
63. Regarding the changing relationship between Frederick William and the Pietists, see Marschke, "Halle Pietism and the Prussian State," pp. 227–228.
64. Again, these steps toward a liturgical union were very much in keeping with Jablonski's strategy for unifying the Protestant confessions.
65. I am indebted to Terence McIntosh (UNC Chapel Hill) for sharing the preliminary results of his research on this subject. See Stolze, ed., "Aktenstücke," pp. 273–288; Delius, "Berliner Kirchliche Unionsversuche," p. 93; Wolfgang Gericke, "Die Herzens- und Vernunftreligion König Friedrich Wilhelms I. und ein apokryphes Glaubensbekenntnis von 1696/1718," in *Glaubenszeugnisse und Konfessionspolitik der brandenburgischen Herrscher bis zur Preußischen Union, 1540–1815* (Bielefeld, 1977), pp. 53–67, here p. 58; and Luh, "Zur Konfessionspolitik," pp. 319–320.
66. A Catholic priest recorded this statement by the Prussian king in 1739: "meine Vorfahren haben [die Reformirte Religion] hier eingeführt; aber ich glaube nicht Alles, was die Reformirten glauben, z.B. von der Prädestination; ich glaube auch Vieles, was die Lutheraner und Vieles, was die Katholiken glauben. Was ich nämlich immer auf Grund der heiligen Schrift und nach der gesunden Vernunft glaubwürdig finde, das glaube ich; denn ich kann nicht all' die verschiedenen religiösen Meinungen prüfen und untersuchen"; Beyer, "König Friedrich Wilhelm I.," p. 6.

CHAPTER EIGHT

Pietist Conversion Narratives and Confessional Identity

JONATHAN STROM

The Pietist conversion narrative has become a central feature in depictions of Pietism. The dramatic account in which a nominal or lukewarm Christian despairs of his or her faith, struggles mightily with repentance, and finally breaks through to an assurance of grace and new life is almost a cliché popularized by the vivid account of August Hermann Francke.[1] This intensification mode of conversion, as some sociologists of religion characterize it, is distinct from other forms of early modern conversion, which have typically centered on a model in which the "convert" moves from one religious confession to another, or from outside Christianity to one of the Christian confessions.[2] This chapter considers the development of Pietist conversion narratives in the late 1730s and 1740s. These narratives became the most prominent artifact of Pietist conversion experiences. While we cannot read these highly stylized accounts of conversion experiences as literal expressions of the experiences themselves, we are nevertheless able to learn much about the direction and function of the narratives in German Pietism, including their use in inculcating confessional identity, by examining how these accounts developed and were communicated.

Until the late seventeenth century there were very few conversion narratives in German Protestantism—in contrast to English Puritanism, in which the written tradition of conversion narratives began much earlier.[3] This is not to suggest that there were no powerful religious experiences but rather that these were rarely framed as conversion experiences. In part the lack of a narrative tradition had doctrinal roots. Lutheran doctrine connected spiritual rebirth or regeneration to baptism, a sacrament almost always conducted in infancy.[4] Because of the close connection of conversion with notions of spiritual rebirth, the description of a specific conversion "experience" after baptism was problematic until some Lutherans, especially Pietists, weakened the connection between baptism and regeneration.[5] The first published collections of conversion-type narratives from the end of the seventeenth century are better described as spiritual autobiographies that sought to portray the lives of true Christians, and the narratives did not necessarily focus on a particular conversion experience.[6] Indeed, Philipp Jacob Spener, often considered the patriarch of German Pietism, did not include an account of his own conversion in his *Lebenslauf*.[7] Accounts that revolved around the conversion experience itself became much more common in Halle Pietism after August Hermann Francke's death in 1727, when his own dramatic conversion story was first published.[8]

Two sets of narratives from the ecclesial Pietist tradition of Spener and Francke form the basis of the discussion here. The first were produced in Mecklenburg during the 1730s and 1740s in the wake of a revival there. These narratives remained largely unpublished, although they circulated within Pietist networks in manuscript form.[9] The second set was published by Johann Jacob Moser, a prominent Württemberg jurist and advocate of Pietism, as a collection of conversion narratives of prisoners awaiting execution, *Seelige letzte Stunden einiger dem zeitlichen Tode übergebener Missethäter* (The Blessed Final Hours of Several Miscreants Sentenced to Death) (1740). The first edition, published anonymously, included an introduction and four narratives and was followed by several other editions and supplements in the 1740s.[10] Moser published a greatly expanded collection in his own name in 1753 that included thirty-one narratives.[11] These two sets of conversion accounts narrate religious experience in ways that were foreign to German Lutheran spirituality prior to the end of the seventeenth century. Especially, the Mecklenburg accounts reveal the divisions and disruptions that could occur in parishes or communities with a strong emphasis on conversion experiences. At the same time, these narratives nonetheless played a significant role in inculcating a specific confessional identity within the Lutheran Pietist context, especially against strains of heterodox, "radical" Pietists. They further reinforced the authority of the Pietist clergy by emphasizing their role in effecting and assessing "true" conversion. The valorization of conversion, especially in the narratives of condemned prisoners, could have unexpected consequences, and both supporters and opponents of Pietism worried that some accounts could pose an inducement to suicide by proxy.

The Mecklenburg narratives were created following an "awakening" or "revival" that began in the mid 1730s. Mecklenburg lay outside the direct orbit of Franckean Pietism, and while strains of radical Pietism ran throughout the duchy, redoubts of anti-Pietistic orthodoxy were to be found in the cities, at court, at the University of Rostock, and in the established church. Pietism, however, gained its strongest foothold in Mecklenburg at the court of Princess Augusta, the unmarried daughter of the last duke of Mecklenburg-Güstrow. Augusta had gained a high measure of autonomy in church matters and become an ardent Pietist with radical leanings in the 1720s and early 1730s.[12] In 1733 she began importing Pietist preachers to her court in Dargun and the parishes in the outlying villages; they drew especially on conversion themes from Francke, in particular the *Bußkampf* or repentance struggle as a preliminary step to a true conversion. The preachers sponsored by Augusta sparked a series of conversions throughout the area, not least at court, resulting in a revival in which the narration of the conversion experience became central. To Mecklenburg, lacking a tradition of revival, this Pietist revival presented a thorough challenge to the established religious culture.

The stories of conversions began around 1733 shortly after the arrival of the first two of the new preachers from the Harz, and they grew especially quickly after 1735 when these Pietists were joined by a third, more senior minister who became the preacher to the court (*Hofprediger*).[13] As accounts of the conversions began to circulate outside Pietist circles, an intriguing set of explanations for these intense experiences developed. Some mixed idolatry with quasi-magical means, reporting that the Pietists venerated a painting of a calf on one of the walls of a parsonage and that when the image bellowed, it would signal a true conversion had taken place.[14] Others attributed the conversions to the effects of elixirs and powders. Accounts of a so-called Quaker powder, which supposedly had the power to induce ecstatic experiences, had circulated widely since the end of the seventeenth century, propagated by opponents of religious dissent, especially anti-Pietist clergy and theologians.[15] In Mecklenburg, stories of Quaker powders and elixirs especially persisted in attributing sudden Pietist conversions to medicinal concoctions.[16] A favorite method was said to be mixing a powder into the bread and butter of an unsuspecting individual in order to convert him or her. A young servant girl from Wismar, for instance, excitedly told the authorities of how two spinster women who had employed her sought to convert her surreptitiously by mixing a black powder into the butter on her bread.[17] Most of the allegations remained on the level of rumor, but it would be a mistake to assume that authorities gave them no credence. In another case, a Pietist cantor was accused of "converting" a condemned woman in Malchin by allegedly giving her magical words written on slips of paper to eat. When the complaints reached the ducal authorities in nearby Dömitz, the unfortunate cantor was arrested and, in turn, tortured before the duke and his counselors ruefully recognized that the cantor's actions were more likely benign than magical.[18]

These accusations were distorted but not perhaps pure confabulations. The Pietist practice of employing elixirs such as the *essentia dulcis*—the most common of the medicines produced at the Halle Foundations—and other powdered medicines for general health likely fueled accusations of Quaker powders and elixirs, just as drawing random Bible verses and other pious sayings from the Pietist *Spruchkästlein* (Little Box of Aphorisms) likely encouraged the stories of magical words written on slips of paper among the Pietists.[19] The strong reactions and casting about for "plausible" explanations underscore what a difficult time orthodox Protestants—lay and learned—in Mecklenburg had in explaining the new phenomenon of Pietist conversion. There were some theological objections, especially on the basis of ecclesiology and the lack of an explicit Biblical warrant for the *Bußkampf*, but even on strict confessional grounds the theological case of the opponents was not especially strong. Even though they summoned some of the Dargun Pietists before the Mecklenburg consistory, they failed to convict them on doctrinal grounds.[20] Allegations of powders, elixirs, and magical slips of paper were much more effective in fomenting opposition, at times inciting parishioners to violence in objecting to the appointment of additional Pietist clergy. This was the case at Jördensdorf, where the parishioners blocked the entrance to the church at a clerical installation of a candidate associated with the Dargun movement, shouting "Beat them! Beat the Quaker priests dead!"[21] For the parishioners at Jördensdorf, rumors surrounding the conversions were easily conflated with older views of Quakers as religious enthusiasts and *Schwärmer*.

Pietists communicated manuscript narratives of conversion experiences through their networks in letters and other means. Typically, the narrative was not composed by the one who converted but by respected members of the Pietist circles, especially Pietist clergy. The narratives could vary in length—in general, the more prominent the position of the converted, the lengthier the account, although there were important exceptions for particularly dramatic stories. In Mecklenburg, the conversions followed a classic *Bußkampf* model of conversion, a model that is often treated as the paradigmatic form of Pietist conversion. It involved at first a period of "stirring" or "awakening" and then an extended *Buße* or "repentance," in which the individual expressed deep distress over his or her sinfulness. According to this understanding of conversion, heartfelt repentance needed to be distinguished from mere stirrings of the soul, and Pietist leaders often encouraged the individual to persist in an extended period of repentance and not mistakenly to assume true conversion was at hand on the basis of these first stirrings.[22] Rather, it was while the individual was in the throes of repentance that a particular sermon, hymn, or Bible verse would trigger sudden insight into God's unmerited grace. The converted joyfully described the experience as a comfort and peace in their soul.[23] The culmination of the narratives in Dargun was invariably the moment of conversion. While occasionally the strength of faith following the conversion would be emphasized with a telling vignette, most of the Mecklenburg accounts end quite quickly after the conversion experience.

Without question, this form of conversion disrupted traditional parish settings like those in Mecklenburg. It split parishes between the converted and unconverted, threatening to rupture a traditional parish structure that sought to include all members of a community within the church. Pietists were exposed to the claim that they ignored many congregants and furthered a sense of melancholy among those who had not experienced a conversion by concentrating unduly on the need for conversion.[24]

But the ways that these conversion experiences inculcated a confessional identity despite the opposition they aroused are also worthy of note. In Dargun and nearby areas, the dominant form of Pietism prior to the arrival of this conversion-oriented Pietism was a radical, much more heterodox Pietism that emphasized universal salvation, spiritualism, and prophecy, largely along the lines of Johann Wilhelm and Johanna Eleonora Petersen, who were early followers of Spener but later diverged from Spener's church-oriented reforms and turned to more heterodox positions on ecclesiology and soteriology. The Petersens were the most prominent representatives of radical Pietism in northern Germany in the early eighteenth century.[25] The new conversion-oriented Pietism derived from Francke and Halle explicitly targeted the more heterodox forms of Pietism and sought to drive these radicals out. While the emphasis on the conversion experience per se in this form of Pietism was hardly traditional in Lutheran orthodoxy, it did retain strong confessional overtones. The long period of *Buße* or repentance afforded an intimate opportunity to catechize the one struggling with faith. Repeatedly, individuals in the throes of conversion were directed to the Bible and Luther's catechism for a short course of confessionally colored instruction. Literacy among the converted was highly prized, and there were several accounts of illiterate individuals who suddenly learned to read in the process of their conversion, testifying both to the eager desire of these individuals to join the converted and to the miraculous power of the Holy Spirit.[26] Further, the schematic form of conversions followed here heightened the authority of the Pietist clergy, since they were the ultimate arbiters of a conversion's authenticity.

The conversion narratives were circulated among Pietists in various forms. Some were parts of letters exchanged with other Pietists, in which the author described a particular conversion experience.[27] Some were extended accounts, composed as a specific conversion narrative or as part of a collection of conversion narratives.[28] They were read and collected within the communities where the narratives arose, but they were also sent throughout networks of sympathetic Pietists in Germany from Mecklenburg to the Harz to Württemberg.[29] Surprisingly few of these accounts were ever printed, despite these Pietists' frequent publication of tracts and sermons, many of which dealt explicitly with conversion.[30] I have found only two from Mecklenburg in this period: one of a murderer about to be executed, and the other from a child who died shortly after his dramatic conversion.[31] Death, it would seem, enhanced the chances that one's conversion story would be published, which should not be entirely surprising since the dead are no longer in the position of causing the editor embarrassment by falsifying the genuine nature of a conversion narrative with subsequent backsliding behavior.[32] It points, too, to the largely internal function of most of these narratives in reinforcing the particular character of conversion within a predominately Pietist audience and network that was not geographically local.

One of the more prominent collections of published conversion narratives from this Hallensian background was the *Seelige letzte Stunden einiger dem zeitlichen Tode übergebener Missethäter*, published anonymously by Württemberg jurist and Pietist Johann Jacob Moser in 1740, in which Moser initially included four conversion narratives along with an extended introduction.[33] Despite an emphasis on conversion in the theology of Francke and others in the Halle tradition, published conversion narratives were not an especially strong feature of Hallensian Pietism until after Francke's death in 1727. The title of Moser's collection clearly echoes Erdmann Heinrich Graf Henckel's *Die letzten Stunden* (The Final Hours, 1720–1733), which portrayed the spiritual biography and death of dozens of exemplary Pietists, but Moser differs from Henckel in that he invariably highlighted conversion as the focal point of each account.[34] Several additional reprints and editions of Moser followed in the 1740s, and in 1753 Moser published a much larger edition of conversion stories of both men and women whose crimes ranged from murder and infanticide to robbery, treason, arson, and counterfeiting.[35]

According to his introduction, Moser had two explicit goals in publishing the collection. First, he wanted to encourage the authorities to provide the book to prisoners facing execution, so as to encourage their heartfelt conversions.[36] Secondly, and much more importantly, Moser wanted this collection to be an example to those who felt themselves superior to these wretches and yet were not truly converted. He argued that "in God's eyes, they are at root not one whit better than the most terrible Sodomites, murderers, adulterers, and blasphemers; rather these criminals have only revealed in concrete outbursts that which, following its secret lusts, lies so well concealed in the power of every human heart."[37]

Consequently, these narratives are by no means morality tales about the dangers of crime, though gruesome descriptions of the offenses often accompanied them and were undoubtedly part of their popular appeal. Rather, the narratives were designed to show that grace was open to all, even the most despicable criminals, if they would but repent thoroughly. Here the narratives focused much less on contrition for the specific crimes of the condemned and much more on their utter, inherent sinfulness and need for a divine redeemer. In none of the Moser narratives did the condemned contest the criminal charges against them, but many were initially resistant to admitting their utter human depravity.[38] In the case of Andreas Lepsch, who was facing execution for *viehische Unzucht* (bestiality), he at first protested to the pastor counseling him that he had not otherwise lived a sinful life and had avoided most vices. This led the Pietist Pastor Heinrich Schubert to cite Bible verse after Bible verse at him to convince him of his wretchedness, warning him that Jesus knew his heart better than anyone.[39] The intent was not to achieve regret for the crime itself, but to drive the individual to a profound repentance for his or her fundamental depravity. Having broken any hope that the condemned could rescue themselves from sin, the Pietist pastor (or in some cases Pietist lay person) could offer the condemned the possibility of the grace that could lead them to a complete change of heart and mind (*Herzens und Sinnes*), thus bringing them to the classic Pietist breakthrough (*Durchbruch*) and true conversion.

Moser's narratives followed a pattern similar to that of the Mecklenburg narratives discussed earlier. A profound *Bußkampf* in which the individual struggled with his or her repentance was critical to the narrative's structure. The temporal duration of the *Bußkampf* was less important than its intensity and the self-recognition it afforded. And in the introduction, as in many of his narratives, Moser warns against the dangers of an insufficient conversion, in which individuals might be falsely comforted with a hymn or Bible passage and erroneously believe that they had been converted when it fact they had experienced only the initial stirrings and not complete repentance.[40]

The captive nature of those awaiting execution and the access the Pietist preachers had to them created a kind of laboratory for quasi-coercive conversion. The narratives describe in detail the intense catechizing work the Pietists undertook to instruct the prisoners awaiting execution. In the case of a brutal Magdeburg tobacconist who had killed his own child in order to punish his wife, the narrative describes how the clergy, who found him utterly ignorant in spiritual matters, instructed him mornings and afternoons, one after the other, in order to teach him the catechism of Luther, the order of salvation, and the fundamentals of Scripture.[41] The narrative describes their efforts at great length, and here they led, as in nearly all the other cases in the Moser collection, to a successful *Durchbruch* and righteous conversion, in which the condemned accepted Jesus Christ as redeemer and demonstrated true faith in the face of death. Often the high point of a narrative is the extended description of the condemned as they were brought to the place of execution: despite the jeers from the crowd and the terrors of their impending execution, they expressed constancy in their faith. Some narratives recount the gruesome details of the execution in order to demonstrate how, even as they were broken on the wheel and left to a slow and agonizing death, the converted criminals would continue to praise Christ, thus testifying to the power and truth of their conversions.[42] A number of accounts describe how a convicted criminal joyously awaited his or her death and gladly went to the place of execution, calling out pious words of encouragement to the onlookers. One narrative described how a woman named Anne Marthe Hungerland willingly placed herself on the execution block and cried out to the crowd: "Oh, I see the heaven open above. Lord Jesus! Take up my soul." And the narrator continues: "she received among these the last of her words the happy stroke. All the words, which she spoke, she enunciated with great power and joyfulness all the while so movingly that most of the spectators broke out in tears."[43]

All the major narratives in the Moser collection depict successful instances of conversion.[44] Cases in which the method of conversion failed or the prisoner strongly resisted the clergy's attempts are not portrayed, suggesting that energetic efforts on the part of the clergy and Pietist laypeople would inevitably lead to conversion. But it is extremely difficult to estimate how common such conversions might have been, since Pietists were generally loath to describe attempts in which they failed, although they occasionally published an admonitory tale.[45] Nor is it easy to judge the accuracy of accounts that were composed largely by the clergy who were intimately involved.[46] Unlike many other conversion narratives—most of the eighteenth-century narratives from Britain and North America were autobiographical—those in the Moser collection and from Mecklenburg were not in the first person.[47] In these accounts, the converted did not describe their own experiences directly; rather they were narrated for them by Pietist insiders, both lay and clerical.

The strong "confessional" context of Moser's narratives is quite striking in the way they inculcated a version of Lutheran identity. The stories Moser presents came from a wide geographic swatch from South Germany to Scandinavia, but thirty of the thirty-one are Lutheran—which, given the profusion of conversion narratives in the Reformed tradition, could hardly have been a coincidence. They reveal a clear confessional selection on Moser's part. They also present a notable contrast to the ecumenical nature of the spiritual biographies and autobiographies in Reitz's *Historie der Wiedergebohrnen* (History of the Reborn) or even the *Closter-Bergische Sammlung Nützlicher Materien zur Erbauung im Wahren Christenthum* (The Berge Monastery Collection of Useful Materials for Edification in True Christianity), published by Johann Adam Steinmetz, who had close ties to Halle Pietism.[48] Here as in Mecklenburg, the elements reinforcing a confessional identity—albeit a Pietist one—were not incidental to the stories. By presenting a particular model of conversion based on the Lutheran Pietist *Bußkampf*, with its distinctive elements of the stirring or awakening, repentance struggle, and then the conversion moment of the breakthrough to grace, the collection explicitly located these narratives within the Lutheran tradition of conversion theology articulated by Francke and others in the Hallensian tradition.[49]

The clergy figured prominently in nearly all the accounts. The participating ministers were in many cases authors of the accounts themselves who often depicted themselves playing a critical role as the subject moved toward the goal of conversion. In those conversion narratives associated with execution, clergy enjoyed special access to the prisoners. They instructed them, challenged facile assumptions about their spiritual condition, gave comfort to them when they despaired, and accompanied them as they went to the place of execution. The active involvement of the clergy, the catechetical preparation, the directed study of Scripture, and administration of the Eucharist were all presented as integral elements of the process leading up to conversion. This put high expectations on the character of the clergy, and in his foreword, Moser appealed for truly converted ministers to take on these cases.[50] The structure of the narratives signaled the centrality of the clergy throughout the process and enhanced their authority in matters of conversion.

The Moser collection went through multiple editions and spurred similar print collections. Without question, conversion accounts of prisoners awaiting execution found an eager readership in print form.[51] The manner in which the composers of the Moser narratives valorized the conversion and subsequent execution of the criminals as true exemplars of Christian witness suggested to some critics that the published narratives appeared to urge imitation to the point that they were implicated in cases of "suicide by proxy."[52] These were instances in which an individual would commit a capital crime with the intent of being executed by the authorities, thus avoiding the religious consequences of suicide, for which repentance was not possible.[53] The Moser collection includes, in fact, one case that is quite clearly an instance of suicide by proxy, in which a woman, Gertrude Magdalene Bremmel, deliberately killed an innocent child in her care in order to effect her execution at the hand of the authorities.[54] Bremmel made no attempt to conceal the crime and immediately afterward presented herself to the *Vogt* and confessed her actions "freely and without any excuses."[55] Later, according to the narrator, Bremmel acknowledged that by murdering the child, she had hoped to achieve salvation: "Thus she thought: when you just do what you have planned, you will be executed, and through the shedding of your blood, everything will be repaid, and you will be saved. Such thoughts were first aroused in her when she had previously seen an execution in person and imagined at that point that whoever dies in this manner cannot but become saved."[56] In the process of her conversion, Bremmel came to see this as an "abominable action" that she deeply regretted. The clergy had criticized the presumption of salvation that she hoped to achieve with her execution, but they worked fervently to bring her to a proper understanding of repentance and true conversion.[57]

Wernigerode, where Bremmel lived, was along with Dargun one of the centers of Pietism that strongly advocated an extended repentance struggle in conversion, and the clergy's views of the conversion process there corresponded closely with those presented elsewhere in the Moser narratives.[58] To be sure, Bremmel claimed no intimate familiarity with Pietist beliefs prior to her incarceration—she claimed repeatedly that she had never understood true repentance and conversion before.[59] That she was deeply moved by the example of a previous execution in which a conversion was implied, though, signals that she was not entirely unfamiliar with aspects of Pietist conversion.[60] Moreover, the bulk of the narrative is given over to Bremmel's successful conversion and faithful death. In the end, she achieved precisely what she had set out to do initially: to die in assurance of grace and salvation.[61]

The prior influence of Pietist conversion ideas on Bremmel remains unclear, but other sources indicate that both Pietists and non-Pietists worried that such narratives could spark imitation. In the preface to the 1753 edition, Moser added a paragraph that explicitly warned against such a "misuse," a recognition that narratives could be misunderstood by some readers.[62] Arguing from a different theological position, Gotthilf Samuel Steinbart, a rationalist who was nonetheless familiar with the Pietist milieu, contended that the publication of narratives like those found in Moser were indeed an inducement to suicide by proxy, and he urged their suppression.[63] The comments of both Moser and Steinbart suggest that contemporaries from different theological perspectives feared that the published narratives were able to affect how individuals framed their own conversions.[64]

The Dargun narratives and the Moser collection reinforced elements of Lutheran confessional identity in the Pietist traditions. Especially in comparison with collections of Pietist biographies and autobiographies published in the early 1700s and featuring many conversion-type stories, including those by Reitz and Arnold, that were ecumenical in nature, these collections of narratives reflect a much more deliberate, confessionalized point of view.[65] Fred van Lieburg has pointed to an analogous role of confessional or doctrinal elements in the way that conversion narratives were fashioned in the Netherlands.[66] Likewise for eighteenth-century Britain, Bruce Hindmarsh noted that conversion narratives often functioned to reinforce doctrinal distinctions among groups, such as Presbyterians or Methodists.[67] Not all Pietist conversion narratives were as strongly confessional as Dargun or Moser, but these two collections as well as those from outside Germany indicate that conversion narratives were not unstructured representations of religious experience but were implicated in doctrinal definition and confessional identity.[68] Stories about conversion played a central role in developing group cohesion and establishing boundaries against competing religious views.

The two collections of conversion narratives that we have examined here differ from each other in important ways. Those from Mecklenburg were intended primarily for an internal, Pietist audience, circulated from hand to hand, and remained unpublished. The Moser collection, by contrast, was framed for a public readership and stylized as theological apologetics. The Mecklenburg manuscript accounts tended to be much shorter and were centered on the *Bußkampf* and the moment of conversion, showing little interest in the individual's subsequent life. Even in manuscript, these accounts were shared and read widely within specific Pietist networks, sometimes as far-flung as Württemberg and Mecklenburg; in most cases they never found their way into print. The Moser narratives may have served discussion within Pietist networks, but their publication presented them to a much broader public as well. For the most part, they were longer than the unpublished Mecklenburg texts, devoted considerable space to the description of the individuals after conversion (even if their lives were cut short by the gallows), and were structured to convince outsiders of the genuine nature of these experiences. Furthermore, they added a final emphasis missing in most of the manuscript narratives: the expression of faith in the face of certain and often gruesome death. Constancy of faith up until death would become one of the hallmarks of the conversion narratives printed after the 1730s.

Finally, these sources raise interesting questions about the fashioning of narratives. Because the subjects of these German texts generally did not compose the accounts of their own experiences, the stories represent ways in which others—particularly Pietist clergy—sought to channel conversion experiences into a confessional framework. The narratives of the condemned tell us little about their inner lives, nor do they offer details about the context of what must have been considerable coercion. These were not the purposes of the writers. Although there is little evidence that conversion experiences were deliberately falsified, we still must be careful in drawing conclusions from the narratives about those experiences. Nevertheless, as the stories of suicide by proxy particularly suggest, the published and unpublished narratives had considerable influence in shaping how eighteenth-century Germans understood and sought conversion, even in unexpected ways.

Notes

1. For a recent treatment that emphasizes the centrality of Francke's conversion, see Hans-Martin Kirn, "The Penitential Struggle ('Busskampf') of August Hermann Francke (1663–1727): A Model of Pietistic Conversion?" in Jan N. Bremmer et al., eds., *Paradigms, Poetics, and Politics of Conversion* (Louvain, 2006), pp. 123–132. Kurt Aland sees Francke's conversion as representative of a "zeitlich genau festzulegendes Bekehrungserlebnis" in Halle Pietism. Aland, "Bemerkungen zu August Hermann Francke und seinem Bekehrungserlebnis," in: *Kirchengeschichtliche Entwürfe* (Gütersloh 1960), p. 563. Likewise, Ulrike Witt understands Francke's conversion experience as forming the basis of a systematic theology of conversion at Halle: Ulrike Witt, *Bekehrung, Bildung und Biographie: Frauen im Umkreis des halleschen Pietismus* (Tübingen, 1995), pp. 71ff. Bill Widén and Markus Matthias both view the normative function of Francke's conversion experience in Pietism more skeptically: Bill Widén, *Bekehrung und Erziehung bei August Hermann Francke* (Åbo, 1967), pp. 4–5 and Markus Matthias, "Bekehrung und Wiedergeburt," in Hartmut Lehmann, ed., *Glaubenswelt und Lebenswelten, Geschichte des Pietismus*, vol. 4 (Göttingen, 2004), p. 61. The critical edition

of Francke's conversion experience is found in Markus Matthias, *Lebensläufe August Hermann Franckes* (Leipzig, 1999).

2. Lewis Rambo develops a detailed typology of religious conversion in his *Understanding Religious Conversion* (New Haven, 1993)—in overview, pp. 13–14. The classic description of this form of religious conversion is found in William James, *The Varieties of Religious Experience* (London, 1902; reprint London, 1911), pp. 189ff.

3. Edmund Morgan, *Visible Saints: The History of a Puritan Idea* (New York, 1963) and Patricia Caldwell, *The Puritan Conversion Narrative: The Beginnings of American Expression* (Cambridge, 1983). For an overview of early English conversion narratives, see D. Bruce Hindmarsh, *The Evangelical Conversion Narrative: Spiritual Autobiography in Early Modern England* (Oxford, 2005), pp. 35–52.

4. On baptism as "the bath of rebirth" or regeneration, see, for instance, Luther's "Small Catechism" in Timothy Wengert and Robert Kolb, *The Book of Concord: Confessions of the Evangelical Lutheran Church* (Minneapolis, 2001), p. 359.

5. Theophil Großgebauer (d. 1661) was one of the earliest Lutherans to abandon the idea of baptismal regeneration and develop an idea of a datable conversion, which he identified with regeneration. Theophil Großgebauer, *Treuer Unterricht von der Wiedergeburt* (Frankfurt, 1661), pp. 13, 57, 94. Spener characteristically remained closer to traditional Lutheran doctrine than Großgebauer and retained baptismal regeneration, but he developed an understanding in which regeneration could be lost and therefore regained later in life. On Spener and regeneration, Johannes Wallmann, *Philipp Jakob Spener und die Anfänge des Pietismus*, 2nd ed. (Tübingen, 1986), pp. 172–174.

6. The well-known collection published by Reitz at the turn of the century comprised spiritual autobiographies and biographies, including translations of English conversion narratives in the first volume but relatively few depictions of explicit conversion experiences from the German context. Johann Henrich Reitz, *Historie der Wiedergebohrnen*, edited by Hans-Jürgen Schrader, 7 vols. in 4 (Tübingen, 1982, originally published 1698–1745). For a good discussion of the purposes of Reitz's narratives and the diversity they represent, see Dorothea von Mücke, "Experience, Impartiality, and Authenticity in Confessional Discourse," *New German Critique* 79 (2000): pp. 5–35, here pp. 16–21.

7. On this point see Wallmann, *Philipp Jakob Spener*, pp. 89–90. In a telling move, some later Pietists nonetheless sought to impute a conversion experience to Spener. See "Merckwürdiger Anfang der Bekehrung des sel. D. Speners," *Sammlung auserlesener Materien zum Bau des Reichs Gottes* 2 (1732): 216–218.

8. Francke's conversion story was not widely known during his lifetime and was only published posthumously. Even after that point, its model character should not be overemphasized. On the publishing history of the conversion story, see Matthias, *Lebensläufe*, pp. 73–75.

9. Many of these conversion accounts—forty—were compiled in a single document, likely by a member of the court of Stolberg-Wernigerode, and are preserved in the archive there: Landesarchiv Magdeburg, Landeshauptarchiv, Außenstelle Wernigerode (hereafter LHA Wernigerode), St-W, Rep. H. Nachlaß Sophie Charlotte VII, No. 9.

10. [Johann Jacob Moser], *Seelige letzte Stunden einiger dem zeitlichen Tode übergebener Missethäter* (Leipzig, 1740); *Selige letzte Stunden einiger dem zeitlichen Tode übergebener Missethäter* (Leipzig, 1742); *Selige Letzte Stunden Einiger dem zeitlichen Tode übergebener Missethäter, Mit einer Vorrede…* (Jena, 1742); *Selige letzte Stunden einiger dem zeitlichen Tode übergebener Missethäter, Erste Forsetzung…* (Leipzig, 1745).

11. Johann Jacob Moser, *Seelige Letzte Stunden 31 Personen, so unter des Schafrichters Hand gestorben* (Stuttgart, Frankfurt, and Leipzig, 1753). An additional unrevised edition appeared in 1767. A final edition was published in 1861.

12. Wilhelmi discusses Augusta's radical background: Heinrich Wilhelmi, "Augusta, Prinzessin von Meklenburg-Güstrow, und die Dargunschen Pietisten," *Jahrbücher des Vereins für Mecklenburgische Geschichte und Altertumskunde* 48 (1883): pp. 110–127. On the revival at Dargun, see Jonathan Strom, "Conversion, Confessionalization, and Pietism in Dargun," in Fred van Lieburg, ed., *Confessionalism and Pietism: Religious Reform in Early Modern Europe* (Mainz, 2006), pp. 149–168.

13. Strom, "Conversion," pp. 157–158.

14. These allegations also suggested that "Krähen und Teuffelsfüße," apparently signs of magical implements, were present in the rooms where conversions occurred, LHA Schwerin, eccl. gen. 1572, protocol of 25 April 1735.

15. See Ehregott Daniel Colberg, *Das platonisch-hermetisches* [sic] *Christenthum: begreiffend die historische Erzehlung vom Ursprung und vielerley Secten der heutigen fanatischen Theologie* (Erfurt, 1690), p. 295 as well as Samuel Morgenbessern, *Prüfung Des Holländischen Qvaker-Pulvers* (Sorau, 1697) and Johann Heinrich Feustking, *Gynaeceum haeretico fanaticum oder Historie und Beschreibung der falschen Prophetinnen, Quäkerinnen, Schwärmerinnen und andern sectirischen und begeisterten Weibes-Personen* (Frankfurt and Leipzig, 1704), pp. 38, 506, 665.

16. See Peter Zorn, *Dissertatio historica Theologicade Philtris enthusasticis anglico batavis H.E. von dem Englisch- und Holländischen Qvaker-Pulver* (Rostock, [1707]).

17. "Protokoll über das Verhör der Marie Elisabeth Salome Fleißner über den Versuch der Schwestern Duve in Wismar, sie zum Dargunschen Glauben zu bekehren." (1747) LHA Schwerin, eccl. gen. 1577.

18. A summary of the case is found in Strom, "Conversion," pp. 162–63. Jacob Rudolph in Dargun described the Beatus case in a series of letters to Gotthilf August Francke in 1744. Staatsbibliothek Preussischer Kulturbesitz in Berlin (StBPK), Francke Nachlaß, 18,2:12/2–5. See also LHA Schwerin eccl. spec., 6215 Malchin. 3r–4r, 20r; eccl. spec. Malchin Kantorat 6226, 44r–45r.

19. On the medicinal products from Halle, see Renate Wilson, *Pious Traders in Medicine: A German Pharmaceutical Network in Eighteenth-Century North America* (University Park, PA, 2000). For the use of *Spruchkästlein* in Pietist conversions, see Moser, *Letzte Stunden 31 Personen*, p. 303. See also instances of its use in Mecklenburg: LHA Schwerin, Unterhalt und Leibgedinge 389, Ausgaben Osterquartal 1735, and Jacob Rudolph's letter to GA Francke, 25 January 1744, StBPK, Francke Nachlaß, 18,2:12/2–5.

20. Wilhelmi, "Augusta," p. 177.

21. "Schlagt zu! Schlagt die Quäker-Priester todt!" Quoted in Wilhelmi, "Augusta," p. 190. See also LHA Schwerin, eccl. spec. 4900.

22. The Dargun Pietists were often careful to distinguish the initial *Rührungen* or stirrings from the actual conversion itself and warned against misjudging them as a completed conversion. See for instance, Henning Christoph Ehrenpfort, *Eine Predigt Von der Heil. Tauffe* (Alten-Stettin, 1735), pp. 39–40 and *Bekehrung und seliges Ende eines eilfjährigen Kindes, August Ernst Friederich Zachariä* (Stettin, [1747]), p. 11.

23. LHA Wernigerode. Rep. H. St-W, Nachlaß Henrich Ernst II. B Nr. 62, which describes the conversion of a cowherd in such terms; also *Bekehrung und seliges Ende eines eilfjährigen Kindes*, pp. 13–14.

24. These charges were made by one of the opponents of the revival at Dargun, presumably the former court preacher Georg Friedrich Stieber, in "Prüfung des Geistes zur deutlicheren Entdeckung einer neuen, doch übel genandten Secte der Bekehrten," Universitätsbibliothek Rostock, Mss. theol. 134, Nr. 6, esp. pp. 68ff.

25. The Petersens were closely connected with the Philadelphian movement and other heterodox streams within radical Pietism. On "radical Pietism" and the Petersens, see Hans Schneider, *German Radical Pietism* (Lanham, MD, 2007), pp. 3–10, 67–74. For works and further literature on Johanna Eleonora Petersen, especially from a literary perspective, see Barbara Becker-Cantarino, ed. and trans., *The Life of Lady Johanna Eleonora Petersen, Written by Herself: Pietism and Women's Autobiography in Seventeenth-Century Germany* (Chicago, 2005).

26. See for instance, LHA Wernigerode. Rep. H. St-W, Nachlaß Henrich Ernst II. B Nr. 62, where a cowherd learned to read nearly miraculously in the course of his conversion, as well as the case of Christian Ritter, a condemned murderer, who also learned to read almost preternaturally during the course of his conversion. *Bekehrung und herrliches Ende Christian Friedrich Ritters, eines ehemaligen zweyfachen Mörders, der am 18. Sept. 1738 zu Dargun in Mecklenburg gerädert worden* (Magdeburg, 1739).

27. Johann Schmidt briefly described the early conversion of a woman in his community in a 1733 letter to his patron in Wernigerode, Countess Sophie-Charlotte. LHA Wernigerode, Rep. H. St-W, Nachlaß Sophie Charlotte I, Briefe 75, Nr. 1. Duchess Augusta described her conversion in a letter to her nephew, King Christian VI. RA Kopenhagen, Konghusets arkiv, Kong Christian VI, Indkomene Breve, Letter from Augusta dated 25 September 1740.

28. See the narrative sent from Lomersheim in Württemberg to Mecklenburg, UB Rostock Mss Theol 133 (5) as well as the extended account of the cowherd's conversion, which was composed as a narrative and sent from Mecklenburg to Wernigerode, LHA Wernigerode. Rep. H. St-W, Nachlaß Henrich Ernst II. B Nr. 62.

29. Wilhelmi cites a collection from Groß-Metling, a small community in Mecklenburg, which was maintained for use within the parish. These narratives were available to him in the nineteenth century but are no longer extant. Wilhelmi, "Augusta," p. 231.

30. Among others: Carl Heinrich Zachariä, *Der in Gottes Wort und unsern Symbolischen Büchern wohlgegründete Buß-Kampf* (Peina, 1736), Jacob Schmidt, *Eine Predigt Vom Gebet, über die Worte Christi Matth. VI. v. 5. 6. 7. 8. Vor der Dargunischen Hoff-Gemeinde … gehalten* (Alten-Stettin, [1735]), and Ehrenpfort, *Eine Predigt Von der Heil.*

31. *Bekehrung und herrliches Ende Christian Friedrich Ritters* and *Bekehrung und seliges Ende eines eilffjährigen Kinde.*

32. Schrader notes that Reitz removed some accounts from later editions of the *Historie der Wiedergebohrnen* because the individual relapsed. Schrader, "Nachwort des Herausgebers," in Reitz, *Historie der Wiedergebohrnen*, vol. 5, p. 182. Consequently, very few accounts were published before death, and vivid retellings of the last "hours" and death of exemplary Christians became one of the common forms of published Lutheran Pietist conversion accounts. These often incorporated conversion either as a prologue to or a process completed in the throes of dying. The best-known collection was Erdmann Heinrich Graf Henckel, *Die letzten Stunden einiger Der Evangelischen Lehre zugetanen und in diesem und nechste verflossenen Jahren selig in dem Herrn Verstorbenen Personen*, 4 vols. (Halle, 1720–1733).

33. Moser, *Seelige letzte Stunden.* Moser had an extraordinary career as both a publicist of the Pietist movement—he was the editor of the periodical *Altes und Neues aus dem*

Reich Gottes (1733–1739)—and a prolific legal authority. See Mack Walker, *Johann Jakob Moser and the Holy Roman Empire of the German Nation* (Chapel Hill, 1981), and more recently, Andreas Gestrich and Rainer Lächele, eds., *Johann Jacob Moser: Politiker, Pietist, Publizist* (Karlsruhe, 2002).

34. Many of the "last hours" and biographies depicted in Henckel do not include any conversion narratives or contain only a brief allusion to such an experience. See Henckel, *Die letzten Stunden.*

35. Moser, *Seelige Letzte Stunden 31 Personen.* That same year Woltersdorff began publishing monthly installments of such accounts, which appeared sporadically until 1760: Ernst Gottlieb Woltersdorff, *Der Schächer am Kreutz: das ist vollständige Nachrichten von der Bekehrung und seligem Ende hingerichteter Missethäter,* 3 vols. (Görlitz, 1753–1760). This collection includes many of the same narratives found in Moser. Though close to some Pietists and inspired by Moser's earlier publications, Woltersdorff did not share Moser's concern for thorough repentance as part of the conversion process. *Der Schächer am Kreutz,* vol. 1, pp. 25, 26, 414. Cf. Moser, *Letzte Stunden 31 Personen,* pp. 12–15.

36. Moser, *Letzte Stunden 31 Personen,* p. 24.

37. Moser, *Letzte Stunden 31 Personen,* p. 25.

38. Certainly not all narratives of condemned prisoners follow this pattern. The conversion account of a Swiss woman accused of infanticide, reprinted in the *Closter-Bergische Sammlung Nützlicher Materien zur Erbauung im Wahren Christenthum* 31 (1756): 740–776, presents a case where the individual initially denied the accusations. The narrator tied her confession of the crime closely to her spiritual repentance and conversion. The alternate morphology of conversion here and the explicitly Reformed context of this case underscores the selectivity of the narratives presented by Moser.

39. Moser, *Letzte Stunden 31 Personen,* p. 769.

40. Moser, *Letzte Stunden 31 Personen,* p. 12.

41. Moser, *Letzte Stunden 31 Personen,* p. 191.

42. Moser recounts one case of a Danish soldier convicted of murder who survived seventeen excruciating hours on the wheel and continued to testify to his hard-won faith until the point of death. Moser, *Letzte Stunden 31 Personen,* p. 600.

43. "Ach, ich sehe den Himmel offen. Herr Jesu! nimm meinen Geist auf. Und empfieng unter solchen letzten Worten den glücklichen Streich. Alle Worte, so sie geredet, hat sie mit grosser Krafft und Freudigkeit ausgesprochen, und noch auch dabey so bewegend, daß den meisten Zuschauern die Thränen aus den Augen gefallen." Moser, *Letzte Stunden 31 Personen,* p. 268.

44. Moser presents the case of a counterfeiter, a onetime Protestant who had converted to Catholicism, and his wife, a lifelong Catholic. Jailed in Augsburg, they both requested pastoral visits by Lutheran clergy. In this case, the husband's *Bußkampf* was portrayed as insincere and incomplete, whereas the wife's was depicted as successful. Moser, *Letzte Stunden 31 Personen,* pp. 783–796.

45. "Das unselige Ende Joh. Ph. P. gewesenen Schuldieners in Ob. verzeichnet von seinem damaligen Pastore, Hn. M.P." *Fortgesetzte Sammlung auserlesener Materien zum Bau des Reichs Gottes* 29 (1735): 620–631.

46. I have only come across one archival account of such a case that can be corroborated from other documents, that of Beatus and an unnamed woman condemned to death in Malchin, cited above. In any case, those who opposed these conversion narratives for the way they celebrated the last moments of convicted criminals did not contest the

veracity of the accounts themselves; rather they called for the suppression of their publication. [Gotthilf Samuel Steinbart], *Ist es rathsam Missethäter durch Geistliche zum Tode vorbereiten und zur Hinrichtung begleiten zu lassen* (Berlin, 1769), pp. 25–26.

47. Hindmarsh emphasizes the autobiographical character of most English conversions narratives of the eighteenth century. Hindmarsh, *Evangelical Conversion*, pp. 321–326 and passim.

48. On Reitz, see above. For Steinmetz and his publication of the *Closter-Bergische Sammlung* and the increasing amount of international material, particularly England, see Rainer Lächele, *Die "Sammlung auserlesener Materien zum Bau des Reichs Gottes" zwischen 1730 und 1760: Erbauungszeitschriften als Kommunikationsmedium des Pietismus* (Tübingen, 2006) pp. 90–94.

49. Proponents of the *Bußkampf* conversion model emphasized its origins in the older Lutheran tradition of the *Anfechtung* (spiritual struggle) and *Busse* (repentance), which had their roots in Luther. See, e.g., Zachariä, *Der in Gottes Wort und unsern Symbolischen Büchern wohlgegründete Buß-Kampf*. The emphasis on a conversion experience that separated believers from unbelievers was one aspect that distinguished Francke and later Pietists from earlier Lutherans. See Johannes Wallmann, *Der Pietismus* (Göttingen, 1990), p. 64. Francke's conversion theology differed from many Reformed orders of salvation in its rejection of predestination. The Wesleyan understanding of conversion shares many characteristics with Lutheran Pietists, including, some argue, a *Bußkampf*. See Frederick A. Dreyer, *The Genesis of Methodism* (Bethlehem, PA, 1999), pp. 37–44. Francke and Lutheran Pietists in general do not, however, emphasize perfectionism, which became characteristic of the Wesleyan tradition.

50. Moser, *Letzte Stunden 31 Personen*, p. 19.

51. Many of the conversion accounts had appeared several times in print individually before they were collected by Moser. For instance, the narratives of Christian Friedrich Ritter and Gertrude Magdalene Bremmel first appeared as pamphlets: *Bekehrung und herrliches Ende Christian Friedrich Ritters* and *Die Hirten-Treue Christi, welche er an einem seiner verlornen Schafe, nemlich an Gertrude Magdalene Bremmelin, einer vorsetzlichen Kindermörderin, erwiesen: zum Preise desselben unendlicher Menschenliebe, wie auch zur Warnung und Besserung beschrieben; nebst einer auf dem Rabenstein gehaltenen Rede* (Wernigerode, 1744). Broadsheet depictions of these conversions and executions also apparently circulated before they were transformed into longer narratives. Commenting on the aftermath of these executions on some individuals Steinbart wrote facetiously of the ensuing publications: "Hier aber unterricht ihn deutlicher ein gedrucktes Blatt von der schönen Bekehrung und seligem Tode des abgethanen Verbrechers, und muntert ihn zuletzt durch ein Bußlied zur Nachfolge auf. Nicht lange nachher erscheint ein ausführliches Tractätchen, darin die Wunder der Gnade in der schnellen Bekehrung des weiland bösewichts N.N. homiletisch ausgeführt, seine Standhaftigkeit im Tode einem Vorchmack des Himmels zugeschrieben und zuletzt sein Seligkeit authentisch versichert wird." Steinbart, *Missethäter*, p. 14.

52. Steinbart, who strongly advocated the prohibition of these conversion accounts, recounted a case of a woman who was despondent about her chances of salvation if she were not executed by the authorities, and, according to Steinbart, resolved therefore to kill a child or a pious preacher, neither of whose souls she considered to be in danger, so that she could die at the hands of the executioner. Steinbart, *Missethäter*, pp. 15–16.

53. Kathy Stuart explores the legal, cultural, and religious context of this phenomenon in her article: "Suicide by Proxy: The Unintended Consequences of Public Executions in

Eighteenth-Century Germany," *Central European History* 41 (2008): 413–445. "Suicide by proxy" is Stuart's term; other historians refer to it as "capital punishment suicide," "concealed suicide," and "suicidal murders." In overview, see ibid., pp. 419–420. In the eighteenth century, the jurist Carl Ferdinand Hommel referred to it as "mittelbarer Selbstmord" and considered it far more dangerous than typical suicide. C.F. Hommel, *Rhapsodia qvaestionvm in foro qvotidie obventivm neqve tamen legibvs decisarvm*, vol. 5 (Bayreuth, 1769), pp. 1454–1455.

54. "Bekehrung und Glaubens-volles Ende Gertrude Magdalene Bremmelin, welche wegen an einem fremden Kinde verübten Mordes A. 1744 in Wernigerode enthauptet worden ist." Moser, *Letzte Stunden 31 Personen*, pp. 269–326. The first few pages provide a brief description of the crime, investigation, and execution, but the bulk of the narrative focuses on the process of conversion that began with her detention.

55. Moser, *Letzte Stunden 31 Personen*, p. 270.

56. "So aber hatte sie gedacht: Wann du es nur thust, was du dir vorgenommen, so wirst du gerichtet, und durch dein Blutvergiessen wird alles bezahlt, und du wirst selig. Dergleichen Gedanken sich zuerst in ihr gereget, da sie ehemals eine Execution mit angesehen, und sich dabey vorgestellet, daß wer also stürbe, nicht anders als selig werden müsse." p. 276.

57. Stuart sees Bremmel's language of doing "good penance" and paying with her blood as clashing with the views of the clergy and indicating the long-term difficulty of inculcating Lutheran ideas of justification after the Reformation. Stuart, "Suicide by Proxy," pp. 443–444. Woltersdorff—who does not emphasize extended forms of repentance—adds a commentary on this passage that is missing in the original and in Moser, thereby shifting its meaning in a more Lutheran orthodox direction. Woltersdorff, *Schächer am Kreutz*, vol. 1, p. 414. Cf. Moser, *Letzte Stunden 31 Personen*, pp. 275, 276. Given the strongly Pietist orientation of the clergy in Wernigerode at this time, another interpretation of Bremmel's convictions may lie in the context of strict Pietist demands for an extended struggle in repentance (*Bußkampf*). Certainly, from the point of view of the clergy Bremmel's view was distorted, but it may very well reflect the Pietist celebration of conversion prior to execution and the demands for a profound personal repentance, which—despite the qualifications of the clergy—would not have appeared entirely passive.

58. Martin Brecht et al., *Der Pietismus im achtzehnten Jahrhundert*, vol. 2 of *Geschichte des Pietismus* (Göttingen, 1995), pp. 346–348.

59. Moser, *Letzte Stunden 31 Personen*, pp. 275, 277.

60. Bremmel's views as recorded by the narrator are obliquely stated, but she emphasized "daß wer also stürbe, nicht anders als selig werden müsse," which suggests that the condemned's behavior was particularly pious and likely expressed some sort of conversion or conversion-type experience. Moser, *Letzte Stunden 31 Personen*, p. 276.

61. The narrator leaves little doubt in the mind of the reader of the genuine nature of Bremmel's subsequent conversion and her steadfast faith even as her death at the hand of the executioner is imminent. Moser, *Letzte Stunden 31 Personen*, pp. 323–326.

62. Moser wrote: "Der Herr verhüte es, daß Niemand so blind, thorecht und verwegen seye, dise Exempel dahin zu mißbrauchen, daß er etwas worauf die Todes-Straffe gesetzet ist, zu dem Ende begehe, damit er auch so erbaulich sterben möge: Das stehet ja nicht weder in eines armen Sünders, noch auch in eines Predigers Macht, er seye auch so redlich und begabt, als er wolle." Moser, *Letzte Stunden 31 Personen*, pp. 27–28. Woltersdorff acknowledged that some had objected that such conversion narratives

could incite some to "wol gar zu Begehung grober Uebelthaten," but he dismissed them as ignorant of the contents of the narratives. Woltersdorff, *Schächer am Kreutz*, p. [*3r].

63. Steinbart, *Missethäter*, pp. 25–26. On Steinbart, including his early education in Pietist institutions, see Richard Hildenbrand, *Gotthilf Samuel Steinbart: Ein Beitrag zur Geschichte der Popularphilosophie im achtzehnten Jahrhundert* (Herne, 1906).

64. Martschukat's discussion of suicide by proxy within larger discourses on salvation of souls and juridical punishment is particularly relevant on this point, though he does not discuss published narratives such as these. Jürgen Martschukat, "Ein Freitod durch die Hand de Henkers. Erörterungen zum Komplementarität von Diskursen und Praktiken am Beispiel von 'Mord aus Lebens-Überdruß' und Todesstrafe im 18. Jahrhundert," *Zeitschrift für historische Forschung* 27 (2000): 53–74.

65. For Reitz, see above. Gottfried Arnold, *Das Leben Der Gläubigen Oder Beschreibung solcher Gottseligen Personen, welche in denen letzten 200. Jahren sonderlich bekandt worden* (Halle, 1701).

66. Fred van Lieburg, "Reformed Doctrine and Pietist Conversion: The Historical Interplay of Theology, Communication and Experience," in Jan N. Bremmer et al., *Paradigms, Poetics and Politics of Conversion* (Louvain, 2006), pp. 133–148.

67. On the way narratives at Cambuslang reflected Reformed theological principles, Hindmarsh, *Evangelical Conversion*, pp. 212–218; Methodists, in contrast, inculcated Arminian principles, pp. 242–247.

68. These narratives work in a very different direction from the radical Pietist biographies and autobiographies cited by von Mücke, which expressed indifference to official doctrine. Their portrayal of individual experience, she argued, signaled "impartiality and tolerance towards others who cannot be judged by external forms and doctrine, insofar as it also refuses sectarian camps." Von Mücke, "Experience, Impartiality, and Authenticity," p. 35.

CHAPTER NINE

Conversion and Sarcasm in the Autobiography of Johann Christian Edelmann

DOUGLAS H. SHANTZ

Johann Christian Edelmann (1698–1767) has been called "the most brilliant representative of the radical German Enlightenment in the eighteenth century."[1] His *Moses mit aufgedecktem Angesichte* (Moses with Uncovered Face) of 1740 immediately gained him infamy. There he promoted views associated with Spinoza and frankly denied Christian faith and dogma. "Never before," observes Emmanuel Hirsch, "had a book appeared in the German language such as Edelmann's Moses, that denied the entire biblical faith and Christian dogma from beginning to end, openly confessed Spinoza's teachings on God and the world, and recklessly questioned traditional Christian views on miracles, God's providence, and prayer."[2] In his 1746 *Confession of Faith*, Edelmann promoted freedom of thought in deciding all religious matters. By the time he began writing his autobiography in 1749, Edelmann was the most notorious German heretic of his day, his name synonymous with atheism, freethinking, and opposition to true religion. In his *Autobiography*, which was finished in 1752, he attacked traditional doctrines of the fall, evil, and Jesus as Messiah as well as his redemptive death for humankind. His *Autobiography* describes a conversion, but not one in the traditional sense of the term. Edelmann's book describes the religious foundations of his awakening to Enlightenment reason in such a way that his experiences were framed, as scholars like Günter Niggl suggest, in the style of Pietist conversion narratives.

During his lifetime, Edelmann was the focus of intense theological controversy, with over 160 pamphlets and books directed against him.[3] Persecuted by secular and church authorities alike, he was constantly on the road, seeking refuge in cities and villages throughout western and northern Germany. Fortunately, Edelmann was able to rely upon a network of disciples and supporters in Hamburg, Leipzig, Frankfurt, and Berlin that included poor peasants, wealthy merchants, and nobles.[4] During his Pietist phase, he found acceptance among Pietist separatists in Berleburg, Hachenburg, and Neuwied. In the early 1740s in Hachenburg he had such a flood of visitors during the day that he worked through the night and "went to bed when others were rising."[5] Toward the end of his life, Edelmann reflected on the widespread attention his writings received both within Germany and beyond: "The great stir that my writings have attracted," he wrote, "shows that my countrymen too are finally beginning to open their eyes and to grow tired of all the horrid books of sermons and catechisms."[6]

Among a host of early modern conversion accounts, Edelmann's autobiography is in a class of its own, offering valuable insight into "the making of a radical [Enlightenment] thinker."[7] Yet it has received comparatively little attention in modern scholarship. In one of the few discussions of the work, Günter Niggl pointed to a surprising feature of Edelmann's account. Niggl writes,

> With a tone of irony and sarcasm Edelmann seeks to justify his speaking and writing on behalf of free thought. It is noteworthy, however, that although he engages in sharp attacks upon the doctrine of new birth of the Pietists, his autobiography takes over the Pietist conversion formula (*das pietistische Bekehrungsschema*) in order to describe his intellectual progress, as Edelmann charts his way from Bible believer to the search for true Christianity, to realizing the divinity of reason, to the battle for true belief, to the "mighty breakthrough of a new birth."[8]

The present study seeks to test Niggl's claim. It examines Edelmann's autobiography in order to shed light on the following questions and issues: To what extent is his account of his journey to skepticism and rationalism marked by a sarcastic critique of Pietist Christianity joined with a Pietist conversion scheme? Why would Edelmann use such a paradoxical way of writing? These questions touch on important aspects of the relation between Pietism and Enlightenment in early modern Germany.

Edelmann's *Selbstbiographie*

The very act of writing an autobiography was a typically Pietist endeavor; the spiritual memoir or conversion story was widespread within the Pietist movement.[9] The purpose of these accounts was to acknowledge the leading hand of God in one's life and to provide encouragement to others in their own journey. Memoirs and conversion accounts became a routine part of self-examination and growth in holiness. By the end of the eighteenth century, autobiography was one of the most widely read literary forms.[10]

The circumstances in which Edelmann wrote his life story were unusual. He was spurred into writing an autobiography by an account of his life rendered by Johann Hinrich Pratje, superintendent of churches and schools in the Duchies of Bremen and Verden. Pratje's work appeared in Frankfurt in installments between 1749 and 1755.[11] Edelmann felt compelled to correct Pratje's unwelcome description of his life and to address a host of rumors that were circulating. "There must be as many untrue accounts of my life flying about the world as Gospels of our Lord Jesus,"[12] Edelmann surmised. Yet Edelmann's *Selbstbiographie* did not see the light of day until a century after he wrote it.[13] The tolerant Friedrich II had granted him permission to reside in Berlin, on the condition that he publish no more books. During Edelmann's eighteen years there from 1749 to 1767, he suffered in silence under Friedrich's publication ban.

The autobiography is structured as a point-by-point refutation of Pratje's account.[14] Edelmann began each chapter by citing a passage from Pratje's work and then critiqued and supplemented it. At one point Edelmann noted, "This passage [of Pratje's], just like the Bible, has an element of truth and an element of falsehood..."[15] He further pursued the analogy between Pratje and the Gospel writers:

> It seems that the spirit of the Evangelists has taken up residence in my author [Pratje]. They relate a mountain of things about the Lord Jesus that they cannot verify and that the Lord Jesus, were he still alive and could confront his inconsiderate biographers, would reveal to be bold-faced lies. It is the same with those writing about my life.[16]

The historical-critical method, then being used on the life of Jesus by early Enlightenment thinkers such as Spinoza, became the model for Edelmann's critique of his "Evangelist" Pratje.[17]

The *Selbstbiographie* has three parts that can be briefly summarized. Part I covers his birth in 1698, early family life in Weißenfels, student life in Jena, and encounters with a variety of sects up to 1736.[18] It includes accounts of Edelmann's meetings with some Mennonites, with some followers of the Protestant mystic Johann Georg Gichtel, and with the Herrnhuters and their leader Count Zinzendorf.[19] From this period stem the beginnings of his work, *Unschuldige Wahrheiten* (Innocent Truths, 1735–1743). Part II deals with Edelmann's experiences while working with Pietists in Berleburg between 1736 and 1741. He began reading Spinoza in 1740 and moved to a mystical, rationalist view of God and his immanence in the world. Under Spinoza's influence, Edelmann gained "a critical distance from the Bible," no longer viewing it as an infallible book.[20] Edelmann published *Moses mit aufgedecktem Angesichte* in 1740 and *Christus und Belial* (Christ and Belial) in 1741. In Part III Edelmann describes his time in Hachenburg from 1741 to 1744 and in Neuwied from 1744 to 1746.[21] In 1743 he published *Die Göttlichkeit der Vernunfft* (The Divinity of

Reason), a discussion of the meaning of *Logos* in the New Testament and the place of reason in Christianity.[22] The *Glaubens-Bekentniss* (Confession of Faith) appeared in Neuwied in 1746. The editor of Edelmann's autobiography, C.R.W. Klose, continued the story from Edelmann's departure from Neuwied in 1746 to his arrival in Berlin in 1749 up to his death in 1767.

Edelmann's Attack on Christianity

W.R. Ward referred to "the sparkling vocabulary of abuse" that Edelmann poured upon the German Christianity of his day.[23] From the very outset of Edelmann's autobiography, the reader is struck by the sarcasm and cutting remarks to which Niggl referred. In recounting his baptism, he wryly observed:

> I was baptized shortly after my birth, and the miserable old devil (with or without horns, I didn't know) was cast out of me using the customary formalities.... Whether he really heeded the command of the cleric I cannot be sure; it is sufficient that my dear parents believed firmly and without question that he had left. But I now know that he had never been in me, and that the whole comedy with which they still today seek to drive him out of innocent children is just a laughable game of deception.[24]

A mood of dark humor reigns over the work, reflecting Edelmann's melancholy as he sat in silent exile in Berlin. His account is not so much about setting the record straight as it is about venting his deeply cynical perspective on German Christianity, both Orthodox Protestant and Pietist. Edelmann's attacks focused respectively on Lutheran theologians and clergy, the Gospel writers and early Christian martyrs, key Christian dogmas, and separatist Pietist groups and leaders. These will be considered in Edelmann's order of treatment.

Looking back on his student days in Jena, Edelmann was bemused by his disciplined devotion to his studies and the esteem in which he held his theology professors. "I took everything my teachers said as if it were an oracle from God."[25] In retrospect, Edelmann realized that he would have done better to study languages such as English and Italian rather than waste his time on theological foolishness. He tried with limited success to master Hebrew grammar, laboring under the misguided notion that Hebrew was the language in which God had revealed himself. He had greater success with Greek and was soon able to read the New Testament and the Septuagint. But Edelmann considered this wasted time as well, observing that it was the least gifted students who seemed to do best in language study. He compared himself to the French healer who was gifted in curing people but had never mastered Latin. When a physician rebuked one of the man's patients for entrusting himself to someone who knew neither Greek nor Latin, the patient replied, "He cured me in French."

Edelman reflected: "I likewise have sought to cure my countrymen in German, because those who understand Greek and Hebrew offer no real help."[26] He dismissed theologians as a class and made it a point of pride that he wrote in German for Germans.

Edelmann was equally unimpressed with the clergy of the day and expressed his anger against "the tyrannical priestly class."[27] In Edelmann's experience, whenever he was forced to defend himself before the preachers, reason fell away and superstition reigned supreme. He described a Swiss poet who wrote: "It is in vain that reason discovers the errors of faith: for when the priest speaks, error becomes truth."[28] On the last page of his autobiography, Edelmann's disgust turns to anger as he compares the clergy to murderers and robbers. "Reason, understanding and sense perception are the properties that my Creator has entrusted to me for the provision of my happiness.... But before I could learn to use them properly, I fell among murderers who sought to rob me of these treasures completely."[29] So much for the clergy.

Edelmann was no more impressed by the early Gospel writers and Christian martyrs. The foundation of the Christian faith lay in the lies and deceptions of the Gospel accounts.[30] The Evangelists of old created their accounts of Jesus's life long after his death. How could one trust the writings of such simple and superstitious people?[31] Rather than seeing the martyrs as heroes and saints, Edelmann suggested they were in fact guilty of hating their own life and committing suicide.[32] This deeply cynical language was calculated to offend, and in this he succeeded admirably.

Edelmann found traditional Christian doctrines of sin and redemption to be offensive. He summed up the typical Protestant sermon with a line of verse: "When you look into your heart, There you find a veritable nest of sin."[33] He was disgusted by the many confessional differences within Christendom. Christ, he suggested, might have done better to remain on earth; maybe then he could have prevented the divisions from taking place.[34] Edelmann observed that Christians talked much of love, but in fact "there is no more hateful and hostile religion in the world than the Christian faith."[35] Christians felt justified in using the most extreme measures in dealing with the enemies of Christ, as was amply proven by Christian history as well as more recent events such as the Thirty Years' War and the Habsburg defeat of the Ottoman Turks in the 1680s and 1690s.

Finally, Edelmann wrote as bitterly against Pietist separatists as he did against Lutheran clergy and theologians. The behavior of the leader of the Pietist Inspirationists, J.F. Rock (1678–1749), reminded him of the Pope.[36] "I have found no sect," Edelmann observed,

> that raves more against reason than the sect of the Inspired....To be perfectly truthful, I must say that never in my life have I heard more miserable, distasteful, uninspired praying than among these inspired brethren.[37]

At one time he considered the Mennonites to be the best sect because they were among the smallest. He thought that the truth was not likely to be found among the larger groups. He naively hoped to settle the matter of infant baptism by studying the Bible, but that proved fruitless because "the Biblical writers are as opposed to each other as their interpreters."[38]

The sarcasm half of Niggl's equation is amply borne out by the evidence offered above. Edelmann was unsparing in the scorn he poured upon the various groups, leaders, and teachings among Christians in his day, including the Pietists. It now remains to consider Niggl's suggestion that there is a remnant of Pietism in the autobiography—specifically, that Edelmann used the Pietist conversion formula to describe his evolving life experience and intellectual progress.

Edelmann's Use of the Pietist Conversion Formula

It is necessary first to identify key features of the Pietist understanding of conversion. From the early 1730s to the mid 1750s, various Pietist communities developed highly schematized forms of conversion and a rich tradition of conversion accounts. These narratives typically focused on the penitential struggle or *Bußkampf*, a drawn-out process of gradually realizing one's failings and shortcomings and a subsequent breakthrough to grace—a dramatic turning point in which a new mind and self-understanding asserted itself.[39]

In 1690, the leader of the Halle Pietists, August Hermann Francke, wrote an account of his struggle with reason and pride and his breakthrough to assurance of faith. By the 1730s many Pietists regarded this account as a model of the Christian conversion experience. Like Edelmann, Francke found that years of theological study did not bring inner satisfaction or change of life. He reflected on his life prior to his spiritual awakening: "It was as if I had spent my whole life in a deep sleep, and had done everything in a dream."[40] During his time of searching, Francke described himself as "ensnared," "caught in deep mire," "bound hand and foot."[41] In his time of crisis he prayed that God would reveal himself.

> Then the Lord heard me, the living God, from his throne as I knelt.... For as someone might turn over their hand, so all my doubts vanished and I was assured in my heart of the grace of God in Christ Jesus. I could address God not only as God but as my Father. *In an instant all my sadness and unrest of heart were taken away, and I was suddenly overwhelmed as if by a stream of joy, so that I praised and magnified God with a full heart,* who had shown me such wonderful grace.... I stood up *with a completely different mind* than when I had knelt down. When I had got down on my knees, I did not believe that there was a God; when I got up I would, without any fear and doubt, have confirmed [it] with the spilling of my blood.[42]

Francke's account concludes with the words, "from this point on" ("von da an"), suggesting the key significance of this event in Francke's life.

Edelmann too went through a long period of wrestling and gradual awakening, culminating in a dramatic new self-understanding—a period that lasted from 1728 to about 1739. Edelmann reflected on the superstition and blindness in which he had been raised: "I will recount, out of my own experience, the troubled circumstances into which a poor soul can fall, who must ever keep before his mind a God prone to anger and a hell full of devils, into which He casts the poor sinner in his wrath."[43] He then described the "important and noteworthy changes" that he experienced on the way to his deliverance.[44]

When he was still a young man of thirty, says Edelmann, he thought that to be a good Lutheran meant to quarrel and engage in disputes on matters of belief.[45] He believed that Christendom was God's means of grace and would have given his life in defense of the infallibility of the Bible. He trembled whenever he heard mention of atheists, naturalists, deists, and freethinkers.[46] But he became increasingly restless. "The more eagerly I began to consider with my own eyes the content of my theological study, the less confident I became."[47] He sought the truth with his whole heart and entrusted himself to God and his grace.

Sometime in 1732 Edelmann obtained and read a copy of Gottfried Arnold's *Unparteyische Kirchen- und Ketzer-Historie* (Impartial History of Churches and Heretics, 1700). Arnold's work brought about a spiritual awakening in Edelmann, drawing him toward Arnold's Spiritualism and toward Pietism.[48]

> In this book I now found, to my great astonishment, so much indecent and irresponsible behavior among the clerical class, who prided themselves on presenting the proper understanding of Christian things, that I developed a great loathing for so-called Orthodoxy. I began to turn more and more to the side of the so-called Pietists because, although they had their failings, they seemed outwardly to do more to encourage a godly life than the Orthodox who emphasized faith but would hear nothing of good works.[49]

According to his recollection, at this point Edelmann was "three quarters Lutheran," but was more Pietist and "half-Separatist" than Orthodox.[50]

In 1734, while in Dresden, his turmoil increased. "I prayed, I fasted, I confessed, I took the sacrament," Edelmann recalled.

> In short, I did everything that one could ask of a true and strict church Christian. But with all these so-called means of grace my inner being remained unchanged.... Meanwhile it became my intention to become a real and honest Christian and so I sought out people who looked the way the first Christians would have looked.[51]

His all-consuming desire was to discover the truth, wherever it might lead him. After encountering Mennonites, Herrnhutters, and the true Inspiration, he finally realized that God's greatest gift to humanity was not religion but reason. Edelmann came to see "the divinity of reason" while in Berleburg in 1739–1740. He awoke one morning and heard the words of John's Gospel, chapter 1, "theos ēn ho logos," and the explanation of the words: "In the beginning was reason, and reason was with God, and reason was God." Reason was the true light that illumines every human being. "It is impossible," Edelmann continued, "for me to describe the strength and quickening that I derived from these ideas. It was as if I were called back from the gates of death to life again."[52]

Like Francke, he experienced a joy unlike anything he had experienced before: "The Lord had mercy upon me in such a joyous and uplifting way that I cannot recall ever in my life experiencing a more sweet pleasure in my inmost being than I had at that time."[53] He compared himself to a shackled slave who had lain captive in complete darkness but was finally granted freedom. In Edelmann's case this was an intellectual freedom: "Reason, which up till now I had not been permitted to heed, because of my ignorance, now had complete freedom to speak and set me all at once in a broad space."[54] Edelmann was now a free man—free to think and free to speak. He shared his new insight with his friends, and they too were encouraged by the truth concerning the light of reason. That day, said Edelmann, was the start of their new birth. "We could see the sunny disposition in each other's eyes. That day was for us nothing else than our birthday, but it was only the beginning of a powerful breakthrough of a new birth."[55] The words in John's Gospel concerning the divinity of reason delivered Edelmann from the Lutheran faith and superstition in which he had been raised.[56]

Edelmann's new birth contrasted starkly with the Pietist experience because of the way it exalted reason and diminished and ridiculed faith. Francke's conversion came through faith and study of Scripture and brought about a humbling of his reason. Francke wrote: "my reason stood as it were at a distance; the victory was snatched out of its hand for the power of God had made it subordinate to faith."[57] Here is the image of faith as victorious and reason as subservient. His conversion brought with it a new attitude toward academic life and scholarship. Francke now saw faith as a mustard seed that was "worth more than a hundred bushels of scholarship."[58] It is not surprising that his critics accused him of being anti-intellectual.[59] For Edelmann, on the other hand, reason triumphed over faith. Reason showed that the foundation of the Christian faith lay in the lies and deceptions of the Gospel accounts and that the Evangelists had created their accounts of Jesus's life long after his death.[60]

By 1740 Edelmann had become "a radical eclectic," teaching a unique syncretism of ideas and experiences that combined an Enlightenment exaltation of reason found in Spinoza, Neoplatonic ideas of the Logos, and a Pietist conviction of God's leading and providence.[61] He became a spokesman for the German Enlightenment, a prophet of reason, in the full confidence that he did so at God's bidding. Edelmann's discovery reflected a growing distance from his Pietist associates in Berleburg, resulting in his move to Hachenburg in 1741.[62]

> The more free and alone I stood in relation to all human company, the more happy and confident I was.... I would never have been able to attain the degree of understanding to which God has assisted me if I had continued in association with my brothers in Frankfurt and Berleburg. I would have rotted in the dark and would never have found those friends who contributed the most to my progress.[63]

Edelmann considered his falling out with the separatists in Frankfurt and Berleburg to be a necessary stage on his journey toward intellectual freedom.

Edelmann persisted in using the language of new birth and God's providence long after he had forsaken his Pietist connections. In Brandenburg, the king asked if he were one of those "born-again" people. Edelmann answered, "No. I have made a great leap beyond this [form of religion]." When the king asked if he attended church services and took the Lord's Supper, Edelmann answered: "I have my church within me. When I find Christians who are planted with Christ in his death, then I will be ready to join them in the Lord's Supper."[64] Yet, time and again, Edelmann used Pietist language in attributing his breakthrough and discovery to God's providential leading. "I abandoned myself to God who had so wonderfully led me," he wrote; and later, "I thank God from my heart ... that he had brought me securely to this point." He concluded the account of his time in Berleburg by thanking his Creator for his "miraculous, gracious, and loving guidance."[65] He expressed gratitude that, "in the matter of my increase in understanding, God dealt with me slowly and in stages."[66]

Edelmann saw evidence of God's care in the many friends who helped to support him with their generous gifts. One example was the provision of his travel expenses. He preferred to avoid traveling by postal-wagon because of the mockery he often encountered from fellow passengers, but travel by private coach was costly. A friend assured Edelmann that he need only let him know when he was setting out and he would cover the travel costs.[67] God also gave him a friend from Leipzig who was so delighted with Edelmann's writings that he promised to send him twenty thaler annually.[68] Another friend paid for publication of his *Moses* book.[69] God's providence was clear to him.

Edelmann's discovery and new birth included a sense of calling as a writer to make the "deficiencies in religion" as widely known as possible.

> I sought to investigate as carefully as I could the exact talent that had been given me. I could think of nothing for which I had more desire and inclination than making known through my writing, for the benefit of my neighbor, the great deficiency which I had discovered in Religion.[70]

Edelmann began writing the *Unschuldige Wahrheiten* in 1735 because he felt God had instructed him to do so.[71] Between 1738 and 1740 this calling intensified and "he wrote as one possessed."[72] He saw himself as a second Luther, not only in his experience of religious crisis and discovery but also in his prolific writing. When someone asked Edelmann why he wrote so much, Edelmann replied, "I learned this from our blessed father Luther."[73] His editor, Klose, mocked Edelmann for his delusions of grandeur: "We cannot ascribe to him the great significance that he attributed to himself, as the trailblazer of freedom.... He saw himself as a second Luther; indeed he saw comparisons with the Lord himself."[74] This sense of calling would have made the publication ban under which Edelmann suffered after 1749 all the more painful. Edelmann's calling also included confronting people such as J.F. Rock and the Inspirationists. On one occasion Edelmann traveled to Homburghausen to debate Rock, anticipating that it would be a battle between reason and faith.[75] At the conclusion of the gathering a hymn was sung that included the verse:

> Zion, test the spirits.
> As for the one who opposes you on both sides,
> Do not heed what he commands of you;
> Simply follow your own star.
> Zion, test what is crooked and evil,
> Test it, test it.[76]

Edelmann reflected, "It was as if these words were addressed to me from heaven, to strengthen me in my new beginning."[77]

He also rated his experiences among the disciples of Mme. Guyon and Mme. Bourignon, leading mystics of the day, as deficient. Their distinctive form of piety involved guiding people to a place of quiet within themselves so that they could hear the inner voice of God. But Edelmann found that he derived little benefit from an hour of silence: "I remained as empty of true contentment as I had been before." He came to see that it was wrong to model one's experience on that of others; one must allow God to act freely. "One sees," Edelmann argued, "that people do not change according to one model, for God must be allowed to act with a free hand. His ways with us are not always the same."[78] Over time Edelmann encountered dozens of forms of misguided "pious" self-denial and "holy foolishness."[79] God gradually showed him how indecent their zeal really was.

Edelmann measured every place, event, and experience by its contribution to his freedom of mind and will. He described, for example, how the pleasant region of the Wetterau lightened his spirits: "the further I ventured into it, the more I discovered of its natural and unforced beauty." In the imperial free city of Friedberg, wrote Edelmann, "I began to find something of the noble and inestimable treasure of freedom."[80] His experiences in the Wetterau stood in sharp contrast to Regensburg, Nürnberg, and "the sad and unfortunate land of Hessen." He judged the character of people he met by how much they demonstrated freedom of mind. The man whom Edelmann most admired in Berleburg was Dr. Cantz, court physician to Count Casimir. "He was a man who had seen the world and who possessed a solid education in many subjects, especially theology."[81] Cantz's broad experience impressed Edelmann. On the other hand were separatist preachers who proclaimed the fearful judgment of God upon those who did not heed their words: "Swabian heads" such as J.F. Rock were proudly anti-intellectual and opposed to reason.[82] Edelmann lamented that Jews and Christians put so much emphasis upon the "dead letters" of the Bible and gave so much trust to those who claimed to speak for God that they neglected the natural reason and goodness that God had placed within them.[83]

Edelmann came to understand that the highest worship of God came through the experience of his majesty in nature. He heard God speak "in the shadows of the forest, or in the meandering brook in a pleasant valley, and in the varied music of the birds."[84] During a journey by ship up the Main River from Offenbach, in the company of Andreas Groß and some separatist brothers and sisters from Frankfurt, Edelmann was moved to tears of joy. They enjoyed a warm summer's day out on the river with many other boats, drank some costly wine, had some coffee and *Vesper-Brodt*, and sang some songs. "This freedom pleased me to no end."[85] At one point as they drifted down the river they encountered another boat with a group of men and women enjoying each other's company while completely naked, with as little shame as Adam and Eve in their condition of innocence in the garden of Eden. Edelman was reminded of the "innocent and free life of the wild in America."[86]

Conclusion

Bernd Neumann insisted that Edelmann's *Selbstbiographie* bore not even the remotest resemblance to Pietist autobiographies of the day.[87] This chapter has argued that Neumann overstates his case and that Niggl is closer to the truth when he suggests that, despite sarcastic attacks on German Protestants and Pietists, Edelmann retained the Pietist conversion scheme in his account. In Edelmann, as with Francke, there was a period of wrestling and gradual awakening, culminating in a dramatic new self-understanding. The former Pietist retained the Pietist sense of God's leading and providence and retained the Pietist language of conversion, new birth, and deliverance in describing his discovery of rationalism and reason. He became a radical German Enlightenment spokesman, a kind of Enlightenment prophet, in the full confidence that he did so at God's bidding. This conviction accounts for Edelmann's paradoxical way of writing in the *Selbstbiographie*.

Under the guiding hand of God, Edelmann discovered the beauty of nature, reason, and freedom. He moved away from Lutheran superstition and separatist perfectionism toward a life marked by "freedom to think and to speak." According to Edelmann's new mindset, "Reason, understanding, and sense perception are the properties that my Creator has entrusted to me for the provision of my happiness."[88] Reason and the wisdom of experience replaced the Bible, Protestant tradition, and separatist preachers.

It is not surprising that remnants of Pietist discourse should persist in the Enlightenment thought and writing of Johann Christian Edelmann. A couple of factors that help to account for this are receiving growing attention in the historiography. One is that scholars now recognize in evangelical conversion discourse "an instrument of modernization."[89] They find the logic of modern subjectification in Pietism and Methodism and their stress upon feeling, emotion, and a living faith.[90] Second, recent scholarship has found that both Pietist and Enlightenment thinkers were attracted to alchemical notions of transformation and renewal.[91] This alchemic-hermetic tradition, rooted in German courts and princely patronage, represented a common background to Pietist conversion ideals and Enlightenment notions of progress and reform.[92] Edelmann's writing and experience reflect this lively intersection of traditions and ideals between German Pietism and Enlightenment in eighteenth-century Europe.[93]

Notes

1. Bernd Neumann, "Nachwort," *Johann Christian Edelmann Selbstbiographie* (Stuttgartt, 1976), p. 553.
2. Emmanuel Hirsch, *Geschichte der neueren evangelischen Theologie II* (Gütersloh, 1951), p. 413.
3. Walter Grossmann, "Johann Christian Edelmann's Idea of Jesus," *Harvard Theological Review* 60 (1967): 375–389, here p. 376.
4. "Edelmann's widespread circle of contacts covered much of Germany and included people of diverse classes and social standing." See Bernd Neumann, "Nachwort," pp. 489, 506, 508.
5. Johann Christian Edelmann, *Joh. Chr. Edelmann's Selbstbiographie, geschrieben 1752*, edited by Carl Rudolph Wilhelm Klose (Berlin, 1849; reprint Stuttgart, 1976), pp. 420–421.
6. "Daß aber meine Schriften in und außerhalb Deutschland so großes Aufsehen gemachet, zeiget wenigstens, daß meine Landsleute endlich auch einmal anfangen die Augen aufzuthun, und nachgrade des Eckelhaften Postillen-Krams, der Catechismen und Himmelswege müde zu werden beginnen"; Edelmann, *Selbstbiographie*, p. 10.
7. Grossmann, "Edelmann's Idea of Jesus," p. 378.
8. Günter Niggl, *Geschichte der deutschen Autobiographie im 18. Jahrhundert* (Stuttgart, 1977), pp. 12–13.
9. Martin H. Jung, *Frauen des Pietismus* (Gütersloh, 1998), pp. 61f. As Karl Weintraub observed, "Around the middle of the seventeenth century, writings that are clearly au-

tobiographies in intent and form appear in great numbers among English Puritans and sectarians and later among German Pietists." Weintraub, *The Value of the Individual: Self and Circumstance in Autobiography* (Chicago, 1978), p. 229. Autobiography was "a peculiarly seventeenth century phenomenon." See David Cornick, "Starting with Oneself: Spiritual Confessions," *The Expository Times* 101, no. 9 (June 1990): 259–263, here p. 259.

10. See Douglas H. Shantz, "The Harvest of Pietist Theology: F.C. Oetinger's Quest for Truth as Recounted in his *Selbstbiographie*," in Michel Desjardins and Harold Remus, eds., *Tradition and Formation: Claiming an Inheritance. Essays in Honour of Peter C. Erb* (Kitchener, 2008), pp. 121–134; and Richard van Dülmen, *Die Entdeckung des Individuums 1500–1800*, 2nd ed. (Frankfurt, 2002), pp. 85–87.

11. Edelmann, *Selbstbiographie*, p. 3. The final, complete version of Johann Hinrich Pratje's work was entitled *Historische Nachrichten von Joh. Chr. Edelmanns, eines berüchtigten Religionspötters, Leben, Schriften und Lehrbegrif, wie auch von den Schriften, die für und wider ihn geschrieben worden, gesamlet und mitgetheilet von Joh. Hinr. Pratje, General-Superintendens der Kirchen und Schulen in den Herzogthümern Bremen und Verden. Zwote verbesserte und sehr vermehrte Auflage* (Hamburg, 1755).

12. Edelmann, *Selbstbiographie*, pp. 1–2.

13. Composed between 1749 and 1753, the work was finally published in 1849 under the editorship of C.R.W. Klose. Edelmann's writings and publications were largely restricted to a twelve-year period between 1735 and 1747; Neumann, "Nachwort," p. 555.

14. Edelmann, *Selbstbiographie*, p. 5.

15. Edelmann, *Selbstbiographie*, p. 202.

16. Edelmann, *Selbstbiographie*, p. 204.

17. Neumann, "Nachwort," p. 557. Edelmann makes numerous references to Pratje as "my Evangelist"; see Edelmann, *Selbstbiographie*, pp. 204, 213, 394.

18. W.R. Ward noted that Jena was cheaper than Leipzig, and so attracted poorer students; W.R. Ward, "Johann Christian Edelmann: A Rebel's Pilgrimage," in Stuart Mews, ed., *Modern Religious Rebels* (London, 1993), p. 31 n. 5.

19. Edelmann, *Selbstbiographie*, pp. 141–155.

20. Scholars disagree on the degree of Edelmann's debt to Spinoza. Rüdiger Otto suggested that Edelmann's concept of God has Neoplatonic and vitalist elements that are foreign to Spinoza's philosophy. See Rüdiger Otto, "Johann Christian Edelmann's Criticism of the Bible and its Relation to Spinoza," in Wiep van Bunge and Wim Klever, eds., *Disguised and Overt Spinozism around 1700* (Leiden, 1996), pp. 171–190, here pp. 171f., 188.

21. Edelmann, *Selbstbiographie*, pp. 429, 439.

22. Walter Grossmann, *Johann Christian Edelmann: From Orthodoxy to Enlightenment* (The Hague and Paris, 1976), p. 200.

23. Ward, "Johann Christian Edelmann," pp. 30, 35 n. 95.

24. Edelmann, *Selbstbiographie*, p. 6.

25. Edelmann, *Selbstbiographie*, p. 35.

26. Edelmann, *Selbstbiographie*, p. 38.

27. Edelmann, *Selbstbiographie*, p. 210.

28. Edelmann, *Selbstbiographie*, p. 396.

29. Edelmann, *Selbstbiographie*, p. 437.

30. Edelmann, *Selbstbiographie*, p. 389.

31. Edelmann, *Selbstbiographie*, p. 213.
32. Edelmann, *Selbstbiographie*, p. 74.
33. Edelmann, *Selbstbiographie*, p. 215.
34. Edelmann, *Selbstbiographie*, p. 59.
35. Edelmann, *Selbstbiographie*, p. 133.
36. Edelmann, *Selbstbiographie*, p. 280.
37. Edelmann, *Selbstbiographie*, p. 259.
38. Edelmann, *Selbstbiographie*, pp. 127, 131f.
39. Jonathan Strom, "The Development of Conversion Narratives in Halle Pietism and Pietist Movements up to the early 1750s," paper given at the Third International Congress on Pietism Research in Halle, Germany, on 2 September 2009.
40. Markus Matthias, ed., *Lebensläufe August Hermann Franckes* (Leipzig, 1999), p. 29.
41. *Herrn M. August Hermann Franckens vormahls Diaconi zu Erffurt, und nach dem er daselbst höchst unrechtmäßigst dimittiret, zu Hall in Sachsen Churf. Brandenburg. Prof. Hebraeae Linguae, und in der Vorstadt Glaucha Pastoris Lebenslauff* (1691), in Matthias, *Lebensläufe August Hermann Franckes*, p. 23.
42. *Herrn M. August Hermann Franckens Lebenslauff*, p. 29. See Markus Matthias, "Bekehrung und Wiedergeburt," in Hartmut Lehmann, ed., *Glaubenswelt und Lebenswelten. Geschichte des Pietismus*, vol. 4 (Göttingen, 2004), p. 29.
43. Edelmann, *Selbstbiographie*, p. 109.
44. "...die Zeiten der wichtigen und merckwürdigen Veränderungen"; Edelmann, *Selbstbiographie*, p. 391.
45. Edelmann, *Selbstbiographie*, pp. 107, 126.
46. Edelmann, *Selbstbiographie*, p. 128.
47. Edelmann, *Selbstbiographie*, p. 130.
48. Annegret Schaper, *Ein langer Abschied vom Christentum: Johann Christian Edelmann (1698–1767) und die deutsche Frühaufklärung* (Marburg, 1996), pp. 105–106, 150.
49. Edelmann, *Selbstbiographie*, p. 131.
50. Edelmann, *Selbstbiographie*, p. 138.
51. Edelmann, *Selbstbiographie*, p. 139.
52. Edelmann, *Selbstbiographie*, pp. 273–274. Edelmann suggests that this was sometime in 1738 (p. 283). Annegret Schaper and others place it in 1739 or 1740; see Annegret Schaper, *Ein langer Abschied vom Christentum*, pp. 150–152.
53. Edelmann, *Selbstbiographie*, p. 273.
54. Edelmann, *Selbstbiographie*, p. 275.
55. "Wir konnten einander den heiteren Zustand unsers Gemüths an Augen ansehen, wir betrachteten diesen Tag nicht anders, als unsern Geburths-Tag, er war aber nur noch ein Anfang zu einen Kräftichen Durchbruch einer neuen Geburth"; Edelmann, *Selbstbiographie*, p. 276.
56. Edelmann, *Selbstbiographie*, p. 109. Edelmann could see God's wisdom in bringing him to freedom only after many long years. As a young man, his Lutheran faith had kept him from the foolishness that he might otherwise have fallen into. See also Edelmann, *Selbstbiographie*, p. 39.
57. *Herrn M. August Hermann Franckens Lebenslauff*, p. 30.
58. *Herrn M. August Hermann Franckens Lebenslauff*, p. 31.
59. *Gerichtliches Leipziger Protocoll in Sachen die so genandten Pietisten betreffend; samt. Hn. Christian Thomasii berühmten J.C. Rechtlichem Bedencken darüber; und zu Ende beygefügter Apologi oder Defensions-Schrifft Hr. M. Augusti Hermanni Franckens an Ihro*

Chur-Fürstl. Durchl. zu Sachsen; ... von einem vornehmen Freund communicirt und herauß gegebenen (1692).

60. Edelmann, Selbstbiographie, pp. 213, 389.

61. Jonathan Israel, Radical Enlightenment: Philosophy and the Making of Modernity 1650–1750 (Oxford, 2001), p. 660. On Edelmann's eclecticism, see also Schaper, Ein langer Abschied vom Christentum, pp. 156, 164.

62. The last meeting of the Inspirationsgemeinde that Edelmann attended in Berleburg was the Sunday after Easter, 1738; see Schaper, Ein langer Abschied vom Christentum, p. 159.

63. Edelmann, Selbstbiographie, p. 232.

64. Edelmann, Selbstbiographie, p. 328.

65. Edelmann, Selbstbiographie, pp. 377, 382, 385.

66. "...deßwegen hat Gott in dem Wachsthum meiner Erkänntniß sehr langsam und stufenweiß mit mir gehen müßen"; Edelmann, Selbstbiographie, p. 436.

67. Edelmann, Selbstbiographie, pp. 319, 411.

68. Edelmann, Selbstbiographie, p. 317. Schaper observes that Edelmann's main supporters were disciples of Johann Georg Gichtel; see her Ein langer Abschied vom Christentum, p. 163.

69. Edelmann, Selbstbiographie, p. 358.

70. Edelmann, Selbstbiographie, pp. 297–298.

71. Edelmann, Selbstbiographie, pp. 157–158.

72. Schaper, Ein langer Abschied vom Christentum, p. 160.

73. Edelmann, Selbstbiographie, p. 422.

74. See C.R.W. Klose's introduction to Edelmann, Selbstbiographie, p. xvii.

75. Edelmann, Selbstbiographie, p. 277.

76. Edelmann, Selbstbiographie, p. 281.

77. Edelmann, Selbstbiographie, p. 281.

78. "...daraus siehet man, daß man sich einem andern nicht nach modeln, sondern Gott seine freye Hand mit sich laßen muß. Denn seine Wege mit uns sind nicht einerley"; Edelmann, Selbstbiographie, p. 234.

79. Edelmann, Selbstbiographie, pp. 234f.

80. Edelmann, Selbstbiographie, pp. 219, 382.

81. Edelmann, Selbstbiographie, p. 242.

82. Edelmann, Selbstbiographie, pp. 275, 280.

83. Edelmann, Selbstbiographie, pp. 250f.

84. Edelmann, Selbstbiographie, p. 300.

85. Edelmann, Selbstbiographie, p. 224.

86. Edelmann, Selbstbiographie, p. 223.

87. Bernd Neumann, "Nachwort," p. 556.

88. Edelmann, Selbstbiographie, p. 437.

89. Bret E. Carroll, Review of Rodger M. Payne, The Self and the Sacred: Conversion and Autobiography in Early American Protestantism (1998) in Church History 69 (2000): 213–214.

90. Charles Taylor, A Secular Age (Cambridge, 2007), pp. 77, 300, 488; and Albrecht Beutel, Kirchengeschichte im Zeitalter der Aufklärung. Ein Kompendium (Göttingen, 2009).

91. See W.R. Ward, Early Evangelicalism: A Global Intellectual History, 1670–1789 (Cambridge, 2006); Anne-Charlott Trepp, "Hermetismus oder zur Pluralisierung von Religiositäts- und Wissensformen in der Frühen Neuzeit: Einleitende Bemerkungen,"

in Anne-Charlott Trepp and Hartmut Lehmann, eds., *Antike Weisheit und kulturelle Praxis: Hermetismus in der Frühen Neuzeit* (Göttingen, 2001), p. 11; and Christopher McIntosh, *The Rose Cross and the Age of Reason: Eighteenth-Century Rosicrucianism in Central Europe and Its Relationship to the Enlightenment* (Leiden, 1992).

92. Tara Nummedal, *Alchemy and Authority in the Holy Roman Empire* (Chicago, 2007).

93. Hermann Stockinger, *Die hermetisch-esoterische Tradition unter besonderer Berücksichtigung der Einflüsse auf das Denken Johann Christian Edelmanns (1698–1767)* (Zürich, 2004).

Afterword

JARED POLEY

In 1897 Max Weber had a fight with his father that appeared to precipitate the older man's death some seven weeks later, which led in turn to a nervous breakdown on the part of the son. The collapse left Weber "so utterly exhausted that his back and arms failed him when he tried to trim the Christmas tree," and he was unable to work for the next five years.[1] Only after he was able to produce "three major essays in different fields as well as an important lecture" did it seem as if a major change had occurred, and by 1904 the crisis appeared to have passed. In her biography of her husband, Marianne Weber reports that the "dark pressure that had been weighing upon Weber during the previous year gradually lifted. From time to time a sky became visible through the shifting clouds in which the star of the productive man shone again."[2] This period of darkness in Max Weber's life, punctuated at the end by a time of light and of intense creativity and productivity, recalls the conversion narratives that have often appeared in the Western canon: Augustine's envelopment in a loving God, Paul's blinding vision on the road to Damascus, Luther's night of terror while caught in the lightning storm on the road from Erfurt, or his time of darkness and light in the tower.

Max Weber experienced a transformation from sickness to health that found resolution most obviously in the essays that were finally published as *The Protestant Ethic and the Spirit of Capitalism*. This study of the religious history of early modern Europe examined the social and economic implications of what Weber called the "emotional act of conversion," and it is a tantalizing indication of the degree to which the transformations discussed in this volume continued to play out in German minds centuries later.[3] The essays in the current volume demonstrate that early twentieth-century Germans' fascination with understanding the links between religion, cognition, and emotion was preceded by an early modern interest in determining how religion inflected action.[4] Max Weber's famous investigation of the religious history of early modern Europe, and the robust transformations of selfhood that were entangled in the culture wars of that time, indicates the continuing strength of those problems in the modern period.

David M. Luebke argues in the introduction to this volume that what he calls the "circle of conversion" was complete by time of the Enlightenment and that confessional identity and popular religiosity had been unified in powerful ways. These nine essays, which cover the long period from the sixteenth to the eighteenth century, provide evidence for that argument. Together, the essays achieve something remarkable: an intense exploration of the ways that religious conversions created a set of problems and opportunities for secular authorities in the early modern period. The vitality of these debates from early modern Germany recall the argument that has informed so much of gender studies and feminist scholarship: the "personal is the political." The claim is also appropriate to the history of religion and of religious change in early modern Germany, and these essays raise a general point that continues to produce interesting analysis: the early modern debates about what to believe and how to practice religion presage a nineteenth-century critique—still deeply embedded in religious traditions—of religion per se. When the personal is political, the political also becomes personal.

The most significant impact of the Reformation's invention of confessions within a single religious tradition was to reify the points of theological difference, reducing complex questions into a range of practices simple enough that non-elites could assimilate them. Previous approaches to the religious history of early modern Germany are challenged in these essays, not only by the critique of statism inherent in many of the contributions but also in descriptions of the syncretic, pluralistic, or irenic practices that even in failure provided an experimental background to the ethos of toleration that informed Enlightened or Romantic thinkers in later periods. Because these essays reveal the ways that conversion was as much personal as it was political, we see better how even the intensely interior demands of Luther and Calvin were always situated in social and political contexts that were about more than just confessionalization. As Luebke reminds us in the introduction: conversion narratives and practices were "inescapably bound up with the formation of confessional blocs."

The early modern German debates about how to negotiate between the secular and the religious, the local and the global, and the confessional and the plural demonstrate that early modern Germans did not just envision the world in terms of truth or doubt, error or certainty, sin or grace, but also took on shaded meanings of difference and sameness, division and unification. Religion and religious change involved questions about state power, the status of society, and the limits of individual autonomy. Conversion was entrenched in the larger dynamic of understanding and enacting the differences between inter- and intrareligious change, and the modes of conversion discussed in this volume allow us to evaluate more carefully the contours of religious change between 1500 and 1800. The "calling" to God, the "turning" of the believer's heart in a different direction, and the "intensification" of his or her religious feeling indicate that Germans both made and manifested historical change.

An unarticulated but ever-present theoretical perspective informs these essays: conversion is implicated—almost in psychological ways—in the larger production of a historically aware self. Many of these authors ask us to imagine conversion as a framework within which a person highlights the importance of change. In other words, the conversion narrative is a discursive mode used to excuse or legitimize past actions or selfhoods as erroneous. The speaker posits differences between error and truth, past and present, and this dynamic highlights again the essentially political nature of conversion narratives in early modern Germany. Conversion narratives are notable for their essential didacticism. These tales are told for a reason. What lessons about the past were encoded in conversion narratives? Which utopias existed at their center? Max Weber, of course, found no utopia in early modern religious history but located instead the historical embryo of the hatefully spiritless emotional "nullity" within which he existed.[5] Yet the fact remains that the conversion experience— so central to early modern theology, civic relations, political interactions, kinship structures, spatial and territorial concepts—also had a determining effect on the imaginations and metaphorical strategies of nonbelievers, indicating the centrality of religious change to the larger culture of early modern and modern Germany alike.

These essays, which employ historical methods as wide-ranging as intellectual, social, cultural, political, and "new world" history, speak to the exciting openness of the questions at hand. The multidisciplinary nature of conversion as a field of study and the range of methods and approaches on display in this volume reflect the vibrancy of German studies as a whole. Never just a tired reaffirmation of national borders, German studies pulls from an interdisciplinary model that unites scholars from multiple disciplines and locations. The particular researchers in this volume, who come from different disciplinary backgrounds as well as from different continents, have produced nine fresh stories about the meaning and practice of conversion in early modern Germany. The richness of the topic and the fascinating analyses offered by these scholars offer not just insight into the historical nature of conversion but also access to a range of meaningful human practices during a time of swift and intensely felt change.

Notes

1. Marianne Weber, *Max Weber: A Biography*, translated by Harry Zohn (New Brunswick, 1988), p. 237.

2. Weber, *Max Weber*, p. 279.

3. Max Weber, *The Protestant Ethic and the Spirit of Capitalism* (London, 2001), p. 89.

4. Max Weber was but one intellectual among many who developed an interest in religion in this period; Georg Simmel ("Zur Soziologie der Religion," 1898) and Sigmund Freud (e.g., *Totem and Taboo, Moses and Monotheism, The Future of an Illusion*) developed their own ideas on the matter. In a larger European context, Émile Durkheim (*Elementary Forms of Religious Life*, 1912) and Marcel Mauss ("Essai sur la Nature et la Fonction du Sacrifice," 1898; "Essai sur le don," 1923) produced novel interpretations of religion around the same time.

5. Weber, *The Protestant Ethic and the Spirit of Capitalism*, p. 124.

~: BIBLIOGRAPHY :~

Adair, E.R. *The Exterritoriality of Ambassadors in the Sixteenth and Seventeenth Centuries*. London, New York, and Toronto, 1929.

Ågren, K. "The Reduktion." In *Sweden's Age of Greatness, 1632–1718*, edited by Michael Roberts, 237–264. London, 1973.

Åkerman, Susanna. *Queen Christina of Sweden and Her Circle: The Transformation of a Seventeenth Century Philosophical Libertine*. Leiden, 1991.

Aland, Kurt. *Kirchengeschichtliche Entwürfe*. Gütersloh, 1960.

Albrecht, Ruth, et al., eds., *Glaube und Geschlecht. Fromme Frauen – spirituelle Erfahrungen – Religiöse Traditionen*. Cologne, 2008.

Allerunterthänigste Repraesentatio Gravaminum Religionis der Römisch- Catholischen im Herzogthumb Cleve, Auch Graffschafft Marck und Ravensberg, Cum Justificationibus, Erstattet Von Ihro Churfürstl. Durchl. zu Pfaltz, Jülich- und Bergischer Regierung. Düsseldorf, 1723.

Allerunterthänigstes Vorstellungs-Schreiben, Welches an Ihre Käyserliche Majestät, Auf Dero über die Religions-Gravamina der Augspurgischen Confessions-Verwandten den 12. Aprilis 1720. erfolgte Commissions-Decret Das Corpus Evangelicorum unterm 16. Novembr. erstbesagten Jahrs allergehorsamst abgelassen. N.p., 1721.

Ammon, Friedrich Wilhelm von, ed. *Gallerie der denkwürdigsten Personen, welche im XVI., XVII. und XVIII. Jahrhunderte von der evangelischen zur katholischen Kirche übergetreten sind*. Erlangen, 1833.

Anderson, Alison D. *On the Verge of War: International Relations and the Jülich-Kleve Succession Crises (1609–1614)*. Boston, 1999.

Anderson, Dana. *Identity's Strategy: Rhetorical Selves in Conversion*. Columbia, 2007.

Anjou, Lars Anton. *Svenska Kyrkans Historia ifrån Upsala Möte år 1593 till Slutet af Sjuttonde Århundradet*. Stockholm, 1866.

Arnade, Peter. *Beggars, Iconoclasts, and Civic Patriots: The Political Culture of the Dutch Revolt*. Ithaca, 2008.

Arnold, Gottfried. *Das Leben Der Gläubigen Oder Beschreibung solcher Gottseligen Personen, welche in denen letzten 200. Jahren sonderlich bekandt worden*. Halle, 1701.

Asch, Ronald G. *The Thirty Years War: The Holy Roman Empire and Europe, 1618–1648*. New York, 1997.

Asselt, Willem van. *The Federal Theology of Johannes Coccejus (1603–1699)*. Leiden, 2001.

Avis, Paul. *Anglicanism and the Christian Church: Theological Resources in Historical Perspective*. Edinburgh, 2002.

Bambauer, Klaus and Hermann Kleinholz, eds. *Geusen und Spanier am Niederrhein: Die Ereignisse der Jahre 1580–1632 nach den zeitgenössichen Chroniken der Weseler Bürger Arnold von Anrath und Heinrich von Weseken*. Wesel, 1992.

Baumgarten, Jens. *Konfession, Bild und Macht: Visualisierung als katholisches Herrschafts- und Disziplinierungskonzept in Rom und im habsburgischen Schlesien (1560—1740)*. Hamburg, 2004.

Becke, Ioannes Carolus von der. *Dissertatio Inauguralis de Die Decretorio Pace Westphalia Posito Maxime ad Paragraphos XXV. et XXVI. Art. V. Instrumenti Osnabrugensis....* Göttingen, 1776.

Becker-Cantarino, Barbara, ed. *The Life of Lady Johanna Eleonora Petersen, Written by Herself: Pietism and Women's Autobiography in Seventeenth-Century Germany.* Chicago, 2005.

Bekehrung und herrliches Ende Christian Friedrich Ritters, eines ehemaligen zweyfachen Mörders, der am 18. Sept. 1738 zu Dargun in Mecklenburg gerädert worden. Magdeburg, 1739.

Bekehrung und seliges Ende eines eilfjährigen Kindes, August Ernst Friederich Zachariä. Stettin, [1747].

Benton, John F., ed. *Self and Society in Medieval France: The Memoirs of Abbot Guibert of Nogent.* Toronto, 1984.

Berger, Peter L. and Thomas Luckmann. "Secularization and Pluralism." *International Yearbook for the Sociology of Religion* 2 (1966): 73–86.

Beutel, Albrecht. *Kirchengeschichte im Zeitalter der Aufklärung. Ein Kompendium.* Göttingen, 2009.

Beyer. "König Friedrich Wilhelm I. und der katholischen Pfarrer Pater Bruns: Auszug aus dem lateinischen geschriebenen Manuscripte des Dominikanerpaters Raymund Bruns." *Mittheilungen des Vereins für die Geschichte Potsdams* 6 (1864): 1–8.

Bierther, Kathrin, ed. "Die Politik Maximilians von Bayern und seiner Verbündeten 1618–1651." In *Der Prager Frieden von 1635,* vol. 10, part 2. Munich and Vienna, 1997.

Bischofberger, Otto, et al. "Bekehrung Konversion." In *Religion in Geschichte und Gegenwart,* edited by Hans Dieter Betz et al., vol. 1, 1228–1241. Tübingen, 1998.

Bock, Heike. *Konversionen in der frühneuzeitlichen Eidgenossenschaft. Zürich und Luzern im konfessionellen Vergleich.* Epfendorf, 2009.

Bodler, Johann. *Fest- und Feyr-täglicher Predigen CURS Als in einem Wett-Rennen zu dem Ring der glückseeligen Ewigkeit.* Dillingen, 1683.

Bogner, Arthur, ed. *Weltmission und religiöse Organisationen. Protestantische Missionsgesellschaften im 19. und 20. Jahrhundert.* Würzburg, 2004.

Böhm, Laetitia. "Konversion. Einige historische Aspekte aus der christlichen Frömmigkeitsgeschichte mit Beispielen von Professoren der alten Universität Ingolstadt." In *Die Weite des Mysteriums: Christliche Identität im Dialog,* edited by Klaus Krämer und Ansgar Paus, 522–548. Freiburg, 2000.

Bölitz, Johannes. *Die evangelischen Pfarrer Wesels.* Wesel, 1978.

Booma, J.G.J. van, and J.L. van der Gouw, eds. *Communio et Mater Fidelium: Acta des Konsistoriums der niederländischen reformirten Flüchlingsgemeinde in Wesel, 1573–1582.* Cologne, 1991.

Böttigheimer, Christoph. *Zwischen Polemik und Irenik. Die Theologie der einen Kirche bei Georg Calixt.* Münster, 1995.

Brady, Thomas A., Jr. "Confessionalization: The Career of a Concept." In *Confessionalization in Europe, 1555–1700: Essays in Honor and Memory of Bodo Nischan,* edited by John M. Headley, Hans J. Hillerbrand, and Anthony J. Papalas, 1–20. Aldershot, 2004.

———. *Zwischen Gott und Mammon: Protestantische Politik und deutsche Reformation.* Berlin, 1996.

———. *Turning Swiss: Cities and Empire, 1450–1550.* Cambridge, 1985.

Brecht, Martin, et al. *Der Pietismus im achtzehnten Jahrhundert.* Vol. 2, *Geschichte des Pietismus.* Göttingen, 1995.

Bremmer, Jan N., Wout Jac. van Bekkum, and Arie L. Molendijk, eds. *Cultures of Conversions*. Louvain, 2006.

———, eds. *Paradigms, Poetics and Politics of Conversion*. Louvain, 2006.

Breuer, Dieter. "Konversionen im konfessionellen Zeitalter." In *Konversionen im Mittelalter und in der Frühneuzeit*, edited by Friedrich Niewöhner and Fidel Rädle, 59–69. Hildesheim, 1999.

Bruce, Steve. "Sociology of Conversion: The Last Twenty-Five Years." In *Paradigms, Poetics and Politics of Conversion*, edited by Jan N. Bremmer, Wout Jac. van Bekkum, and Arie L. Molendijk, 1–12. Louvain, 2006.

Brunner, Daniel L. *Halle Pietists in England: Anthony William Boehm and the Society for Promoting Christian Knowledge*. Göttingen, 1993.

Buckser, Andrew and Stephen D. Glazier, eds. *The Anthropology of Religious Conversion*. Lanham, MD, 2003.

Burns, J.H. "The Idea of Absolutism." In *Absolutism in Seventeenth-Century Europe*, edited by John Miller, 21–42. Basingstoke, 1990.

Caldwell, Patricia. *The Puritan Conversion Narrative: The Beginnings of American Expression*. Cambridge, 1983.

Calvin, John. *Institutiones Christianae Religionis*, ed. by John T. McNeill, transl. by Ford Lewis Battles, 2 vols. Philadelphia, 1960. Reprint, Louisville, 2006.

Carpenter, Edward. *Thomas Tenison, Archbishop of Canterbury: His Life and Times*. London, 1948.

Carroll, Bret E. Review of Rodger M. Payne, *The Self and the Sacred: Conversion and Autobiography in Early American Protestantism* (1998). *Church History* 69 (2000): 213–214.

Carsten, F.L. *Princes and Parliaments in Germany: From the Fifteenth to the Eighteenth Century*. Oxford, 1959.

Christian Fratelli Unpartheyisches Liebes-Schreiben An einen guten Freund Wegen Veringung Derer beyden Protestirenden Religionen. Nemlich, der Evangelisch-Lutherischen und Evangelisch-Reformirten. Regensburg, 1725.

Christophilus, Johannes [Friedrich Kind]. *Höchstnöthige Warnung, Für der recht Socinianischen…Übersetzung…Des XLV. Psalms Davids, Durch einen Studiosum zu Helmstädt*. Wittenberg and Leipzig, 1708.

Claydon, Tony. *Europe and the Making of England 1660–1760*. Cambridge, 2007.

Cnattingius, Hans. *Bishops and Societies: A Study in Anglican Colonial and Missionary Expansion, 1698–1850*. London, 1952.

Cohn, Henry J. "The Territorial Princes in Germany's Second Reformation, 1559–1622." In *International Calvinism, 1541–1715*, edited by Menna Prestwich, 135–166. Oxford, 1985.

Colberg, Ehregott Daniel. *Das platonisch-hermetisches* [sic] *Christenthum: begreiffend die historische Erzehlung vom Ursprung und vielerley Secten der heutigen fanatischen Theologie*. Erfurt, 1690.

Comaroff, Jean and John Comaroff. *Of Revelation and Revolution: Christianity, Colonialism and Consciousness in South Africa*, vol. 1. Chicago, 1991.

Contzen, Adam *Politicorum Libri Decem, in quibus De Perfectae Reipubl. Forma, Virtutibus, Et Vitiis….* 2nd ed. Cologne, 1629.

Cooper, Thompson and William Gibson. "Snape, Andrew (1675–1742)." *Oxford Dictionary of National Biography* 51 (2004): 478–479.

Cornick, David. "Starting with Oneself: Spiritual Confessions." *Expository Times* 101, no. 9 (June 1990): 259–263.

Corpis, Duane J. "Mapping the Boundaries of Confession: Space and Urban Religious Life in the Diocese of Augsburg, 1648–1750." In *Sacred Space in Early Modern Europe,* edited by Will Coster and Andrew Spicer, 302–325. Cambridge, 2005.

Cosmann, Peggy. *Zur Geschichte des Subjektivitätsbegriffs im 19. Jahrhundert.* Würzburg, 1999.

Coster, François de. *Enchiridon Controversiarum.* Cologne, 1595.

Cothenius, Daniel. *Disputatio Catech. XVIII. De Poenitentia seu Conversione Hominis peccatoris ad Deum, ejusque partibus … Sub praesidio.…* Wittenberg, 1602.

Coy, Jason Philip, Benjamin Marschke, and David Warren Sabean, eds. *The Holy Roman Empire, Reconsidered.* New York, 2010.

Cruickshanks, Eveline. "Religion and Royal Succession: The Rage of Party." In *Britain in the First Age of Party 1680–1750: Essays presented to Geoffrey Holmes,* edited by Clyve Jones, 19–43. London, 1987.

Daniel, Ute. *Compendium Kulturgeschichte. Theorien, Praxis, Schlüsselwörter.* Frankfurt, 2001.

Davis, Natalie Zemon. *Society and Culture in Early Modern France.* Stanford, 1975.

Delicatissimum solomoneum epithalamium.… N.p., 1706.

Delius, Walter. "Berliner kirchliche Unionsversuche im 17. und 18. Jahrhundert." *Jahrbuch für Berlin-Brandenburgische Kirchengeschichte* 45 (1970): 7–121.

Deppermann, Klaus. *Der hallesche Pietismus und der preußische Staat unter Friedrich III. (I.).* Göttingen, 1961.

Deventer, Jörg. "Zu Rom übergehen. Konversion als Entscheidungshandeln und Handlungsstrategie. Ein Versuch." In *Staatsmacht und Seelenheil. Gegenreformation und Geheimprotestantismus in der Habsburgermonarchie,* edited by Rudolf Leeb, Susanne Claudine Pils, and Thomas Winkelbauer, 168–180. Vienna, 2007.

Dickmann, Fritz. *Der Westfälische Frieden,* 7th ed. Münster, 1998.

———. *Friedensrecht und Friedenssicherung: Studien zum Friedensproblem in der neueren Geschichte.* Göttingen, 1971.

Dietrich, Richard, ed. *Die politische Testamente der Hohenzollern.* Cologne and Vienna, 1986.

Dietz, Burkhard and Stefan Ehrenpreis, eds. *Drei Konfessionen in einer Region: Beiträge zur Geschichte der Konfessionalisierung im Herzogtum Berg von 16. bis zum 18. Jahrhundert.* Cologne, 1999.

Dingel, Irene. *Concordia controversa. Die öffentlichen Diskussionen um das lutherische Konkordienwerk am Ende des 16. Jahrhunderts.* Gütersloh, 1996.

Dippold, Günter. *Konfessionalisierung am Obermain: Reformation und Gegenreformation in den Pfarrsprengeln von Baunach bis Marktgraitz.* Staffelstein, 1996.

Dithmarus, Iustus Christopherus. "Dissertatio de Anno Decretorio Exercitii Utriusque Religionis in Germania." In *Dissertationum Academicarum atque Exercitationum Varii ex Iure Publico, Naturali et Historia Desumti Argumenti,* edited by Iustus Christopherus Dithmarus. Leipzig, 1737.

Dixon, C. Scott, Dagmar Freist, and Mark Greengrass, eds. *Living with Religious Diversity in Early-Modern Europe.* Farnham, 2009.

Doble, C.E., ed. "Letters of the Rev. William Ayerst, 1706–1721 (Continued)." *English Historical Review* 4, no. 13 (1889): 131–143.

Dohna, Lothar Graf zu. "Alexander Burggraf und Graf zu Dohna-Schlobitten." In *Neue Deutsche Biographie,* vol. 4, 52–53. Berlin, 1971.

———. "Christoph Delphicus zu Dohna." In *Neue Deutsche Biographie*, vol. 4, 48–49. Berlin, 1971.

Dooren, J.P. van. "Der Weseler Konvent 1568. Neue Forschungsergebnisse." *Monatshefte für Evangelische Kirchengeschichte des Rheinlandes* 31 (1982): 41–55.

Dreyer, Frederick A. *The Genesis of Methodism*. Bethlehem, 1999.

Duchhardt, Heinz and Gerhard May, eds. *Union – Konversion – Toleranz. Dimensionen der Annäherung zwischen den christlichen Konfessionen im 17. und 18. Jahrhundert*. Mainz, 2000.

Dünnwald, Achim. *Konfessionsstreit und Verfassungskonflikt: Die Aufnahme der Niederländischen Flüchtlinge im Herzogtum Kleve 1566–1585*. Bielefeld, 1998.

Eaton, Richard. "Comparative History as World History: Religious Conversion in Modern India." *Journal of World History* 8, no. 2 (1997): 243–271.

Edelmann, Johann Christian. *Joh. Chr. Edelmann's Selbstbiographie, geschrieben 1752*, edited by Carl Rudolph Wilhelm Klose. Berlin, 1849. Reprint, Stuttgart, 1976.

Edzardi, Sebastian. *Vindiciae adversus Jo. Fabricii Theologi Helmstadiensis defensionem*. N.p., 1707.

Ehrenpfort, Henning Christoph. *Eine Predigt Von der Heil. Tauffe*. Alten-Stettin, 1735.

Ehrenpreis, Stefan. *'Wir sind mit blutigen Köpfen davongelaufen…': Lokale Konfessionskonflikte im Herzogtum Berg 1550–1700*. Bochum, 1993.

Ehrenpreis, Stefan and Ute Lotz-Heumann. *Reformation und konfessionelles Zeitalter*. Darmstadt, 2002.

Ehrenpreis, Stefan and Bernhard Ruthmann. "Jus reformandi, jus emigrandi. Reichsrecht, Konfession und Ehre in Religionsstreitigkeiten des späten 16. Jahrhunderts." In *Individualisierung, Rationalisierung, Säkularisierung. Neue Wege der Religionsgeschichte*, edited by Michael Weinzierl, 67–95. Vienna, 1997.

Eichfeld, Johannes Fridericus. *De Ordine Modoque Gratiae Divinae in Conversione Hominis Occupatae Aphorismi Theologici … Praeside Johanne Fechtio*. Rostock, n.d.

Eire, Carlos. *War against the Idols: The Reformation of Worship from Erasmus to Calvin*. Cambridge, 1986.

Eisenkopf, Paul. *Leibniz und die Einigung der Christenheit. Überlegungen zur Reunion der evangelischen und katholischen Kirche*. Munich, 1975.

Elliott, J.H. "Power and Propaganda in the Spain of Philip IV." In *Rites of Power: Symbolism, Ritual, and Politics since the Middle Ages*, edited by Sean Wilentz, 145–173. Philadelphia, 1985.

Englische Liturgie, Oder, Das allgemeine Gebeth-Buch… Frankfurt an der Oder, 1704.

Ernst, Albrecht. *Die reformierte Kirche der Kurpfalz nach dem Dreißigjährigen Krieg (1649–1685)*. Stuttgart, 1996.

Erstenberger, Andreas [Franciscus Burghardt]. *De Avtonomia, Das ist, von Freystellung mehrerlay Religion vnd Glauben: Was vnd wie mancherlay die sey, was derhalben biß daher im Reich Teutscher Nation fürgangen, Vnnd ob dieselb von der Christenlichen Obrigkeit möge bewilliget vnnd gestattet werden*, vol. 3. Munich, 1586.

Evangelischer Wanders-Mann, Aufzeichnend, Was Recht-glaubige Wanders-Leuth Auß der Irr-Glaubigen Predigen zu lehrnen haben, so wol zu Hauß, als draus, Lutherisch- als Catholischen, zu sichern Nachricht nutzlich und lustig zu gebrauchen. Augsburg, 1692.

Every, George. *The High Church Party, 1688–1718*. London, 1956.

Ewichius, Hermannus. *Vesalia, Sive Civitatis Vesaliensis Descriptio. Wesel: Oder Beschreibung der Stadt Wesel*. 1668. Reprint, Wesel, 1979.

Fabricius, Johann. *Ioannis Fabricii…ad…A. S. doctorem Anglicanvm epistola qva falsas relationes et impvtationes a se depellit.* N.p., 1708.

———. *Epistola Ad Pios Et Ervditos Britannos: Qua Famam suam contra falsas & ininquas relationes tuetur.* Helmstedt, 1708.

———. *Send–Schreiben an einen guten Freund über die so genannte reiffere Erörterung Hr. Johann Warnefrieds.* Helmstedt, 1707.

———. *Erörterte Frage, Herrn Fabricii…Daß zwischen der Augspurgischen Confession und Catholischen Religion kein sonderlicher Unterscheid seye….* N.p., 1706.

Feustking, Johann Heinrich. *Gynaeceum haeretico fanaticum oder Historie und Beschreibung der falschen Prophetinnen, Quäkerinnen, Schwärmerinnen und andern sectirischen und begeisterten Weibes-Personen.* Frankfurt and Leipzig, 1704.

Flemming, Willi. "Anton Ulrich, Herzog von Braunschweig-Wolfenbüttel, Dichter." *Neue deutsche Biographie* 1 (1953): 315–316.

Flüchter, Antje. "Konfessionalisierung in kulturalistischer Perspektive? Überlegungen am Beispiel der Herzogtümer Jülich-Berg." In *Was heißt Kulturgeschichte des Politischen?* edited by Barbara Stollberg-Rilinger, 225–252. Berlin, 2005.

Förster, Friedrich Christoph. *Friedrich Wilhelm I., König von Preußen.* 3 vols. Potsdam, 1834–1835.

Forster, Marc R. *The Counter-Reformation in the Villages: Religion and Reform in the Bishopric of Speyer, 1560–1720.* Ithaca, 1992.

Fortsetzung des Abdrucks einiger Acten-Stücke, die von Ihro, des regierenden Herrn Marggrafen zu Brandenburg-Onolzbach Hoch-Fürstl. Durchl. als dermahligem ausschreibendem Fürsten des Fränckischen Crayses, auf Requisition eines Hochlöblichen Corporis Evangelicorum, übernommene Restitutions- u. Executions-Commission betreffend in Causa des Gräflich-Hohenlohischen Hauses, Neuensteinischer Linie, contra die Herren Fürsten v. Hohenlohe-Waldenburg. N.p., 1750.

Francisco, Adam S. *Martin Luther and Islam: A Study in Sixteenth-Century Polemics and Apologetics.* Leiden, 2007.

Franck, Caspar. *Catalogus haereticorum, das ist: warhafftige Erzelung der namhafften Irrthumb und Ketzer, welche von Anfang der Welt biß auff unsere Zeit entstanden….* Ingolstadt, 1576.

François, Etienne. *Die unsichtbare Grenze. Protestanten und Katholiken in Augsburg 1648–1806.* Sigmaringen, 1991.

Franzen, August. *Bischof und Reformation: Erzbischof Hermann von Wied in Köln vor der Entscheidung zwischen Reform und Reformation.* Münster, 1971.

———. "Die Herausbildung des Konfessionsbewußtseins am Niederrhein im 16. Jahrhundert." *Annalen des Historischen Vereins für den Niederrhein* 158 (1956): 164–209.

Freeman, David Fors. "Those Persistent Lutherans: The Survival of Wesel's Minority Lutheran Community, 1578–1612." In *The Formation of Clerical and Confessional Identities in Early Modern Europe,* edited by Wim Janse and Barbara Pitkin, 397–407. Leiden, 2006.

———. "Wesel and the Dutch Revolt: The Influence of Religious Refugees on a German City, 1544–1612." Ph.D. dissertation, Emory University, 2002.

Frick, Johann. *Britannia Rectius De Lutheranis Edocta….* Ulm, 1709.

———. *Grund Der Wahrheit, Von grossem Haupt-Unterschied der Evangelischen, und Römisch-Catholischen Religionen….* N.p., 1707.

Frisch, Michael. "Die Normaltagsregelung im Prager Frieden." *Zeitschrift der Savigny- Stiftung für Rechtsgeschichte, Kanonistische Abteilung* 87 (2001): 442–454.

————. *Das Restitutionsedikt Kaiser Ferdinands II. Vom 6. März 1629: Eine rechtsgeschichtliche Untersuchung*. Tübingen, 1993.

Fuchs, Ralf-Peter. *Ein 'Medium zum Frieden': Die Normaljahrsregel und die Beendigung des Dreißigjährigen Krieges*. Munich, 2010.

————. "Für die Kirche Gottes und die Posterität: Kursachsen und das Friedensmedium eines Normaljahres auf dem Frankfurter Kompositionstag 1631." *Mitteilungen des Sonderforschungsbereichs 'Pluralisierung und Autorität in der Frühen Neuzeit'* 1 (2007): 19–27. http://www.sfb-frueheneuzeit.uni-muenchen.de/mitteilungen/M1-2007/fuerdiekirche.pdf

Garstein, Oskar. *Rome and the Counter-Reformation in Scandinavia: The Age of Gustavus Adolphus and Queen Christina of Sweden, 1622–1656*. Leiden, 1992.

Gebauer, Johannes H. *Kurbrandenburg und das Restitutionsedikt von 1629*. Halle, 1899.

Gedicke, Lampertus. *Kurtze Erklärung Der Lutherischen Lehre von der wahren Gegenwart des Leibes und Blutes Christi im heiligen Abendmahl*. Berlin, 1722.

Geertz, Clifford. "Centers, Kings and Charisma: Reflections on the Symbolics of Power." In *Rites of Power: Symbolism, Ritual, and Politics since the Middle Ages*, edited by Sean Wilentz, 13–38. Philadelphia, 1985.

Gericke, Wolfgang. *Glaubenszeugnisse und Konfessionspolitik der brandenburgischen Herrscher bis zur Preußischen Union, 1540–1815*. Bielefeld, 1977.

Gestrich, Andreas and Rainer Lächele, eds. *Johann Jacob Moser: Politiker, Pietist, Publizist*. Karlsruhe, 2002.

Gibbs, Graham C. "Union Hanover/England. Accession to the Throne and Change of Rulers: Determining Factors in the Establishment and Continuation of the Personal Union." In *Die Personalunionen von Sachsen-Polen 1697–1763 und Hannover-England 1714–1837. Ein Vergleich*, edited by Rex Rexheuser, 241–274. Wiesbaden, 2005.

Goeters, J.F.G. "Der katholische Hermann von Wied." *Monatshefte für Evangelische Kirchengeschichte des Rheinlandes* 35 (1986): 1–17.

Gordon, Bruce. *Calvin*. New Haven, 2009.

————. "The Changing Face of Protestant History and Identity in the Sixteenth Century." In *Protestant History and Identity in Sixteenth-Century Europe*, edited by Bruce Gordon, vol. 2, 1–22. Aldershot, 1996.

Gotthard, Axel. "'Politice seint wir Bäpstisch': Kursachsen und der deutsche Protestantismus im frühen 17. Jahrhundert." *Zeitschrift für historische Forschung* 20 (1993): 275–319.

Gouw, J.L. van der. "Herman Herbertz te Wesel." In *In en om de Sint-Jan: bijdragen tot de Goudse kerkgeschiedenis. Een-en-twintigst verzameling: Bijdragen van de Oudheidkundige Kring 'Die Goude*,' edited by P.H.A.M. Abels, 61–74. Delft, 1989.

Greengrass, Mark. *The Longman Companion to the European Reformation, c. 1500–1618*. New York, 1998.

Greyerz, Kaspar von, Manfred Jakubowski-Tiessen, Thomas Kaufmann, and Hartmut Lehmann, eds. *Interkonfessionalität – Transkonfessionalität – binnenkonfessionelle Pluralität: Neue Forschungen zur Konfessionalisierungsthese*. Gütersloh, 2003.

Grochowina, Nicole. "Bekehrungen und Indifferenz in Ostfriesland im 16. Jahrhundert." In *Konversion und Konfession in der Frühen Neuzeit*, edited by Ute Lotz-Heumann, Jan-Friedrich Missfelder, and Matthias Pohlig, 243–270. Gütersloh, 2007.

————. "Confessional Indifference in East Frisia." *Reformation and Renaissance Review* 7 (2005): 111–124.

Großgebauer, Theophil. *Treuer Unterricht von der Wiedergeburt*. Frankfurt, 1661.

Grossmann, Walter. *Johann Christian Edelmann: From Orthodoxy to Enlightenment*. The Hague and Paris, 1976.

————. "Johann Christian Edelmann's Idea of Jesus." *Harvard Theological Review* 60 (1967): 375–389.

Gundermann, Iselin. "Verordnete Eintracht: Lutheraner und Reformierte in Berlin-Brandenburg, 1613–1740." *Herbergen der Christenheit: Jahrbuch für deutsche Kirchengeschichte* 28/29 (2004/05): 141–155.

Günter, Heinrich. *Das Restitutionsedikt von 1629 und die katholische Restauration Altwirtembergs*. Stuttgart, 1901.

Günther, Hans-Jürgen. *Die Reformation und ihre Kinder dargestellt an: Vater und Sohn Johannes Pistorius Niddanus. Eine Doppelbiographie J. Pistorius d. Ä. (1502–1583) und J. Pistorius d. J. (1546–1608)*. Nidda, 1994.

Güthoff, Elmar. "Kanonistische Erwägungen zur eigenständigen Bedeutung der Apostasie." In *Iudicare inter fideles: Festschrift Karl-Theodor Geringer*, edited by Winfried Aymans, Heribert Schmitz, and Stephan Haering, 109–119. St. Ottilien, 2002.

Handlungen und Gebete bey dem öffentlichen Gottesdienste der evangelisch lutherischen Gemeine in der Reichsstadt Kempten. Kempten, 1794.

Harran, Marilyn J. *Luther on Conversion: The Early Years*. Ithaca, 1983.

Hart, Arthur Tindal. *The Life and Times of John Sharp, Archbishop of York*. London, 1949.

Hartmann, Stefan. "Die Polenpolitik König Friedrich Wilhelms I. von Preussen zur Zeit des 'Thorner Blutgerichts' (1724–1725)." *Forschungen zur Brandenburgischen und Preussischen Geschichte* 5 (1995): 31–58.

Hashagen, Justus. *Der rheinische Protestantismus und die Entwicklung der rheinischen Kultur*. Essen, 1924.

Haus, Franciscus. *De anno decretorio M.DC.XXIIII. Opificum Collega non concernente*. Würzburg, 1771.

Headley, John M., Hans J. Hillerbrand, and Anthony Papalas, eds. *Confessionalization in Europe, 1555–1700: Essays in Honor and Memory of Bodo Nischan*. Aldershot, 2004.

Heal, Bridget. *The Cult of the Virgin Mary in Early Modern Germany: Protestant and Catholic Piety, 1500–1648*. Cambridge, 2007.

Hecht, Christian. *Katholische Bildertheologie im Zeitalter der Gegenreformation und Barock. Studien zu den Traktaten von Johannes Molanus, Gabriele Paleotti und anderen Autoren*. Berlin, 1997.

Heckel, Martin. "Die Religionsprozesse des Reichskammergerichts im konfessionell gespaltenen Kirchenrecht." In *Martin Heckel: Gesammelte Schriften: Staat – Kirche – Recht – Geschichte*, edited by Klaus Schlaich, vol. 3, 382–440. Tübingen, 1997.

————. "Das Restitutionsedikt Kaiser Ferdinands II. vom 6. März 1629 – eine verlorene Alternative der Reichskirchenverfassung." In *Wirkungen europäischer Rechtskultur*, edited by Gerhard Köbler and Hermann Nehlsen, 351–376. Munich, 1997.

————. "Die Krise der Religionsverfassung des Reiches und die Anfänge des Dreißigjährigen Krieges." In *Martin Heckel: Gesammelte Schriften*, edited by Klaus Schlaich, vol. 2, 970–998. Tübingen, 1989.

————. "Parität (I)." In *Martin Heckel: Gesammelte Schriften*, edited by Klaus Schlaich, vol. 1, 106–226. Tübingen, 1989.

————. "Parität (II)." In *Martin Heckel: Gesammelte Schriften*, edited by Klaus Schlaich, vol. 1, 227–323. Tübingen, 1989.

Heidemann, Johannes. *Vorarbeiten zu einer Geschichte des höheren Schulwesens in Wesel*. 2 vols. Wesel, 1853–1859.

Helm, Paul. *John Calvin's Ideas.* Oxford 2004.

Heming, Carol Piper. *Protestants and the Cult of the Saints in German-Speaking Europe, 1527–1531.* Kirksville, MO, 2003.

Henckel, Erdmann Heinrich Graf. *Die letzten Stunden einiger Der Evangelischen Lehre zugetanen und in diesem und nechste verflossenen Jahren selig in dem Herrn Verstorbenen Personen.* 4 vols. Halle, 1720–1733.

Hendrix, Scott. "Rerooting the Faith: The Reformation as Re-Christianization." *American Society of Church History* 69, no. 3 (2000): 558–577.

Henshall, Nicholas. *The Myth of Absolutism: Change and Continuity in Early Modern European Monarchy.* London and New York, 1992.

Henze, Barbara. *Aus Liebe zur Kirche-Reform: Die Bemühungen Georg Witzels (1501–1573) um die Einheit der Kirche.* Münster, 1995.

Heshusius, Tilemannus. *Dancksagung zu Gott für die Bekehrung Eduardi Thorni auß Engellandt bürtig, welcher die Gotteslesterliche Sect der Jesuiter....* Lauingen, 1567.

Hibben, C.C. *Gouda in Revolt: Particularism and Pacifism in the Revolt of the Netherlands, 1572–1588.* Utrecht, 1983.

Hildebrandus, Henricus. *Annus decretorius 1624 in Instrumenti Pacis Caesareo-Svecici Articulo V.* Altorf, 1705.

Hildenbrand, Richard. *Gotthilf Samuel Steinbart: Ein Beitrag zur Geschichte der Popularphilosophie im achtzehnten Jahrhundert.* Herne, 1906.

Hillmann, Johannes. *Die Evangelische Gemeinde Wesel und ihre Willibrordkirche.* Düsseldorf, 1896.

Hindmarsh, D. Bruce. *The Evangelical Conversion Narrative: Spiritual Autobiography in Early Modern England.* Oxford, 2005.

Hinrichs, Carl. *Preußentum und Pietismus: Der Pietismus in Brandenburg-Preußen als religiös- soziale Reformbewegung.* Göttingen, 1971.

Hirsch, Emmanuel. *Geschichte der neueren evangelischen Theologie II.* Gütersloh, 1951.

Hirten-Treue Christi, welche er an einem seiner verlornen Schafe, nemlich an Gertrude Magdalene Bremmelin, einer vorsetzlichen Kindermörderin, erwiesen: zum Preise desselben unendlicher Menschenliebe, wie auch zur Warnung und Besserung beschrieben; nebst einer auf dem Rabenstein gehaltenen Rede. Wernigerode, 1744.

Hodler, Beat. "Konfessionen und der Handlungsspielraum der Untertanen in der Eidgenossenschaft im Zeitalter der Reformierten Orthodoxie." In *Gemeinde, Reformation und Widerstand: Festschrift für Peter Blickle zum 60. Geburtstag,* edited by Heinrich R. Schmidt, André Holenstein, and Andreas Würgler, 281–291. Tübingen, 1998.

Hoeck, Wilhelm. *Anton Ulrich und Elisabeth Christine von Braunschweig-Lüneburg-Wolfenbüttel. Eine durch archivalische Dokumente begründete Darstellung ihres Übertritts zur römischen Kirche.* Wolfenbüttel, 1845.

Höfele, Andreas, Stephan Laqué, Enno Ruge, and Gabriela Schmidt, eds. *Representing Religious Pluralization in Early Modern Europe.* Münster, 2007.

Hoffmannus, Godofredus Daniel. *Commentatio Iuris Publici Ecclesiastici de Die Decretorio Kalendis Ianuarii Anni 1624 Omnique ex Pace Westphalica Restitutione.* Ulm, 1750.

Hommel, C.F. *Rhapsodia qvaestionvm in foro qvotidie obventivm neqve tamen legibvs Decisarvm,* vol. 5. Bayreuth, 1769.

Hotson, Howard. "Irenicism in the Confessional Age: The Holy Roman Empire, 1563–1648." In *Conciliation and Confession: The Struggle for Unity in the Age of Reform, 1415–1648,* edited by Howard P. Louthan and Randall C. Zachman, 228–285. Notre Dame, 2004.

Hsia, R. Po-Chia. *Society and Religion in Münster, 1535–1618*. New Haven, 1984.

Hulsemann, Johannes. *Disputatio Theologica de vocatorum conversione per poenitentiam, quam in collegio Theologico publice aperto…*. Leipzig, 1706.

Iserloh, Erwin. *Geschichte und Theologie der Reformation im Grundriß*, 3rd ed. Paderborn 1985.

Israel, Jonathan. *Radical Enlightenment: Philosophy and the Making of Modernity 1650–1750*. Oxford, 2001.

Jacobi, Jacob. *Summarische Relation. Von der Lutherischen Freystellung, derselbigen Hundert-järigen Verlauff, und derentwegen Newlich gehaltenem JubelJahr, und von Bruder Josemans ernewertem alten PredicantenLatein, von deß Römischen Bischoffs Alter, Lehre, Wandel, Raht, und Anschlag. Zu Erleuterung dieser Zeit Streittigkeiten in dem Religionswesen sehr dienstlich und nothwendig, Auß den furnembsten Romanischer und Luterischer Seiten HistoriSchreibern … zusammen getragen*. Straßburg, 1618.

Jacobson, G. and Bengt Hildebrand. "Christoff Delphicus Dohna." In *Svenskt Biografiskt Lexikon*, vol. 11, 328–333. Stockholm, 1945.

Jacobson, Heinrich Friedrich, ed. *Urkunden-Samlung von bisher ungedruckten Gesetzen nebst Uebersichten gedructkter Verordnung für die evangesliche Kirche von Rheinland und West-falen*. Königsberg, 1844.

James, William. *The Varieties of Religious Experience*. London, 1911 [1902].

Johnson, Carina. "Idolatrous Cultures and the Practice of Religion." *Journal of the History of Ideas* 67 (2006): 597–621.

Johnson, Christine R. *The German Discovery of the World: Renaissance Encounters with the Strange and Marvelous*. Charlottesville, 2008.

Johnson, Christopher H. and David Warren Sabean, eds. *Sibling Relations and the Transfor-mations of European Kinship, 1300-1900*. New York, 2011.

Jordan, Stefan. *Theorien und Methoden der Geschichtswissenschaft*. Paderborn, 2009.

Jung, Martin H. *Frauen des Pietismus*. Gütersloh, 1998.

Kaplan, Benjamin J. *Calvinists and Libertines: Confession and Community in Utrecht, 1578–1620*. Oxford, 1995.

Kathrein, Werner, et al., eds. *Im Dienst um die Einheit und die Reform der Kirche zum Leben und Werk Georg Witzels*. Frankfurt, 2003.

Kaufmann, Thomas. *"Türckenbüchlein": Zur christlichen Wahrnehmung "türksicher Religion" in Spätmittelater und Reformation*. Göttingen, 2008.

———. "Matthias Flacius Illyricus." In *Mitteldeutsche Lebensbilder. Menschen im Zeitalter der Reformation*, edited by Werner Freitag, 177–199. Cologne, 2004.

———. "Die Konfessionalisierung von Kirche und Gesellschaft: Sammelbericht über eine Forschungsdebatte." *Theologische Literaturzeitung* 121 (1996): 1008–1012, 1112–1121.

Keene, Nicholas. "John Ernest Grabe, Biblical Learning and Religious Controversy in Early Eighteenth-Century England." *Journal of Ecclesiastical History* 58 (2007): 656–674.

Keller, Dieter. "Herzog Alba und die Wiederherstellung der katholischen Kirche am Rhein." *Preußische Jahrbücher* 48 (1881): 586–606.

Kessel, Heinrich. "Reformation und Gegenreformation im Herzogtum Cleve (1517–1609)." *Düsseldorfer Jahrbuch* 30 (1920): 1–160.

Kessler, Andreas . *Methodus Haereticos convertendi: Außführlicher Tractat von der Ketzer Bekehrung, in zweyen Theilen verfasset…*. Coburg, 1631.

Kiefl, Franz Xaver. *Der Friedensplan des Leibniz zur Wiedervereinigung der getrennten christ-lichen Kirchen*. Paderborn, 1903.

Kipp, Herbert. *"Trachtet zuerst nach dem Reich Gottes":* Landstädtische Reformation und Rats-Konfessionalisierung in Wesel (1520–1600). Bielefeld, 2004.

Kirn, Hans-Martin. "The Penitential Struggle ('Busskampf') of August Hermann Francke 1663–1727: A Model of Pietistic Conversion?" In *Paradigms, Poetics, and Politics of Conversion,* edited by Jan N. Bremmer, Wout Jac. van Bekkum, and Arie L. Molendijk, 123–132. Louvain, 2006.

Klepper, Jochen, ed. *Der König und die Stillen im Lande. Begegnungen Friedrich Wilhelms I. mit August Hermann Francke, Gotthilf August Francke, Johann Anastasius Freylinghausen, Nikolaus Ludwig Graf von Zinzindorf.* Witten and Berlin, 1962.

Klingebiel, Thomas. "Pietismus und Orthodoxie. Die Landeskirche unter den Kurfürsten und Königen Friedrich I. und Friedrich Wilhelm I. (1688 bis 1740)," In *Tausend Jahre Kirche in Berlin–Brandenburg,* edited by Gerd Heinrich, 293-324. Berlin, 1999.

Klueting, Harm. *Das konfessionelle Zeitalter 1525–1648.* Stuttgart, 1989.

———, ed. *Irenik und Antikonfessionalismus im 17. und 18. Jahrhundert.* Hildesheim, 2003.

Koch, Ernst. "Victorin Strigel (1524–1569): Von Jena nach Heidelberg." In *Melanchton in seinen Schülern,* edited by Heinz Scheible, 391–404. Wiesbaden, 1997.

Koch, Ernst and Johannes Wallmann, eds. *Ernst Salomon Cyprian (1673–1745) zwischen Orthodoxie, Pietismus und Frühaufklärung. Vorträge des Internationalen Kolloquiums vom 14. bis 16. September 1995 in der Forschungs- und Landesbibliothek Gotha Schloß Friedenstein.* Gotha, 1996.

Koch, H.W. "Brandenburg-Prussia." In *Absolutism in Seventeenth-Century Europe,* edited by John Miller, 123–155. Basingstoke, 1990.

Köhn, Mechtild. *Martin Bucers Entwurf einer Reformation des Erzstiftes Köln.* Witten, 1966.

Kolb, Robert. *Bound Choice, Election, and Wittenberg Theological Method: From Martin Luther to the Formula of Concord.* Grand Rapids, 2005.

Koller, Edith. "Die Rolle des Normaljahrs in Konfessionsprozessen des späten 17. Jahrhunderts vor dem Reichskammergericht." *Zeitenblicke* 3 (2004), http://deposit.ddb .de/ep/netpub/43/37/61/976613743/_data_stat/koller/index.html.

König, Daniel. *Bekehrungsmotive: Untersuchungen zum Christianisierungsprozess im römischen Westreich und seinen romanisch-germanischen Nachfolgern (4.–8. Jahrhundert).* Husum, 2008.

Kreiner, Armin. "Pluralismus (fundamentaltheologisch)." In *Lexikon für Theologie und Kirche,* edited by Walter Kasper, vol. 8, 362–363. Freiburg, 1999.

Kurze doch gründtliche Anzieg und Unterricht woher die Uneinigkeiten so heutigs tags im Römischen Reich schweben, entsprungen, und wem die Zerrüttung desselben zuzumessen sey. N.p., 1615.

Lächele, Rainer. *Die "Sammlung auserlesener Materien zum Bau des Reichs Gottes" zwischen 1730 und 1760: Erbauungszeitschriften als Kommunikationsmedium des Pietismus.* Tübingen, 2006.

Lademacher, Horst, Renate Loos, and Simon Groenveld, eds. *Ablehnung – Duldung – Anerkennung: Toleranz in den Niederlanden und in Deutschland. Ein historischer und aktueller Vergleich.* Münster, 2004.

Lanzinner, Maximilian and Dietmar Heil, eds. *Deutsche Reichstagsakten: Reichsversammlungen 1556–1662. Der Reichstag zu Augsburg 1566,* vol. 2. Munich, 2002.

Lau, Franz. "Anbruch und Wildwuchs der Reformation." In *Reformationsgeschichte Deutschlands bis 1555,* edited by Franz Lau and Ernst Bizer, 2nd ed., 17–43. Göttingen, 1969.

Leibniz, Gottfried Wilhelm. *Allgemeiner politischer und historischer Briefwechsel*, vol. 16. Berlin, 2000.

Lentz, Christel. "Das kurze dramatische Leben des Grafen Gustav Adolph von Nassau-Saarbrücken-Idstein (1632–1664): Erbgraf, Konvertit und Türkenkämpfer." *Nassauische Annalen* 116 (2005): 281–300.

Leone, Massimo. *Religious Conversion and Identity: The Semiotic Analysis of Texts.* London and New York, 2004.

Lermen, Blasen auch Ursachen und Ausschlag, deß besorgten innerlichen Kriegs zwischen den Catholischen und Calvinisten in Teutschlandt. Das ist: Kurtze und gründtliche anzeig unnd erleuterung, welchem theil der Krieg lieber sey alß der Friedt: was ein jeder für tringende Ursachen zum Krieg hab: und was der ein oder ander für einen Außschlag zugewarten. N.p., 1616.

Leyser, Polycarp. *Ad Virum Illustrem....* Hanover, 1707.

Lieburg, Fred van. "Reformed Doctrine and Pietist Conversion: The Historical Interplay of Theology Communication and Experience." In *Paradigms, Poetics and Politics of Conversion*, edited by Jan N. Bremmer, Wout Jac. van Bekkum, and Arie L. Molendijk, 133–148. Louvain, 2006.

Lohse, Bernhard, ed. *Der Durchbruch der reformatorischen Erkenntnis bei Luther: Neuere Untersuchungen.* Stuttgart, 1988.

Lotz-Heumann, Ute. "The Concept of 'Confessionalization': A Historiographical Paradigm in Dispute." *Memoria y Civilización* 4 (2001): 93–114.

Lotz-Heurnann, Ute, Jan-Friedrich Mißfelder, and Matthias Pohlig, eds. *Konversion und Konfession in der Frühen Neuzeit.* Gütersloh, 2007.

Lucius, Johann. *Disputatio de arbitrii servitute circa conversionem hominis, aliosque actus spirituales, in inclyta Witteberg. Academia ad disputandum proposita sub Praesidio Balth. Meisneri....* Dresden and Wittenberg, 1615.

Luebke, David M. "Confessions of the Dead: Interpreting Burial Practice in the Late Reformation." *Archiv für Reformationsgeschichte* 101 (2010): 55–79.

———. "Customs of Confession: Managing Religious Diversity in Late Sixteenth- and Early Seventeenth-Century Westphalia." In *Religion and Authority: Rethinking Central Europe from the Middle Ages to the Enlightenment*, edited by Howard Louthan, Gary Cohen, and Franz Szabo. New York, 2010.

Luh, Jürgen. *Unheiliges Römisches Reich. Der konfessionelle Gegensatz 1648–1806.* Potsdam, 1995.

Luria, Keith. *Sacred Boundaries: Religious Coexistence and Conflict in Early-Modern France.* Washington, DC, 2005.

Luther, Martin. "Preface to the Latin Writings (1545)," translated by Lewis Spitz. In *Luther's Works*, edited by Jaroslav Pelikan and Helmut T. Lehmann, vol. 34, 327–343. Philadelphia, 1960.

———. "Vorrede zum ersten Bande der Gesamtausgabe seiner lateinischen Schriften" (1545). In *Martin Luthers Werke: Kritische Gesamtausgabe*, 65 vols. Weimar, 1883–1966. Reprint vol. 54, 177–187, Weimar, 2000–2007.

———. "Von der Bekehrung Pauli." *Martin Luthers Werke. In einer das Bedürfniß der Zeit berücksichtigenden Auswahl*, vol. 9, 2nd ed. Hamburg, 1828.

Lutzenburgensis, Bernardus. *Catalogus Haereticorum omnium penè, qui ad haec usque tempora passim literarum monumentis proditi sunt, illorum nomina errores, & tempora quibus vixerunt ostendens....* Cologne, 1522.

MacCulloch, Diarmaid. *Reformation: Europe's House Divided, 1490–1700.* London, 2003.

————. *The Later Reformation in England, 1547–1603.* Basingstoke, 1990.

Mader, Eric-Oliver. "Konfessionalität im Hause Pfalz-Neuburg: Zur Bedeutung des Faktors 'Konversion' für das konfessionelle Profil einer Herrscherdynastie." In *Barocke Herrschaft am Rhein um 1700: Kurfürst Johann Wilhelm und seine Zeit,* edited by Benedikt Mauerer et al., 95–115. Düsseldorf, 2009.

————. "Fürstenkonversionen zum Katholizismus in Mitteleuropa im 17. Jahrhundert: Ein systematischer Ansatz in fallorientierter Perspektive." *Zeitschrift für Historische Forschung* 34, no. 3 (2007): 403–440.

————. "Adam Contzen, S.J. (1571–1635)." In *Encyclopedia of Witchcraft: The Western Tradition,* edited by Richard Golden, vol. 1, 214–215. Santa Barbara, 2006.

Magdeburg, Joachim. *Widerlegung, Des Grewlichen und Gottslesterlichen Papistischen Irthumbs, vom Merito Congrui, oder Freyen willen, Welchen nu die Synergisten mit ihrer Lere von der mit hülffe des Menschen inn der Bekerung als vom Todt widerumb aufferwecken, unnd in die Kirchen einfüren wollen.* Regensburg, 1566.

Marschke, Benjamin. "'Lutheran Jesuits': Halle Pietist Communication Networks at the Court of Friedrich Wilhelm I of Prussia." *Covenant Quarterly* 65, no. 4 (November 2006): 19–38.

————. *Absolutely Pietist: Patronage, Factionalism, and State-Building in the Early Eighteenth-Century Prussian Army Chaplaincy.* Tübingen, 2005.

Martens, Wilhelm. *Das Kirchenregiment in Wesel zur Zeit der letzten klevischen und der ersten brandenburgischen Fürsten.* Göttingen, 1913.

Martschukat, Jürgen. "Ein Freitod durch die Hand des Henkers. Erörterungen zum Komplementarität von Diskursen und Praktiken am Beispiel von 'Mord aus Lebens-Überdruß' und Todesstrafe im 18. Jahrhundert." *Zeitschrift für historische Forschung* 27 (2000): 53–74.

Matheus, Ricarda. "Mobilität und Konversion. Überlegungen aus römischer Perspektive." *Quellen und Forschungen aus italienischen Archiven und Bibliotheken* 85 (2005): 170–213.

Matthias, Markus. "Bekehrung und Wiedergeburt." In *Glaubenswelt und Lebenswelten, Geschichte des Pietismus,* edited by Hartmut Lehmann, vol. 4. Göttingen, 2004.

————. *Lebensläufe August Hermann Franckes.* Leipzig 1999.

————. "Merckwürdiger Anfang der Bekehrung des sel. D. Speners." *Sammlung auserlesener Materien zum Bau des Reichs Gottes* 2 (1732): 216–218.

McClanahan, Grant V. *Diplomatic Immunity: Principles, Practices, Problems.* New York, 1989.

McIntosh, Christopher. *The Rose Cross and the Age of Reason: Eighteenth-Century Rosicrucianism in Central Europe and Its Relationship to the Enlightenment.* Leiden, 1992.

"Merckwürdiger Anfang der Bekehrung des sel. D. Speners." *Sammlung auserlesener Materien zum Bau des Reichs Gottes* 2 (1732): 216–218.

Metzler, Joseph, ed. *Sacrae Congregationis de Propaganda Fide memoria rerum.* Vol. 2, 1622–1700. Rome, 1971.

Mills, Kenneth and Anthony Grafton, eds. *Conversion: Old Worlds and New.* Rochester, 2003.

Miskimin, Patricia Behre. *One King, One Law, Three Faiths: Religion and the Rise of Absolutism in Seventeenth-Century Metz.* Westport, CT, 2002.

Mennecke-Haustein, Ute. *Conversio ad ecclesiam. Der Weg des Friedrich Staphylus zurück zur vortridentinischen katholischen Kirche.* Heidelberg, 2003.

————. "Die Konversion des Friedrich Staphylus (1512–1564) zum Katholizismus – eine conversio?" In *Konversionen im Mittelalter und in der Frühen Neuzeit,* edited by Friedrich Niewöhner and Fidel Rädle, 71–84. Hildesheim, 1999.

————. "Konversionen." In *Die katholische Konfessionalisierung*, edited by Wolfgang Reinhard and Heinz Schilling, 242–257. Gütersloh, 1995.

Mensing, Johannes. *Bescheidt Ob der Glaube alleyn, on alle gute wercke dem menschen genug sey zur seligkeyt etc.* N.p., 1528.

Moerner, Theodor von. *Kurbrandenburgs Staatsverträge von 1601 bis 1700.* Berlin, 1867.

Morgan, Edmund. *Visible Saints: The History of a Puritan Idea.* New York, 1963.

Morgenbessern, Samuel. *Prüfung Des Holländischen Qvaker-Pulvers.* Sorau, 1697.

Morrison, Karl F. *Conversion and Text: The Cases of Augustine of Hippo, Herman-Judah, and Constantine Tsatsos.* Charlottesville, 1992.

————. *Understanding Conversion.* Charlottesville, 1992.

Moser, Johann Jacob. *Von der Landeshoheit im Geistlichen, nach denen Reichs-Gesetzen und dem Reichs-Herkommen, wie auch aus denen Teutschen Staats-Rechts-Lehrern und eigener Erfahrung….* Frankfurt and Leipzig, 1773.

————. *Seelige Letzte Stunden 31 Personen, so unter des Schafrichters Hand gestorben.* Stuttgart, Frankfurt, and Leipzig, 1753.

————. *Selige letzte Stunden einiger dem zeitlichen Tode übergebener Missethäter, Erste Forsetzung….* Leipzig, 1745.

————. *Selige letzte Stunden einiger dem zeitlichen Tode übergebener Missethäter.* Leipzig, 1742.

————. *Selige Letzte Stunden einiger dem zeitlichen Tode übergebener Missethäter, Mit einer Vorrede….* Jena, 1742.

————. *Seelige letzte Stunden einiger dem zeitlichen Tode übergebener Missethäter.* Leipzig, 1740.

[Mothe, Claude Groteste de La]. *Memoires sur la pretendue declaration de l'Université de Helmstad Touchant le changement de Religion de la Reine d'Espagne.* Rotterdam, 1710.

Mücke, Dorothea von. "Experience, Impartiality, and Authenticity in Confessional Discourse." *New German Critique* 79 (2000): 5–35.

Muldoon, James, ed. *Varieties of Religious Conversion in the Middle Ages.* Gainesville, 1997.

Müller, Gerhard, Horst Balz, and Gerhard Krause, eds. *Theologische Realenzyklopädie*, vol. 19. Berlin and New York, 1990.

Musaeus, Johannes. *De Conversione Hominis Peccatoris ad Deum Tractatus Theologicus quo de Conversionis appelationibus, natura, actibus, & speciatim de actibus fidei….* Jena, 1659.

Mutzenbecher, Johann Friedrich. "Sebastian Edzardi." *Zeitschrift des Vereins für Hamburgische Geschichte* 5 (1866): 210–223.

Mylius, Christian Otto, ed. *Corpus constitutionum marchicarum: oder, Königl. Preussis. und Churfürstl. Brandenburgische in der Chur- und Marck Brandenburg, auch incorporirten Landen publicirte und ergangene Ordnungen, Edicta, Mandata, Rescripta, etc.* Berlin, 1737–1751.

Neumann, Bernd. "Nachwort." In Johann Christian Edelmann, *Selbstbiographie.* Stuttgart, 1976.

Neuser, Wilhelm H. *Johann Calvin: Leben und Werk in seiner Frühzeit, 1509–1541.* Göttingen, 2009.

Niewöhner, Friedrich and Fidel Rädle, eds. *Konversionen im Mittelalter und in der Frühen Neuzeit.* Hildesheim, 1999.

Niggl, Günter. *Geschichte der deutschen Autobiographie im 18. Jahrhundert.* Stuttgart, 1977.

Nischan, Bodo. *Prince, People and Confession: The Second Reformation in Brandenburg.* Philadelphia, 1994.

Nørgaard, Anders. *Mission und Obrigkeit. Die Dänisch-hallische Mission in Tranquebar 1706– 1845.* Gütersloh, 1988.

Nöthiger und kurtzgefaßter Unterricht Theils von der Historie und Innhalt Des Auf einen drey-ßig jährigen Krieg endlich in dem Jahre 1648. erfolgten und durch GOttes Gnade bereits hundert Jahre daurenden Westphälischen Friedens, Besonders auch zu Ansehung der hieran Theil nehmenden des H.R.R. Freyen Stadt Augsburg, Und der darinnen, Krafft solchen Friedens und dessen Executions-Recesses auf immer vestgestellten Regiments-Paritaet: Theils von Christschuldiger Begehung Eines auf den 8ten August. 1748. als auf das ohnehin wegen dieses Friedens jährlich gewohnliche Evangelische Friedens-Fest Obrigkeitlich verordneten Hunderjährigen Jubel-Angedenckens zum Besten anderer, sonderlich der Lateinischen und Deutschen Schulen unsers Evangelischen Augspurgs abgefasset. Augsburg, 1748.

Nummedal, Tara. *Alchemy and Authority in the Holy Roman Empire.* Chicago, 2007.

Oakey, Niall. "Fixtures or Fittings: Can Surviving Pre-Reformation Ecclesiastical Material Culture Be Used as a Barometer of Contemporary Attitudes to the Reformation in England?" In *The Archaeology of Reformation,* edited by David Gaimster and Roberta Gilchrist, 58–72. Leeds, 2003.

Oberman, Heiko A. "*Subita Conversio:* The Conversion of John Calvin." In *John Calvin and the Reformation of the Refugees,* with introduction by Peter A. Dykema, 131–148. Geneva, 2009.

———. *Luther: Man Between God and the Devil.* New York, 1989.

O'Brien, Charles H. "Ideas of Religious Toleration at the Time of Joseph II: A Study of the Enlightenment among Catholics in Austria." *Transactions of the American Philosophical Society,* New Series, 59 (1969): 1–80.

Ogdon, Montell. *Juridical Bases of Diplomatic Immunity: A Study of the Origin, Growth and Purpose of the Law.* Washington, DC, 1936.

Ohst, Martin. "Späte Helmstedter Irenik zwischen Politik und Theologie." *Jahrbuch der Gesellschaft für Niedersächsische Kirchengeschichte* 92 (1994): 139–170.

Olin, John C., ed. *A Reformation Debate: Sadoleto's Letter to the Genevans and Calvin's Reply.* New York, 1966.

O'Rourke, David K. "The Experience of Conversion." In *The Human Experience of Conversion: Persons and Structures in Transformation,* edited by Francis A. Eigo, 1–30. Villanova, PA, 1987.

Oschmann, Antje. *Der Nürnberger Exekutionstag 1649–1650: Das Ende des Dreißigjährigen Krieges in Deutschland.* Münster, 1991.

———, ed. *Die Friedensverträge mit Frankreich und Schweden,* vol. 1. Münster, 1998.

Otto, Rüdiger. "Johann Christian Edelmann's Criticism of the Bible and its Relation to Spinoza." In *Disguised and Overt Spinozism around 1700,* edited by Wiep van Bunge and Wim Klever, 171–190. Leiden, 1996.

Ozment, Steven. *Protestants: The Birth of a Revolution.* New York, 1991.

Parker, David. *The Making of French Absolutism.* London, 1983.

Parker, Geoffrey. *The Dutch Revolt.* New York, 1977.

Partee, Charles. *Calvin and Classical Philosophy.* Leiden, 1997.

Peper, Ines. *Konversionen im Umkreis des Wiener Hofes um 1700.* Vienna, 2010.

Pettegree, Andrew. *Reformation and the Culture of Persuasion.* Cambridge, 2005.

Pistorius, Johann and Jakob von Baden-Hachberg, *Vnser, Von Gottes Genaden, Jacobs, Marggrafen zu Baden vnd Hachbergk....* Cologne, 1591.

Pleijel, Hilding. *Karolinsk Kyrkofromhet, Pietism och Herrenhutism 1680–1772.* Vol. 5, *Svenska Kyrkans Historia.* Stockholm, 1935.

Pollack, Detlef. "Überlegungen zum Begriff und Phänomen der Konversion aus religionssoziologischer Perspektive." In *Konversion und Konfession*, edited by Ute Lotz-Heumann, Jan-Friedrich Missfelder, and Matthias Pohlig, 33–58. Gütersloh, 2007.

Pratje, Johann Hinrich. *Historische Nachrichten von Joh. Chr. Edelmanns, eines berüchtigten Religionspötters, Leben, Schriften und Lehrbegrif....* Hamburg, 1755.

Pree, Helmut. "Die Konversion als Rechtsakt." In *Kirchenrecht und Theologie im Leben der Kirche: Festschrift Heinrich J. F. Reinhardt*, edited by Heinrich J.F. Reinhardt, Rüdiger Althaus, Klaus Lüdicke, and Matthias Pulte, 347–353. Essen, 2007.

Press, Volker. "Das Haus Dohna in der europäischen Adelsgesellschaft des 16. und 17. Jahrhunderts." In *Reformatio et Reformationes. Festschrift für Lothar Graf zu Dohna zum 65. Geburtstag*, edited by Andreas Mehl and Wolfgang Christian Schneider, 371–402. Darmstadt, 1989.

Prieur, Jutta, ed. *Geschichte der Stadt Wesel.* 2 vols. Düsseldorf, 1991.

Pütter, Johann Stephan. *Historische Entwickelung der heutigen Staatsverfassung des Teutschen Reichs.* 3 vols. Göttingen, 1786–1787.

Queller, Donald E. *The Office of the Ambassador in the Middle Ages.* Princeton, 1967.

Rambo, Lewis. *Understanding Religious Conversion.* New Haven, 1993.

Ranke, Leopold von. *Deutsche Geschichte im Zeitalter der Reformation*, vol. 2. Meersburg, 1933.

Räss, Andreas. *Die Convertiten seit der Reformation nach ihrem Leben und aus ihren Schriften dargestellt*, 13 vols. Freiburg, 1866–1880.

Redslob, Gustav Moritz. "Frick, Johann." *Allgemeine deutsche Biographie* 7 (1878): 379–380.

Reinhard, Wolfgang. "Pressure toward Confessionalization? Prolegomena to a Theory of the Confessional Age." In *The German Reformation: Essential Readings*, edited by C. Scott Dixon, 172–192. Oxford, 1999.

———. "Was ist katholische Konfessionalisierung?" *Die katholische Konfessionalisierung*, edited by Wolfgang Reinhard and Heinz Schilling, 419–452. Heidelberg, 1995.

———. "Zwang zur Konfessionalisierung? Prolegomena zu einer Theorie des konfessionellen Zeitalters." *Zeitschrift für historische Forschung* 10 (1983): 257–299.

Reitz, Johann Henrich. *Historie der Wiedergebohrnen: Vollständige Ausgabe der Erstdruck aller sieben Teile der pietistischen Sammelbiographie*, edited by Hans-Jürgen Schrader, 4 vols. Tübingen, 1982.

Repgen, Konrad. "Die westfälischen Friedensverhandlungen: Überblick und Hauptprobleme." In *1648: Krieg und Frieden in Europa.* Vol. 1, *Politik, Religion, Recht und Gesellschaft*, edited by Klaus Bußmann and Heinz Schilling, 335–372. Münster, 1998.

Riches, Daniel. "The Culture of Diplomacy in Brandenburg-Swedish Relations, 1575–1697." Ph.D. dissertation, University of Chicago, 2007.

———. "The Rise of Confessional Tension in Brandenburg's Relations with Sweden in the Late Seventeenth Century." *Central European History* 37, no. 4 (2004): 568–592.

Riedel-Spangenberger, Ilona. "Konversion, Konvertiten." In *Lexikon für Theologie und Kirche*, edited by Walter Kasper, vol. 6, 338–340. Freiburg, 1997.

Ritter, Moriz. *Deutsche Geschichte im Zeitalter der Gegenreformation und des Dreissigjährigen Krieges (1555–1648)*, vol. 2. Darmstadt, 1962.

Roberts, Michael. *Essays in Swedish History.* Minneapolis, 1967.

Roelen, Martin Wilhelm, ed. *Ecclesia Wesele: Beiträge zur Ortsnamenforschung und Kirchengeschichte.* Wesel, 2005.

Roensch, Manfred. "Die Konkordienformel in der Geschichte des deutschen Luthertums." *Lutherische Theologie und Kirche* 2, no. 79 (1979): 37–52.

Rohls, Jan. *Geschichte der Ethik*. 2nd ed. Tübingen, 1999.

Rotscheidt, Wilhelm. "Übergang der Gemeinde Wesel von dem lutherischen zum reformierten Bekenntnis im 16. Jahrhundert." *Monatshefte für Rheinische Kirchengeschichte* 13 (1919): 225–256.

Rystad, Göran. *Karl XI: en biografi*. Lund, 2003.

Sardemann, Gerhard. "Johannes Brantius, Rektor an den Höhen Schule in Wesel, 1594–1620." *Zeitschrift des Bergischen Geschichtsvereins* 4 (1867): 115–206.

Schaper, Annegret. *Ein langer Abschied vom Christentum: Johann Christian Edelmann (1698–1767) und die deutsche Frühaufklärung*. Marburg, 1996.

Schäuffele, Wolf-Friedrich. *Christoph Matthäus Pfaff und die Kirchenunionsbestrebungen des Corpus Evangelicorum 1717–1726*. Mainz, 1998.

Schauroth, Eberhard Christian Wilhelm von, ed. *Vollständige Sammlung aller Conclusorum, Schreiben Und anderer übrigen Verhandlungen des Hochpreißlichen Corporis Evangelicorum…*, vol. 1. Regensburg, 1751.

———, ed. *Vollständige Sammlung aller Conclusorum, Schreiben und anderer übrigen Verhandlungen des Hochpreißlichen Corporis Evangelicorum vom Jahr 1663, biß 1752…*, vol. 3. Regensburg, 1752.

Scherer, Georg. *Rettung der Jesuiter Unschuld wider die Giftspinnen Lucam Osiander*. Ingolstadt, 1586.

Scheutz, Martin. "Die 'fünfte Kolonne': Geheimprotestanten im 18. Jahrhundert in der Habsburgermonarchie und deren Inhaftierung in Konversionshäusern (1752–1775)." *Mitteilungen des Instituts für österreichische Geschichtsforschung* 114 (2006): 326–380.

Schilling, Heinz. "Die Konfessionalisierung von Kirche, Staat und Gesellschaft-Profil, Leistung, Defizite und Perspektiven eines geschichtswissenschaftlichen Paradigmas." In *Die katholische Konfessionalisierung*, edited by Wolfgang Reinhard and Heinz Schilling, 1–49. Heidelberg, 1995.

———. "Dortmund im 16. und 17. Jahrhundert – Reichstädtische Gesellschaft, Reformation und Konfessionalisierung." In *Dortmund: 1100 Jahre Stadtgeschichte Festschrift*, 151–202. Dortmund, 1982.

———. *Konfessionskonflikt und Staatsbildung: eine Fallstudie über das Verhältnis von religiösem und sozialem Wandel in der Frühneuzeit am Beispiel der Grafschaft Lippe*. Gütersloh, 1981.

———. *Niederländische Exulanten im 16. Jahrhundert*. Gütersloh, 1972.

———, ed. *Reformierte Konfessionalisierung in Deutschland: Das Problem der 'Zweiten Reformation*. Gütersloh, 1986.

Schilling, Johannes. *Gewesene Mönche. Lebensgeschichten in der Reformation*. Munich, 1990.

Schmidlin, Josef. "Die Gründung der Propagandakongregation." *Zeitschrift für Missionswissenschaft* 12 (1922): 1–14.

Schmidt, G.L. *Georg Witzel, ein Altkatholik des XVI. Jahrhunderts*. Vienna, 1876.

Schmidt, Hans. "Konversion und Säkularisation als politische Waffe am Ausgang des konfessionellen Zeitalters. Neue Quellen zur Politik des Herzogs Ernst August von Hannover am Vorabend des Friedens von Nymwegen." *Francia* 5 (1977): 183–230.

Schmidt, Heinrich Richard. *Dorf und Religion: Reformierte Sittenzucht in Berner Landgemeinden der Frühen Neuzeit*. Stuttgart, 1995.

Schmidt, Jacob. *Eine Predigt Vom Gebet, über die Worte Christi Matth. VI. v. 5. 6. 7. 8. Vor der Dargunischen Hoff-Gemeinde...gehalten.* Alten-Stettin, [1735].

Schnath, Georg. *Geschichte Hannovers im Zeitalter der neunten Kur und der englischen Sukzession 1674–1714,* vol. 4. Hildesheim, 1982.

Schneider, Bernd Christian. *Ius reformandi: Die Entwicklung eines Staatskirchenrechts von seinen Anfängen bis zum Ende des Alten Reiches.* Tübingen, 2001.

Schneider, Hans. *German Radical Pietism.* Lanham, MD, 2007.

Schorn-Schütte, Luise. "Konfessionalisierung als wissenschaftliches Paradigma?" In *Konfessionalisierung in Ostmitteleuropa,* edited by Joachim Bahlcke and Arno Strohmeyer, 63–77. Stuttgart, 1999.

Schulze, Winfried. "Pluralisierung als Bedrohung: Toleranz als Lösung." In *Der Westfälische Friede: Diplomatie – politische Zäsur – kulturelles Umfeld – Rezeptionsgeschichte,* edited by Heinz Duchhardt, 115–140. Munich, 1998.

———. "Kanon und Pluralisierung." In *Kanon und Zensur,* edited by Aleida Assmann and Jan Assmann, 317–325. Munich, 1987.

Schunka, Alexander. "Brüderliche Korrespondenz, unanständige Korrespondenz. Konfession und Politik zwischen Brandenburg–Preußen, Hannover und England im Wendejahr 1706." In *Daniel Ernst Jablonski. Religion, Wissenschaft und Politik um 1700,* edited by Joachim Bahlcke and Werner Korthaase, 123–150. Wiesbaden, 2008.

———. "Daniel Ernst Jablonski, Pietism, and Ecclesiastical Union." In *Pietism, Revivalism and Modernity: 1650–1850,* edited by Fred van Lieburg and Daniel Lindmark, 23–41. Newcastle, 2008.

———. "Zwischen Kontingenz und Providenz. Frühe Englandkontakte der halleschen Pietisten und protestantische Irenik um 1700." *Pietismus und Neuzeit* 34 (2008): 82–114.

———. *Gäste, die bleiben: Zuwanderer in Kursachsen und der Oberlausitz im 17. und frühen 18. Jahrhundert.* Münster, 2006.

Schwöbel, Christoph. "Pluralismus II." In *Theologische Realenzyklopädie,* edited by Gerhard Müller, vol. 26, 724–739. Berlin, 1996.

Schüssler, Hermann. "Fabricius, Johann." *Neue deutsche Biographie* 4 (1959): 735–736

Seegrün, Wolfgang. "In Münster und Nürnberg: Die Verteilung der Konfessionen im Fürstentum Osnabrück 1648–50." *Blätter für deutsche Landesgeschichte* 134 (1998): 59–93

Shantz, Douglas H. "The Harvest of Pietist Theology: F.C. Oetinger's Quest for Truth as Recounted in his *Selbstbiographie.*" In *Tradition and Formation: Claiming an Inheritance. Essays in Honour of Peter C. Erb,* edited by Michel Desjardins and Harold Remus, 121–134. Kitchener, 2008.

Siebenhüner, Kim. "Conversion, Mobility and the Roman Inquisition in Italy around 1600." *Past & Present* 200 (2008): 5–35.

———. "Glaubenswechsel in der Frühen Neuzeit: Chancen und Tendenzen einer historischen Konversionsforschung." *Zeitschrift für historische Forschung* 34, no. 2 (2007): 243–272.

Snape, Andrew. *A Sermon Preach'd before the Princess Sophia at Hannover, the 13/24th of May, 1706.* Cambridge, 1706.

Soldan, Wilhelm Gottlieb. *Dreißig Jahre des Proselytismus in Sachsen und Braunschweig: Mit einer Einleitung.* Leipzig, 1847.

Spehr, [Ferdinand]. "Anton Ulrich, Herzog von Braunschweig-Wolfenbüttel." *Allgemeine deutsche Biographie* 1 (1875): 487–490.

————. "Charlotte Christine Sophie, Kronprinzessin von Rußland." *Allgemeine deutsche Biographie* 4 (1876): 103–105.

————. "Elisabeth Christine." *Allgemeine Deutsche Biographie* 6 (1877): 11–12.

Spohnholz, Jesse. "Multiconfessional Celebration of the Eucharist in Sixteenth-Century Wesel." *Sixteenth Century Journal* 39 (2008): 705–729.

————. *The Tactics of Toleration: A Refugee Community in the Age of Religious Wars.* Newark, DE, 2010.

Steinbart, Gotthilf Samuel. *Ist es rathsam Missethäter durch Geistliche zum Tode vorbereiten und zur Hinrichtung begleiten zu lassen.* Berlin, 1769.

Steinemann, Holger. *Eine Bildtheorie zwischen Repräsentation und Wirkung: Kardinal Gabriele Paleottis "Discorso intorno alle imagini sacre e profane" (1582).* Hildesheim, 2006.

Steinwascher, Gerd. "Die konfessionellen Folgen des Westfälischen Friedens für das Fürstbistum Osnabrück." *Niedersächsisches Jahrbuch für Landesgeschichte* 71 (1999): 51–80.

Stempel, Walter. *'Unnder beider gestalt': Die Reformation in der Stadt Wesel.* Wesel, 1990.

————. "Die Einführung der Kölner Reformation in der Stadt Wesel." *Monatshefte für Evangelische Kirchengeschichte des Rheinlandes* 34 (1985): 260–268.

Stockinger, Hermann. *Die hermetisch-esoterische Tradition unter besonderer Berücksichtigung der Einflüsse auf das Denken Johann Christian Edelmanns (1698–1767).* Zürich, 2004.

Stolze, Wilhelm, ed. "Aktenstücke zur evangelischen Kirchenpolitik Friedrich Wilhelms I." *Jahrbuch für Brandenburgische Kirchengeschichte* 1 (1904): 264–290.

————, ed. "Die Testamente Friedrich Wilhelms I." *Forschungen zur Brandenburgischen und Preußischen Geschichte* 17 (1904): 221–234.

Ströler-Bühler, Heike. *Das Restitutionsedikt von 1629 im Spannungsfeld zwischen Augsburger Religionsfrieden 1555 und dem Westfälischen Frieden.* Regensburg 1991.

Strom, Jonathan. "The Development of Conversion Narratives in Halle Pietism and Pietist Movements up to the Early 1750s." Conference paper presented at the Third International Congress on Pietism Research, Halle, Germany, 2 September 2009.

————. "Conversion, Confessionalization, and Pietism in Dargun." In *Confessionalism and Pietism: Religious Reform in Early Modern Europe,* edited by Fred van Lieburg, 149–168. Mainz, 2006.

————, ed. *Pietism and Community in Europe and North America: 1650–1850.* Leiden, 2010.

Strom, Jonathan, Hartmut Lehamnn, and James Van Horn Melton, eds. *Pietism in Germany and North America, 1680–1820.* Aldershot, 2009.

Stuart, Kathy. "Suicide by Proxy: The Unintended Consequences of Public Executions in Eighteenth-Century Germany." *Central European History* 41 (2008): 413–445.

Sykes, Norman. *William Wake, Archbishop of Canterbury 1657–1737.* 2 vols. Cambridge, 1957.

Taylor, Charles. *A Secular Age.* Cambridge, 2007.

Teschenmacher, Werner. *Annales ecclesiastici.* Düsseldorf, 1962.

Trepp, Anne-Charlott. "Hermetismus oder zur Pluralisierung von Religiositäts- und Wissensformen in der Frühen Neuzeit: Einleitende Bemerkungen." In *Antike Weisheit und kulturelle Praxis: Hermetismus in der Frühen Neuzeit,* edited by Anne-Charlott Trepp and Hartmut Lehmann. Göttingen, 2001, 7–15.

Trigg, Jonathan D. *Baptism in the Theology of Martin Luther.* Leiden, 1994.

Tüchle, Hermann. *Die Protokolle der Propagandakongregation zu deutschen Angelegenheiten 1657–1667. Diasporasorge unter Alexander VII.* Paderborn, 1972.

————. *Acta SC de Propaganda Fide Germaniam spectantia. Die Protokolle der Propagandakongregation zu deutschen Angelegenheiten 1622–1649.* Paderborn, 1962.

Ullman, Chana. *The Transformed Self: The Psychology of Religious Conversion.* New York and London, 1989.

Ulrichs, Karl Friedrich. "Johann Pfeffinger." In *Biographisch Bibliographisches Kirchenlexikon,* edited by Traugott Bautz, vol. 7, 413–416. Herzberg, 1994.

"Unselige Ende Joh. Ph. P. gewesenen Schuldieners in Ob. verzeichnet von seinem damaligen Pastore, Hn. M.P." *Fortgesetzte Sammlung auserlesener Materien zum Bau des Reichs Gottes* 29 (1735): 620–631.

Upton, Anthony F. *Charles XI and Swedish Absolutism.* Cambridge, 1998.

———. "Sweden." In *Absolutism in Seventeenth-Century Europe,* edited by John Miller, 99– 121. Basingstoke, 1990.

Valentin, Jean-Marie, ed. *'Monarchus poeta'. Studien zum Leben und Werk Anton Ulrichs von Braunschweig–Lüneburg.* Amsterdam, 1985.

Van Dülmen, Richard. *Die Entdeckung des Individuums 1500–1800.* 2nd ed. Frankfurt, 2002.

———. *Religion und Gesellschaft: Beiträge zu einer Religionsgeschichte der Neuzeit.* Frankfurt, 1989.

Van Engen, John. "Conversion and Conformity in the Early Fifteenth Century." In *Conversion, Old Worlds and New,* edited by Kenneth Mills and Anthony Grafton, 30–65. Rochester, 2003.

Van Lieburg, Fred A., and Daniel Lindmark, eds. *Pietism, Revivalism, and Modernity, 1650–1850.* Newcastle upon Tyne, 2008.

Verdrähung des nudi facti possessionis anni normalis 1624. Ungrund der sogenannten Selbst-Hülff. Gesprächs-Weiss zwischen einem Catholischen und zwischen einem Protestanten. Regensburg, 1758.

Vierhaus, Rudolf. "Die Rekonstruktion historischer Lebenswelten. Probleme moderne Kulturgeschichtsschreibung." In *Wege zu einer neuen Kulturgeschichte,* edited by Hartmut Lehmann. Göttingen, 1995.

Voigt, H.G. "Valentin Paceus: Seine *Entwicklung* vom protestantischen Führer zum altgläubigen Konvertiten." *Zeitschrift des Vereins für Kirchengeschichte der Provinz Sachsen* 22 (1926): 1–25.

Volkland, Frauke. *Konfession und Selbstverständnis: Reformierte Ritual in der gemischtkonfessionellen Kleinstadt Bischofszell im 17. Jahrhundert.* Göttingen, 2005.

Von merkwürdigen Bekehrungen zur katholischen Kirche, vom sechszehenten bis achtehenten Jahrhundert; sammt einigen Grundsätzen, die für Rechtglaubigen sehr tröstlich sind, in Neueste Sammlung jener Schriften, die von einigen Jahren her über verschiedene wichtigste Gegenstände der Wahrheit im Drucke erschienen sind, vol. 33. Augsburg, 1787.

Walker, Mack. *The Salzburg Transaction: Expulsion and Redemption in Eighteenth-Century Germany.* Ithaca, 1992.

———. *Johann Jakob Moser and the Holy Roman Empire of the German Nation.* Chapel Hill, 1981.

Wallmann, Johannes. *Der Pietismus.* Göttingen, 1990.

———. *Philipp Jakob Spener und die Anfänge des Pietismus.* 2nd ed. Tübingen, 1986.

Walter, E. "Konversion." In *Lexikon für Theologie und Kirche,* edited by Josef Höfer and Karl Rahner, vol. 6, 2nd ed., 520f. Freiburg, 1961.

Walter, Michel. "Die Konversion des Grafen Johann Ludwig von Nassau-Hadamar im Jahre 1629." *Archiv für Mittelrheinische Kirchengeschichte* 20 (1968): 71–102.

Wandel, Lee Palmer. *Voracious Idols and Violent Hands: Iconoclasm in Reformation Zurich, Strasbourg, and Basel.* Cambridge, 1995.

Wappmann, Volker. *Durchbruch zur Toleranz: Die Religionspolitik des Pfalzgrafen Christian August von Sulzbach, 1622–1708.* Neustadt an der Aisch, 1995.

Ward, W.R. *Early Evangelicalism: A Global Intellectual History, 1670–1789.* Cambridge, 2006.

———. "Johann Christian Edelmann: A Rebel's Pilgrimage." In *Modern Religious Rebels,* edited by Stuart Mews. London, 1993.

Warnefried, Johann [Frick, Johann]. *M. B. H. Reiffere Erörterung der Frage ob zwischen der Augspurgischen Confession, und Römisch-Catholischen Religion kein sonderbahrer Unterschied seye....* N.p., 1707.

Weber, Marianne. *Max Weber: A Biography.* Translated by Harry Zohn. New Brunswick, 1988 [1926].

Weber, Max. *The Protestant Ethic and the Spirit of Capitalism.* London, 2001 [1904].

Weidemann, Heinz. *Gerard Wolter Molanus Abt zu Loccum. Eine Biographie,* vol. 2. Göttingen, 1929.

Weigel, Valentin. *Zwei nützlicher Tractate, der erste von der Bekehrung des Menschen, der andere von der Armut des Geistes oder wahrer Gelassenheit,* edited by Winfried Zeller. Stuttgart-Bad Cannstatt, 1966.

Weintraub, Karl J. *The Value of the Individual: Self and Circumstance in Autobiography.* Chicago, 1978.

Wendland, Walter. "Die Pietistische Bekehrung." *Zeitschrift für Kirchengeschichte* 38 (1920): 193–238.

Wengert, Timothy and Robert Kolb. *The Book of Concord: Confessions of the Evangelical Lutheran Church.* Minneapolis, 2001.

Werner, Manuela. *'Gott geb, daß dis das letzte sey': Alltag in Wesel um 1600.* Wesel, 2003.

Whaley, Joachim. *Religious Toleration and Social Change in Hamburg, 1529–1819.* Cambridge, 1985.

Widén, Bill. *Bekehrung und Erziehung bei August Hermann Francke.* Åbo, 1967.

Wiesner-Hanks, Merry E. *Women and Gender in Early Modern Europe,* 3rd ed. Cambridge, 2008.

Wilentz, Sean. "Introduction: Teufelsdröckh's Dilemma: On Symbolism, Politics, and History." In *Rites of Power: Symbolism, Ritual, and Politics Since the Middle Ages,* edited by Sean Wilentz, 1–10. Philadelphia, 1985.

Wilhelmi, Heinrich. "Augusta, Prinzessin von Mecklenburg-Güstrow, und die Dargunschen Pietisten." *Jahrbücher des Vereins für Mecklenburgische Geschichte und Altertumskunde* 48 (1883): 89–284.

Wilson, Peter H. *Absolutism in Central Europe: Historical Connections.* London and New York, 2000.

Wilson, Renate. *Pious Traders in Medicine: A German Pharmaceutical Network in Eighteenth-Century North America.* University Park, PA, 2000.

Witt, Ulrike. *Bekehrung, Bildung und Biographie: Frauen im Umkreis des halleschen Pietismus.* Tübingen, 1995.

Wohlrab-Sahr, Monika. "Religiöse Bekehrung in soziologischer Perspektive. Themen, Schwerpunkte und Fragestellungen der gegenwärtigen relgionssoziologischen Konversionsforschung." In *Religiöse Konversionen. Systematische und fallorientierte Studien in soziologischer Perspektive,* edited by Hubert Knoblauch, Volkhard Krech, and Monika Wohlrab-Sahr, 7–43. Konstanz, 1998.

Wolters, Albert. *Reformationsgeschichte der Stadt Wesel.* Bonn, 1868.

Woltersdorff, Ernst Gottlieb. *Der Schächer am Kreutz: das ist vollständige Nachrichten von der Bekehrung und seligem Ende hingerichteter Missethäter*. 3 vols. Görlitz, 1753–1760.

Zachariä, Carl Heinrich. *Der in Gottes Wort und unsern Symbolischen Büchern wohlgegründete Buß-Kampf*. Peina, 1736.

Zeaeman, Georgius. *Drey Evangelische Jubel- und Danckpredigen*. Kempten, 1618.

Zedler, Johann Heinrich, ed., *Grosses vollständiges Universal-Lexicon aller Wissenschaften und Künste*. 64 vols. Halle and Leipzig, 1732-1750.

Zeeden, Ernst Walter. *Konfessionsbildung: Studien zur Reformation, Gegenreformation und katholische Reform*. Stuttgart, 1985.

———. *Die Entstehung der Konfessionen: Grundlagen und Formen der Konfessionsbildung im Zeitalter der Glaubenskämpfe*. Munich, 1965.

Zeller, Winfried, ed., *Zwei nützlicher Tractate, der erste von der Bekehrung des Menschen, der andere von der Armut des Geistes oder wahrer Gelassenheit (1570)*. Stuttgart-Bad Cannstatt, 1966.

Zorn, Peter. *Dissertatio historica Theologicade Philtris enthusasticis anglico batavis H.E. von dem Englisch- und Holländischen Qvaker-Pulver*. Rostock, [1707].

Zwierlein, Cornel. "'convertire tutta l'Alemagna' – Fürstenkonversionen in den Strategiedenkrahmen der römischen Europapolitik um 1600: Zum Verhältnis von 'Machiavellismus' und 'Konfessionalismus.'" In *Konversion und Konfession in der Frühen Neuzeit*, edited by Ute Lotz-Heumann, Jan-Friedrich Mißfelder, and Matthias Pohlig, 63–105. Gütersloh, 2007.

❧ NOTES ON THE CONTRIBUTORS ☙

Duane J. Corpis, Assistant Professor, Department of History, Cornell University, received his doctorate in history from New York University (2001). He is currently completing the manuscript of his first book, *The Geographies of Conversion and the Boundaries of Confession in Early Modern Germany, 1648–1800*. He has published two book chapters concentrating on the spatial dynamics of religious difference: "Mapping the Boundaries of Confession: Space and Urban Religious Life in the Diocese of Augsburg, 1648–1750," in *Sacred Space in Early Modern Europe*, edited by Will Coster and Andrew Spicer (Cambridge University Press, 2005) and "Losing One's Place: Memory, History, and Space in Post-Reformation Germany," in *Enduring Loss in Early Modern Germany*, edited by Lyne Tatlock (Brill, 2010). A member of the editorial collective of the journal *Radical History Review*, he has coedited three special issues focusing on world history, global activism, and religion and politics.

Ralf-Peter Fuchs, PD Dr. phil., is Associate of the Institute of Modern History at Ludwig-Maximilians-Universität in Munich and has also held the visiting chair in early modern history at Bochum, Duisburg-Essen, and Saarbrücken. He studied under Winfried Schulze and participated in several research projects. He has published on topics as diverse as the histories of witchcraft, honor, the *Reichskammergericht*, and the history of jazz in postwar Germany. Newer publications probe the stocks of knowledge of early modern farmers and craftsmen who had been interrogated as witnesses in lawsuits and focus on the concept of time in the Early Modern period. His most recent project focuses on peacemaking after the Thirty Years' War through the category of "normative years" and is published as "Ein Medium zum Frieden. Die Normaljahrsregel und die Beendigung des Dreißigjährigen Krieges" (Munich, 2010). His other publications include "Hexerei und Zauberei vor dem Reichskammergericht" (Wetzlar, 1994), "Um die Ehre. Westfälische Beleidigungsprozesse vor dem Reichskammergericht (1525–1805)" (Paderborn, 1999), and "The Supreme Court of the Holy Roman Empire: The State of Research and the Outlook" in *Sixteenth Century Journal* 34 (2003, translated by Thomas A. Brady). He is coeditor with Winfried Schulze of "Wahrheit, Wissen, Erinnerung. Zeugenverhörprotokolle als Quellen für soziale Wissensbestände der Frühen Neuzeit" (Münster, Hamburg, and London, 2002) as well as with Arndt Brendecke and Edith Koller of "Die Autorität der Zeit in der Frühen Neuzeit" (Berlin, 2007).

David M. Luebke is Associate Professor of History at the University of Oregon. His publications include *His Majesty's Rebels: Factions, Communities and Rural Revolt in the Black Forest* (Ithaca: Cornell University Press, 1997) and many articles, most recently "Confessions of the Dead: Interpreting Burial Practice in the Late Reformation," *Archiv für Reformationsgeschichte* 101 (2010).

Eric-Oliver Mader was born in 1968 in Munich. After studying history, Italian philology, and philosophy at the University of Munich, he was a fellow of the Institute für Europäische Kulturgeschichte and received his doctorate from the Ludwig-Maximilians-Universität in Munich with the dissertation "Die letzten Priester der Gerechtigkeit. Die Auseinandersetzung der letzten Generation von Richtern des Reichskammergerichts mit der Auflösung des Heiligen Römischen Reiches Deutscher Nation." As a research fellow at the Gerda Henkel Stiftung in Düsseldorf he studied Count Palatine Wolfgang Wilhelm of Pfalz-Neuburg before joining the staff of Saarland University in Saarbrücken, where his focus was the conversion of protestant princes to Catholicism. He has also been a fellow at Herzog August Bibliothek in Wolfenbüttel, where his research centered on early modern conceptions of conversion. Since February 2010, he has been at the Bayerische Architektenkammer in Munich. His research interests include the Holy Roman Empire, early modern political theory and theology, confession and conversion, and architects and architecture of postwar Germany.

Benjamin Marschke is Associate Professor of History at Humboldt State University in Arcata, California. He holds a Ph.D. in history from UCLA (2003), where he studied under David Warren Sabean and Geoffrey Symcox. Marschke has held fellowships from the DAAD, the Fritz Thyssen Stiftung, and the Max Planck Institut für Geschichte. His publications include *Absolutely Pietist: Patronage, Factionalism, and State-Building in the Early Eighteenth-Century Prussian Army Chaplaincy* (Tübingen, 2005). Among other projects, Marschke is currently working on a revision of the history of the relationship of Halle Pietism and the Prussian monarchy under King Frederick William I of Prussia (1713–1740), from which he has already published tentative results: "Halle Pietism and the Prussian State: Infiltration, Dissent, and Subversion," in *Pietism in Germany and North America, 1680–1820*, edited by Jonathan Strom (Aldershot, 2009) and "'Lutheran Jesuits:' Halle Pietist Communication Networks at the Court of Friedrich Wilhelm I of Prussia," in *The Covenant Quarterly* 65, no. 4 (November 2006).

Jared Poley is Associate Professor of History at Georgia State University (USA). He earned his Ph.D. in 2001 and is author of *Decolonization in Germany: Weimar Narratives of Colonial Loss and Foreign Occupation* (Bern,

2005). His current research focuses on the history of greed in Europe and the Atlantic.

Daniel Riches is Assistant Professor of History at the University of Alabama. He received his undergraduate and graduate degrees from the University of Chicago, where he wrote his dissertation, *The Culture of Diplomacy in Brandenburg-Swedish Relations, 1575–1697* (2007), under the direction of Constantin Fasolt. He has also studied at the Humboldt-Universität zu Berlin. His research interests include the intersections of religion and diplomacy in early modern Europe, the role of interpersonal networks, the history of higher education, and military history. His research has been supported by grants from the Deutscher Akademischer Austauschdienst, Mellon Foundation, Ford Foundation, Allstate Insurance Foundation, and United States Department of Education Jacob K. Javits Fellowship Program. Selected publications include "Italian Travel and the Professors of the University of Frankfurt/Oder in the Sixteenth and Seventeenth Centuries," in *Italien und Deutschland. Austauschbeziehungen in der gemeinsamen Gelehrtenkultur der frühen Neuzeit*, edited by Emilio Bonfatti, Herbert Jaumann, and Merio Scattola (Padua, 2008); "Early Modern Military Reform and the Connection Between Sweden and Brandenburg-Prussia," *Scandinavian Studies* 77, no. 3 (2005); and "The Rise of Confessional Tension in Brandenburg's Relations with Sweden in the Late-seventeenth Century," *Central European History* 37, no. 4 (2004).

Daniel C. Ryan is currently Visiting Assistant Professor at the College of Charleston. He earned his Ph.D. (2008) from the University of California, Los Angeles, where he wrote a dissertation titled "The Tsar's Faith: Conversion, Religious Politics, and Peasant Protest in Imperial Russia's Baltic Periphery, 1845–1870s."

David Warren Sabean is the Henry J. Bruman Endowed Professor of German History at UCLA. He is the author of *Property, Production, and Family in Neckarhausen, 1700–1870* (1990) and *Kinship in Neckarhausen, 1700–1870* (1998). He has recently edited, with Simon Teuscher and Jon Mathieu, *Kinship in Europe: Approaches to Long-Term Development (1300–1900)* and co-edited volumes on sibling relationships in European history, interregional and international families in Europe and beyond, and blood and kinship in European history. His current research is on incest discourse in Europe and America since the Renaissance.

Alexander Schunka is Junior Professor for European Cultures of Knowledge at the University of Erfurt (Forschungszentrum Gotha). He graduated in history and Ottoman studies at the Ludwig-Maximilians-University of Munich, where he also worked as a research associate and received his doctoral degree in 2004. Before joining the Universität Erfurt, he taught early modern history at the University of Stuttgart from 2004 to 2009. His main field of research is early modern European history, with a particular interest in migrations and transfer processes, religious history, the history of communication, and historical anthropology. He has published two books (*Soziales Wissen und dörfliche Welt*, 2000; *Gäste, die bleiben*, 2006), one edited volume (*Migrationserfahrungen*, 2010), and a number of articles in German and English dealing with early modern continental migrations, the Counter-Reformation in the Habsburg Lands, and rural life and social knowledge in sixteenth-century Germany, among other topics. His current book project is on Anglo-German encounters in the early Enlightenment.

Douglas H. Shantz holds the Chair of Christian Thought in the Department of Religious Studies at the University of Calgary, Alberta, Canada. He completed his Ph.D. in history in 1987 under Dr. Werner O. Packull at the University of Waterloo, Waterloo, Ontario. His thesis was published as his first book: *Crautwald and Erasmus: A Study in Humanism and Radical Reform in Sixteenth Century Silesia* (Baden-Baden, 1992). For the last twenty years his main research field has been German Pietism, especially Pietist autobiography and millennialism and relations between Pietism and Enlightenment. He has published numerous articles in this field as well as a book, *Between Sardis and Philadelphia: The Life and World of Pietist Court Preacher Conrad Broeske* (Brill, 2008). Forthcoming are an introduction to Pietism (Johns Hopkins) and "Companion to German Pietism" (Brill).

Jesse Spohnholz is Assistant Professor of History at Washington State University. He has a doctorate in history from the University of Iowa (2004) and an M.Litt. in Reformation Studies from the University of St. Andrews (1998). He has been awarded the 2005 Fritz Stern Prize by the German Historical Institute and the 2009 Harold J. Grimm Prize by the Sixteenth Century Studies Association. Spohnholz's research focuses on the daily practices of religious toleration during the Age of Religious Wars, as well as religion, family, and gender in the Netherlands and northwest Germany. He is the author of *The Tactics of Toleration: A Refugee Community in the Age of Religious Wars* (Newark, DE, 2010). His articles include "Multiconfessional Celebration of the Eucharist in Sixteenth-Century Wesel," in *Sixteenth Century Journal* 39, no. 3 (2008), and "Olympias and Chrysostom: The Debate over Wesel's Reformed Deaconesses, 1568–1609," *Archiv für Reformationsgeschichte* 98 (2007). Currently Spohnholz is preparing a study of the massive dislocations caused by the religious wars tentatively titled *The Reformation of the Refugees.*

Jonathan Strom is Associate Professor of Church History at Emory University in Atlanta. His scholarship focuses on the development of religious culture in Europe after the Reformation. A graduate of the University of Chicago, he has received a Lilly Faculty Fellowship and been a visiting scholar at the Max-Planck-Institut für Geschichte in Göttingen. His earlier work focused on the clergy in the confessional age includes *The Clergy in Seventeenth-Century Rostock* (1999), and more recently he has examined lay religion in work on Pietism and Revivalism. He has published numerous articles and chapters and is the editor of several books, most recently *Pietism in Germany and North America 1680–1820* with James Melton and Hartmut Lehmann (2009) and *Pietism and Community in Europe and North America* (2010). He has two current projects, one nearing completion entitled "Conversion, Conventicles, and Prophecy in North Germany" and a new project on the cultural history of the common priesthood in German and American Protestantism.

∾: INDEX :∾